On the Blanket

*For the Superior and Community of the Redemptorist
Monastery, Clonard at Clonard Street, Belfast
and in particular for Fr. Alex Reid*

On the Blanket

The inside story of the IRA PRISONERS' "DIRTY" protest

by
Tim Pat Coogan

Roberts Rinehart Publishers
Boulder, Colorado

Published in the United States and Canada by Roberts Rinehart Publishers,
5455 Spine Road, Boulder, Colorado 80301

Distributed to the trade by Publishers Group West

First edition published in Ireland in November 1980
by Ward River Press Ltd., Knocksedan House, Swords, Dublin

ISBN 1-57098-133-7 (paperback)

Library of Congress Catalog Card Number 96-72312

© Tim Pat Coogan, 1980, 1997

Typesetting:
Red Barn Publishing, Skeagh, Skibbereen, Co. Cork, Ireland

Printed in the United States of America

Contents

Foreword

I am allowing the original preface to this book to stand. The mood of the period which it reflects has a striking similarity to that of today. The difference is quantitative, not qualitative. Then, I was appealing to London for a restoration of the Special Category Status in Long Kesh prison. Now, to take steps which will help to restore the peace process.

There is an uncanny resemblance between the situation in 1980 and 1997. In 1980, the IRA were apparently outmanoeuvred and weakened. People were saying that it was inconceivable that the Republicans would be heard from again, just as they have argued over the last twelve months that a resumption of war in Northern Ireland was unthinkable. Yet, as we now know, the hunger strike, which I sought to avoid by writing the H Block story, did break out—and it now looks very much as if the war is visibly getting under way again.

The central, inescapable fact of the drama described in these pages is that it led directly to the strength of Sinn Féin today. The so-called "dirty protest" was the first stage in the rocket which propelled Gerry Adams and his colleagues into the leadership of the Republican movement. Eventually, he was able to use his position to organise the ceasefire and was invited to the White House as an honoured guest.

The ceasefire broke down for the same reason that the events described in this book ended in tragedy. In a nutshell, those with the power of initiative, the British Prime Ministers of the respective times, Margaret Thatcher and John Major, exercised it on the side of confrontation, not compromise.

American readers (indeed, readers in many parts of the world including the Republic of Ireland) will find it hard to bring their minds to bear both on the nature of the struggle described here and its intensity.

Golgotha lay along the way, a wrenching hunger strike which cost the lives of ten young men and transformed not only Northern Ireland's politics but the entire approach to the Irish issue in three capitals: Dublin, London and Washington.

Will the present tense and uncertain situation mean that Golgotha will be revisited? Just as at the end of the dirty protest described herein, one's automatic response is to say "I hope not." However, the experience of those years makes it necessary to add "but the possibility is not remote."

The Parliamentary balance at Westminster meant that the Ulster Unionists kept John Major in power for the period 1994 to the British general election of 1997. One of the prices paid for that alliance was peace in Ireland. John Major talked Green to Dublin and acted Orange towards Belfast. The Unionists' votes outweighed the urgings of constitutional Nationalists like John Hume (the leader of the SDLP Party), Gerry Adams, successive Dublin governments and even President Clinton.

It is my hope that American readers of *On the Blanket* will react differently. The Irish peace process needs all the friends it can get. Firstly, to help to ensure that the IRA ceasefire is restored, nothing that I say should be taken as conferring a prescriptive right on anyone to blow up anyone else. Secondly, however, to ensure that this time the ceasefire is acted upon, not merely used for party political advantage as did John Major.

I would ask readers to look in particular at chapter fourteen and the different reasons advanced by the British for not acting in a larger statesman-like way. The faces have changed but the same type of arguments are made still. The spin doctors spin. The PR machine grinds on. Voices are not raised. Nomenclature is sanitised. Sophistries are uttered—but nothing is done. And so the young men go out to die, or take life, and the innocent are caught in the cross-fire.

Activity without movement is useless. I hope, having read this book, that Irish Americans will join those organisations which were so instrumental in helping to bring about the IRA ceasefire of August 31, 1994. Lobbying, calling one's congressmen, publicising: these are methods I commend. The absence of the effective availability of these methods in Ireland's six north-eastern counties led to the horrific events described in this book. If men and women of goodwill do not raise their voices in support of peace in Ireland, I fear even more horrific events may lie ahead.

Tim Pat Coogan
Dublin
January 31, 1997

Acknowledgments

I am particularly indebted to the work of three priests, Fr. Brian Brady, Fr. Denis Faul and Fr. Raymond Murray, especially that of the two last named for research materialised in compiling this book. I have drawn liberally on their published dossiers, in particular "H Block" and "The Castlereagh File" which, along with the rest of their voluminous output on denials of civil rights in Northern Ireland, will be invaluable to all future historians. I also made copious use of the particularly fine document on the economy of Northern Ireland which the SDLP prepared, under the direction of Hugh Logue, for the Atkins Constitutional Conference on Northern Ireland. The remainder of my sources should be acknowledged in the text. My thanks are also due to Mr. Hugh O'Flaherty, S. C, who kindly read the work in manuscript and made a number of valuable suggestions. I wish to thank the Northern Ireland Office for the facilities which they afforded me, and especially for arranging my visits to the prisons at Long Kesh and Armagh. Finally, my thanks to Mr. Andrew Boyd for several last-minute corrections. None of the foregoing is, of course, responsible for any inaccuracies remaining in the text.

Preface

This book was conceived—as so many children are—by accident. At the end of February 1980 Philip MacDermott called on me to discuss a novel I had been thinking about writing, and mentioned that he had become intrigued by the sight of a H Block protest he had witnessed some time earlier. "It was cold and wet and there were these women out in the rain dressed only in blankets. Gosh, I thought to myself, to think I was complaining about the cold!" We began talking about the issue, which both of us knew about only in a general way, wondering what sort of people embarked on such a protest. What drove them to it? How was the H Block issue connected with the shooting of warders?

Philip thought the protest should be written about, and asked me for suggestions as to likely authors. I gave him some names, but on one ground or another he turned them down, and suggested finally that I should do the book. I rejected the idea out of hand instinctively, recoiling from the idea of the excrement-befouled cells. Moreover, having just completed a work spanning the previous troubled decade of Irish history, I felt myself at that time emotionally unable to cope with Northern Ireland and its intensities. However, eventually largely out of politeness to Philip I agreed to think about the proposal, and to do some preliminary research. Almost immediately I was both fascinated and appalled.

There was far more to the issue than met the eye. Broken promises, high level secret diplomacy, political intrigue, an unjust economic and social order that both interacted with and contributed to a terrifying IRA campaign of violence. All these sicknesses grew out of the diseased nature of Northern Irish society itself, along with the "conveyor-belt" system of Castlereagh interrogations and Diplock Courts that put the Northern Ireland prison population up by five hundred percent since the troubles had begun just ten years before. In a faecal society, itself resembling a prison in many respects, the H Block protest began to assume a repellently apt symbolism.

I learned that grievous as had been the toll in suffering to the prisoners and their relatives—and to the relatives and friends of the men and women whose lives were caught up in their destinies and sometimes lost because of the H Block issue, the prison officers— even worse things were in prospect should negotiations to solve the problem fail. Not alone was it planned to resume the campaign of shooting warders, halted since January 1980, but a very savage resumption and intensification of the IRA bombing campaign in England was no remote possibility.

Solving the H Block issue would not of itself solve the Northern agony. That awaited an overall Anglo Irish solution, involving Dublin, London and Belfast. But it would remove one poisonous barb from the bleeding body politic of Northern Ireland. So long as that barb remained it would be a source of continued suffering to those involved in the dilemma, a threat to those as yet unscathed, and an absolutely insuperable obstacle to peace in this island, which had to be removed before the ever-growing tendency towards the destabilisation of our entire society presented by the troubles in Northern Ireland could be halted and cured.

This book is intended to show how and why this should have happened.

Tim Pat Coogan
Dublin
June 5, 1980

PART ONE
The Road to H Block

CHAPTER 1

Inside

Everything goes up your bum. The lads are circling around so that the screws don't see the priest slipping us the cigarette box. We roll up the fags in our hands and cram the tobacco into a biro casing. Then one of your mates comes behind you and you bend down and up it goes. The lads make sure that it's well up so nothing will show when the screws search us after Mass. It's amazing what fits up there—one fellow brought out three pencils that way and another hid a pen, a comb and a lighter. You don't feel it unless the casing is too long, but you do bleed all the time and sometimes pieces of flesh come off. Everyone has piles.

The speaker was a bearded, handsome, young man of about five feet nine inches, aged twenty-seven, called Joseph Maguire. He was dressed in neatly creased slacks with a smart leather jacket. The only unusual thing about him was that he seemed very thin and unhealthily pale. He had come out of prison a few days earlier, having lost two and a half stone of the ten stone he weighed when he began his three years "on the blanket," in one of the H Blocks sited in the Maze prison, formerly known as Long Kesh, west of Belfast, ten miles off the M1 motorway. He had been found guilty of being in possession of arms.

According to Maguire, Mass on Sunday was the high point of his week and that of his comrades still behind bars. "We got out of the cells for an hour—a yarn, news of our families. Father Reid is wonderful."[1]

The reason that Maguire and his colleagues were both forced and enabled to enlarge upon the carrying capacity of the human rectum was that they were all stark naked save for a small towel which was the only clothing worn by them as a result of their protest against being denied political status and the consequent punishment visited upon them by the authorities for so doing. The protest and its consequences had led to a situation being created in the H Blocks unlike anything known in Europe since World War II ended. But with that curious human facility for remembering the good things rather than the bad which one often encounters, I found that in retelling his experience Maguire, married to a pretty, cheerful girl with one child, tended to have the more pleasant aspects of his captivity to the forefront of his mind.

> It's all Gaelic in the H Blocks. It was great the way I was able to learn Irish. You stand at a cell door maybe, with the lead of a pencil, and a man who has Irish shouts out a word. Maybe he was one of the men who learned it in the cages.[2] Anyhow you write down the word and the phonetic spelling beside it, and the meaning, and then you repeat it. That goes on all day. If you haven't a lead you can use your Rosary beads. There is a lot of religion in the Blocks. No Marxism. No way. They never miss the Rosary every night in Gaelic. Gaelic prayers are a great way of learning Irish.
>
>   Then you have stories and songs. Some of the memories are fantastic. One man, Bobby Sands, memorised *Trinity* by Leon Uris. That took eight days to tell. The spirit is fantastic. The lads are very good to each other. I only remember one fight between two of the lads. You are all in there because you want to be there.

"There" meant twenty-four hours a day in a ten by eight cell with no exercise or fresh air, usually enclosed with a companion, because though the cells were designed for only one occupant, numbers grew as the troubles continued. The cells were originally painted white and ran along like two arms of a H connected in the centre by an administration section. Hence the name H Block.

In their protest the prisoners were organised under a command structure which had an OC overall to whom the Blocks OCs were responsible. These in turn controlled the OCs of the individual wings. I remarked to Maguire that he made the regime sound quite cheerful. Was he one of those prisoners who found themselves hankering for the secure confines of prison after their release? He immediately relinquished his hold on the memories of the good times, shuddered and said "No, any place is better than there. I would rather be anywhere." He described the normal day.

> Around 7 o'clock the screws check every cell to ensure that everyone is present and alive. Breakfast is a wee drop of porridge or cornflakes, watery milk or sometimes no milk at all, two rounds of pan bread. Sometimes you could see right through the tea. Either that or they would give you the previous day's tea, thick and black. They give you half of everything to try to starve you into breaking. We always like it when there are visitors coming because then you get good food. Everyone is happy when the visitors come. Then you know you would get what it said on the menu. For instance if it said "creamed potatoes and roast beef" that is what you would get. But normally we used to call the roast meat "razor meat," it would be that thin. You get the vegetables very hard, carrots or peas that have been lifted in and out of the water and they are always cold. The third meal could be a piece of bacon, a boiled egg, a cup of tea and a piece of marge. The fourth meal came at seven o'clock with tea and "cake."

The "cake" was only dough. We used to make chess-
men and draughts out of it. You would scrape a board
on the floor and play on it. We were always hungry and
looking forward to the next meal. I got frightened looking at myself in the mirror when I had a bath when I
came home.

Despite this routine Maguire found that the H Block routine
was preferable to his fifteen months in the "Crum"—the Crumlin
Road jail in Belfast—where the first part of his sentence was served;
one of three in a cell in B Wing, the punishment wing. The bulk of
the prisoners, normal criminal prisoners or ODCs (ordinary decent
criminals)[3] as Mr. Merlyn Rees, the former Secretary of State for
Northern Ireland, used to call them, were dressed in prison clothing
and the handful of Republican prisoners, who were naked, had to
walk through clothed prisoners when slopping out or going to see the
Governor. Because of their protest the prisoners were of course in
constant breach of prison rules, to which they then added other
breaches of their own invention.

For instance, they would be told to stand to attention by the
Governor but instead would stand in front of him naked, with their
arms folded so that warders would have to hold them to attention
standing one on either side of the naked recalcitrant. The visit to the
Governor took place every eleven days when the prisoners would be
informed of a loss of a remission for bad behaviour and sentenced to
"three" days on the boards with the Number One diet. This meant no
bed as the mattress on the floor was taken out all day and the cell furniture contents were thus reduced to a Bible, a slop bucket—and a
prisoner.

The prisoners would remain thus from 7:00 a.m. to 9:00 p.m.
when the bedding would be put back into the cell, subsisting on a
diet of a cup of tea and dried bread in the morning, a lunch of pota-
toes with soup and no meat, and an evening meal of tea and dried
bread. They were not allowed books, cigarettes or permission to
attend Mass. Visits were restricted to one per month with a maximum

of three persons, and the Republicans were sited with three cells between each other, so that the shouted communication of H Block was impossible. Moreover the windows in the "Crumlin" were broken so that both the chill air and the drone from the prison boiler room permeated the cell uncomfortably.

However, in the H Blocks to which Maguire was transferred when he went on the "dirt," he found that "there was strength in numbers" and the "Gaelic was a Godsend. Only for it, we would have been climbing the walls."

At the same time prisoners began darkening those walls with any dirt they could lay their hands on, and scribbling political slogans on the white walls, which, combined with the bright lights in the cells, had been producing complaints about eyestrain. These last might well have been avoided, with all the implications such avoidance would have had for the "dirt" protest, had the prisoners been allowed normal exercise, fresh air and daylight.

The battle of the bowels hotted up when the prisoners started throwing their faeces out the window and the screws, "dressed up like spacemen with bloody big gloves," started throwing it back in to them.

In addition, the authorities employed firemen's hoses to clean down the walls around the windows of the cells, thereby swamping the cells. Then in order to dispose of the faeces and continue with the darkening of the walls the prisoners started smearing the excreta over the white paint. One result of the smearing had been that, despite the fact that the cells were cleaned regularly—as we shall see—the prisoners being forcibly removed to another Block whilst this was done, according to Maguire, there were "millions" of little white maggots in the cells.

"You wake up with them in your hair and your nose and your ears. You lift up the mattress and they are crawling under it." Apart from the maggots, Maguire said that problems of both health and disposal were compounded by the fact that dysentery and diarrhoea were prevalent.

Maguire unconsciously exemplified the particularly Irish characteristic which Seán O'Casey captured so well in his plays:

the tear and the smile syndrome. His recollections of his incarceration were obviously based on the same light-and-shade thought pattern. In the same breath in which he described the retching details of the maggots, for instance, his face lit up and he began without prompting to give the answer to my unspoken question as to what was the mental condition of himself and his colleagues in the midst of all this.

> They gave a concert for me, the night before I was let out. One fellow did the tin whistle with his mouth and another fellow made music by banging on the door with his hands. They sang eight duets and they put on their own version of the New Faces panel game on TV with the host, compère—they had the countrymen[4] on the panel. They were really professional. They really put their hearts into it.

Maguire's account touched on one issue which has been a topic of controversy in Ireland in recent years—the teaching of history—but in a way which shed a new light on it. A sizeable body of Irish scholarly opinion has been advocating revisionism in the teaching of Irish history. That is a turning away from the old hagiographical portrayal of 1916 and the events as seen through nationalist eyes, going on the basis that a new approach would somehow help to bridge the gap between North and South, Catholic and Protestant.

However, the difficulty of achieving anything by this approach, against the reality of the backdrop of the violence in Northern Ireland, was exemplified by Maguire's description of the H Block history lectures. "We did everything. World, European, and the whole history of Ireland, the Irish Clans, everything, from the start right up to today." The "lecturer," as Maguire called the principal history teacher, Tommy McKearney from County Tyrone, was serving a sentence of twenty years for murder. The McKearneys were a famous Republican family who figured in a major contro-

----

versy over mistaken identity during the IRA's bombing campaign in
Britain in 1975.

Margaret McKearney, Tommy McKearney's sister, whom the
police suspected of being one of the couriers who kept the Balcombe
Street raiders supplied with money and briefings, was named as being
probably "the most evil woman in England"—at a time when she was
actually in Ireland—and confusion was compounded when a Protestant assassination squad tried to murder her parents in retaliation, in
response to the publicity generated by Scotland Yard's announcement.
In fact an innocent couple of the same name were shot to death.

It will take some time before Northern Ireland returns to a state
of political activity whereby teaching in tranquil classrooms can
hope to have the effects desired by the advocates of a neutral inter-
pretation of history. The H Block "lectures," for instance, will have
had to become a distant memory before any such process can hope
to have a marked effect.

Maguire's account underlines why "we were under pressure all
the time. When the screws lock up everyone at night, everyone is
relieved. You feel we are away now. But when there is a move on you
are dreading it. A 'move' means beatings."

The moves were occasioned by the necessity of having to transfer the prisoners from one wing to another in order to clean the cells
or to carry out searches. The two types of search most dreaded by the
prisoners, they said, were the table search and the mirror search.

Maguire claims that being taken to the table search involved
being dragged through the corridors by the hair and arms, being run
into iron grilles along the way, until one arrived at the point in the
wing where the table was set up. Here the customary routine was for
the prisoner to refuse the instruction to bend over the table for an anal
inspection—the warders were of course aware of the prisoners'
methods of concealment of contraband—and the prisoner was held
by the arms and legs off the ground, facing down. A warder stood
between the legs, parted the buttocks to see if anything had been
secreted. Mouths were also searched and after (allegedly) more
punching and beating, and a ritualistic bang or two into the grille-

work along the way, the prisoner was finally transferred to a clean cell—which he soon set about filthying.

Even more detested than the table search was the mirror search, in which the prisoners habitually refused to adopt a squatting position, giving rise, they said, to blows and kicks, sometimes with a warder sitting on a prisoner's back. A metal detector was used to inspect the anal area and according to the prisoners this came in handy for beating them on the testicles as well. Other sorts of harassment by some warders were alleged, such as using the same finger to explore a prisoner's mouth as had just been used to investigate his rectum.

Understandably the dialogue which ensued on these occasions was not the stuff of which children's programmes are made.

It was an IRA tactic not to retaliate physically; to accept the beatings, but to resist by gestures such as the refusal to squat or stand to attention when told to do so. The authorities (it was claimed) attempted to break the defiance psychologically as well as physically, by giving the warders detailed information about an individual prisoner and his family, so that they would become dismayed by the seeming omnipotence of the State. Prisoners often suffered bouts of anxiety as to what would befall their families if the threats which were made against them were carried out. Normally the greatest period of anxiety for a prisoner was prior to a visit, because after it a mirror search was mandatory. The prisoner had to contend with both the strain of a visit from a wife or mother who was quite often so horrified at his unkempt appearance as to try to get him off "the blanket," as well as the knowledge that after the visit was concluded, he would be subjected to the treatment associated with a mirror search.

Maguire said that once, while waiting for a visit, he saw another prisoner, Jimmy McMullen, get fifty-two punches after he had received a visit from his mother. "I counted them. I didn't want the same treatment, so I was dreading the visit by the time my wife showed up."

The traditional tirelessness of prisoners in working out methods of conveying messages or cigarettes to each other had been

----

brought to a fine art in the H Block. For instance, to distribute the tobacco smuggled in by the method which Maguire described at the outset, the following technique was employed.

Threads were pulled from the cotton towels, which were the only covering prisoners would wear, in lengths of a foot to a foot and a half long, and put together until a length had been created sufficiently long to reach across the wing from one cell door to another. The Blocks were put up so quickly that the cell doors were often ill-fitting, and left gaps between the wall and jamb. When this was done, further threads were pulled from the towels and chewed until all dye and detergent is removed from them, because these prevented the threads from burning properly. This chewed thread was then wound together to make a wick, and finally bits of thread were chewed and fluffed up to make cotton wool. The cotton wool then ignited easily using flint, or a wheel from a cigarette lighter to strike a spark. The wick was ignited from the burning cotton wool and then blown out so that it smouldered with a dull red glow. Meanwhile a little train of tobacco had been prepared by tying cigarettes together. The cigarettes weren't much bigger than needles; the normal ratio being one ordinary cigarette to five "H Block brand." The glowing wick was securely affixed to the train of tobacco.

The train of tobacco was then guided by instructions shouted by a prisoner in the next cell, or the one across the corridor at an angle, because the Blocks were so designed that the prisoner could not see directly across from him. The prisoner would then try to "shoot" a button, possibly surreptitiously taken from the trousers (which they agreed to wear for visits) tied to the line, across the line to the needy smoker, by banging the button with a Bible. Sometimes the shooters had to "aim and fire" for over an hour, while the prisoner shouting guidance looked through the crack between door and jamb to see whether the button should be shot more to the left or the right, before the button arrived at the delivery point at the facing cell door. The delivery point was where another prisoner could use a "shovel" made from a letter or strip of toilet paper to scoop up the button and then reel across the line and tobacco train.

On one occasion Maguire and his companion "had it all over the floor" as they manufactured a train when a warder appeared at the cell door. He smelled the smoke and shouted at the prisoners through the door but he then had to run to a colleague for keys to open the cell, and by the time he got back, Maguire said, "the cell was full of smoke but we had the stuff up our bum. They brought us up over the mirror but found nothing".

The prisoners' antipathy towards the authorities extended to everyone they came in contact with; members of the Prison Visiting Committee, the medical staff and so on. All the prisoners referred to the official doctor as "Dr. Mengels". Maguire described being brought up before the doctor. "He sat on a chair at the end of a corridor, looked at us and said 'they were walking' or 'he has got lice' or something like that."

The routine which followed varied only in degree, not in kind. He told me it meant having his head shaved with electric shears, being "trailed" back to his cell, (trailing entails being frog-marched off the ground by a warder on either side, cuffed and banged off the grille work), trailed out again for a photograph, trailed out again later for a bath. He says he was lifted by the ears, dropped into scalding water and restrained from turning on the cold tap; that he was scrubbed all over with a wire brush applied with particular vigour to his testicles and told by a warder, "I will give you a good wash."

While this was going on, a warder crept up a small ladder from behind him and emptied a bucket of cold water over him. After being dried off, the medical orderly painted him all over with white calomile lotion. Some prisoners who received the same sort of bathing treatment said that they were plunged into ice cold baths, not boiling hot ones.

The question of bringing a degree of hygiene to the prisoners was obviously extremely difficult, but some warders allegedly made it even more so if they can. For instance, strong chemicals which one prisoner described to me as "smelling like CS Gas—and believe me I would know CS—I had enough of it out on the streets"—was poured under the doors into the cells. Then water followed which made the chemicals fume, and though they probably did succeed in their objective of killing infection, the chemicals made the prisoners retch and cough, and stung their eyes badly. The prisoners alleged that their instructions not to retaliate were tested not alone by these methods but also by the attitude of individual warders coming to the doors of the cells, saying to a silent prisoner "what were you shouting about," and then handing out a beating as a result. However, the prisoners for their part obviously annoyed the warders by refusing to obey orders such as to stand straight with their hands over their heads at full stretch. Sometimes, it was said, the warders felt that the situation had gone beyond the accepted standards of humanity and told the prisoners they were only doing a job or perhaps, after striking a recalcitrant, would say something like "you have me so frustrated that I couldn't help myself."

As the pressure-cooker atmosphere of H Block mounted, it was obvious that common humanity was boiling away. For instance, several prisoners said to me that on hearing of a "screw's death"[5] they had a feeling of elation. One man said to me that after hearing the news of the Deputy Governor Myles's shooting, his cell mate started to shake and then shouted for joy.

"You feel very degraded when you were naked; it lifts you when someone strikes back," he added. Yet despite the ferocity of the encounter between warders and prisoners, feelings of delicacy proved hard to suppress. Prisoners for instance had an unspoken rule that when defecating in a cell with one or more companions, a prisoner would either use his mattress as a screen or else advise his comrades to look out of the window.

But why was the encounter so ferocious? Why would the prisoners not behave like ODCs? Why did men embark on the routine described by Maguire—and readers can be assured that one prisoner's experience varies very little from that of another—even when they were serving life sentences? The answer lies buried both in Ireland's history of recent and not so recent troubles, and in the effect on that history of first the Fenian and later the IRA prison

experience. That history has to be understood if one is to compre-
hend either the attitudes of the prisoners and their jailers or the feelings of those at home, over whom the phrase "on the blanket" had
also thrown a pall of misery and suffering.

1.   A member of the Redemptorist Community of the Clonard Monastery, Clonard Street, off the Falls Road in Belfast, Fr. Alex Reid was one of the panel of priests who were admitted to the H Block complex to minister to the men's spiritual welfare.
2.   The "cages" were what the prisoners call the compounds where men with Special Category status were held in conditions resembling a prisoner-of-war camp.
3.   The term HACs, Honest Average Criminals was, I was told, employed by the Prison Visitors Committee which deals with the H Blocks.
4.   H Block prisoners of course come from all over the Province—not just Belfast.
5.   Nobody connected with the prisoners, that was, family or friends, ever refers to the warders by anything save the prison argot term of "screws."

CHAPTER 2
Those That Can Suffer the Most

Most people are amazed and perturbed when the IRA begin a hunger strike or a jail protest of some sort. What is it all about? Why are they doing it? The questions echo from one generation to another, as the portcullis of the years comes down on each cycle of IRA activity. The IRA's theologians, however, are different, seeing the prison saga as part of a continuous backdrop of cause and effect. "This war will be won in the prisons" was a frequently repeated saying of William McKee, at one time the principal IRA leader in Belfast. In this he was echoing an ancient tradition of the physical force school of Irish nationalism that goes back to the last century. This tradition has been of particular significance to the IRA's prison story in general, and, as we shall see, the H Block situation in particular.

Prison is where society makes its sanctions stick—if it can. The encounter between the warders and the prisoners is the last testing ground. For the IRA it has traditionally been yet another battle-ground in the war, in which the game is not deemed to be up at the moment when the judge passes his sentence, but merely moves to another and time-hallowed plane. The fight is against the forces of the State inside the prison, instead of outside it as formerly.

There is, along with the IRA doctrine of force, a dual standard of endurance as well as infliction which is as old as the separatist movement itself. Sayings embodying this tradition, such as Terence McSwiney's famous remark on the subject of endurance, are rever-entially handed down from one generation of IRA volunteers to the next. Terence McSwiney, a member of the IRA and Sinn Féin Lord Mayor of Cork, died on the seventy-fourth day of his hunger strike in Brixton prison, at the height of the Anglo-Irish war, on October 25, 1920. In the course of his inaugural speech as Lord Mayor he spoke words which epitomised the endurance side of the IRA coin: ". . . the contest on our side is not one of rivalry or vengeance but of endurance. It is not those who can inflict the most but those that can suffer the most who will conquer . . . It is conceivable that the army of occupation could stop us functioning for a time. Then it becomes simply a question of endurance. Those whose faith is strong will endure to the end in triumph."

McSwiney's was a peculiarly Irish[1] form of self-sacrifice. (During the time of the Brehon laws, by which Ireland was governed prior to the coming of the Normans, one of the most telling ways to retaliate against a wrongdoer was for the affronted party to starve himself outside the guilty party's house.) McSwiney's mortal protest caught the imagination of the world at the time, and of the IRA ever since.

But whilst the philosophy of a McSwiney is both lofty and inspiring to militant Republicans, in the dull grey, daily grind of prison conflict they look to other exemplars of survival. An average young IRA volunteer will normally have received a historical indoctrination in the experience and writings of these figures, who generally speaking fall into two categories. First, there are the hero-figures from the Fenian movement, which first sprang up in the second half of the nineteenth century, modelling itself on the continental cell system. Then there are the men, and more latterly the women, too, who suffered in English and Irish jails during the period 1916-21, the years of World War II, and the current phase of hostilities which commenced in 1969.

At the top of the list of names of prison fighters who inspired the volunteers of the 1916–21 period, and who are still recalled admiringly today in *An Phoblacht* (the IRA newspaper), are those of O'Donovan Rossa and Thomas Clarke. Rossa, from County Cork, was one of the earliest members of the Irish Republican Brother-

----

hood, the Fenians. He was condemned to life imprisonment on December 13, 1865, for his part in the dynamite campaign of that era, which was the precursor of the bombing campaign in England at the eve of World War II, and of the attacks against English cities mounted during the 1970s by the IRA.

In September 1870, the Devon Commission of Inquiry into the treatment of Fenian prisoners heard a report by a Dr. Lyons into the case of O'Donovan Rossa who was described to the Commission as being "arrogant, hot tempered, strong-willed" but a man of "integrity, courage and contempt for corruption." However, it was not his character which was of prime interest to the Commission, which had been set up as a result of widespread unease following reports of what was happening to the Irish prisoners in English jails. Amongst other punishments Rossa had been handcuffed behind his back, the manacles only being removed to allow him to eat and sleep, for a period of thirty-four days. Dr. Lyons' report said:

> It is also worthy of note that the almost continuous employment of bread-water punishment diet in the case of O'Donovan Rossa in the months of May and June 1868 did not prevent him from committing the assault already referred to (attempts to strike the Prison Governor) that the handcuffing which followed from 17th to 20th July in punishment also did not prevent him, when liberated from committing a further offence, for which he was, after an interval of two hours and a quarter, again put in handcuffs for two days, and that the infliction of 28 days' bread and water punishment did not prevent him from committing additional offences, for which he was further reported and tried by the visiting director in October 1868.
>
> The marked and immediate effect of the few well chosen words of Captain du Cane, accompanied by a total remission of the punishments undoubtedly incurred by the prisoner's conduct, show in well defined contrast the

influence of moral agency as against the failure of long
continued measures of coercion accompanied with a
total of more than forty days of bread and water diet
spread over the period from May 1 to October, 1868.

Captain du Cane, the Chairman of the prison board of direc-
tors, if he did not concede to Rossa what in present day terms would
be called "political status," had in effect told him that he would wipe
the slate clean and act fairly towards him in future if Rossa would
act accordingly. Rossa accepted the Captain's olive branch and for
the rest of his sentence had to endure no further worsening of the
grim prison conditions of the time.

However, the story of O'Donovan Rossa did not end there.
What really dynamited him into Republican folklore was his funeral
in 1915 when after a lifetime working for separatism he was brought
home to be buried in Dublin.

It was one of the classic demonstrations of the importance of
the funeral to Republican theology. The body lay in state at City Hall,
a huge crowd followed the cortege to Glasnevin Cemetery, and an
extraordinary oration was delivered by Pádraig Pearse. It contained,
after much reference to the sufferings of Rossa and the nobility of
his character, the following burst of grapeshot oratory:

Life springs from death; and from the graves of patriot
men and women spring living nations. The Defenders of
this realm have worked well in secret and in the open.
They think that they have pacified Ireland. They think
that they have purchased half of us and intimidated the
other half. They think that they have foreseen everything, think that they have provided against everything;
but the fools, the fools, the fools! They have left us our
Fenian dead, and while Ireland holds these graves, Ireland unfree shall never be at peace.

The speech was followed by a volley over the grave. A year
later another volley had claimed the life of Pádraig Pearse himself.

He too had gone to a patriot grave via an English firing squad. The Court Martial that condemned him in the wake of the Easter Rising of 1916 was inevitably only a brief legal halt on the route to execution laid out for him and his fellow leaders of the rebellion. It was to one of these, Tom Clarke, that Pearse had been referring by implication in his oration over Rossa's grave when in another celebrated passage he spoke of Rossa being "in spiritual communion with those of his day, living and dead, who suffered with him in English prisons, in communion of spirit with our own dear comrades, who suffer in English prisons today, and speaking on their behalf as well as our own, we pledge to Ireland our love, and we pledge to English rule in Ireland our hate."

Because of what he had "suffered in English prisons" for his dynamiting activities, it was around Clarke that the new generation of Fenians grouped, when he came back to Dublin in 1898, to be welcomed with torchlights and bonfires in that anniversary year of Wolfe Tone's unsuccessful rising. 1798, the "Year of the French," had failed like all the other Irish rebellions, including the seeming failure of 1916, but it bequeathed to Ireland a tradition of militant Republicanism, of striking at England while she was preoccupied elsewhere, and of attempting to unite "Protestant, Catholic and dissenter" in the struggle which persists to this day. That might be called the code of infliction in the name of Republicanism, but Clarke was hailed in his time for his fidelity to the code of endurance. So much so that the Proclamation of 1916, declaring a Republic and containing the revolutionaries' testament of aims and beliefs, carried Clarke's name at the top of the list of signatories.

In his *Irish Felon's Prison Life*,[2] Clarke wrote of his experiences:

> Generally speaking, we were all treated alike, (at
> Chatham Prison) for the authorities deliberately set
> themselves to drive us all mad or to kill us, and they
> succeeded in doing this with most of our numbers.
> Some of us realised the situation early in our impris-

onment, and saw that the mercilessly savage treatment was meant to smash us and three of us Daly, Ryan and myself set ourselves to defeat the officials' design. It was a fight against dreadful odds. On the one side were the prison authorities with all the horrors of the prison machinery, relentlessly striving to accomplish its objects with unlimited ways and means at their disposal. On the other side were the prisoners, each standing alone and friendless, but resolved never to give in, with nothing to sustain him in the fight but his own courage and the pride he had in being an Irish Fenian, without encouragement save the sympathy and cheering words coming to him every now and then, from his plucky and self-reliant comrade fighting the same fight as himself in the same spirit of "No surrender."

Throughout the whole time we stood loyally by each other and as I have said, were in close and constant communication with each other. Never a week passed but I received a note from John Daly—and some weeks two or three notes—and he received the same from me. This went on for eleven years. As with Daly, as with Egan for the eight years he was with us. Tell that to the prison authorities and they would say that it was utterly impossible. But, we too had reduced our business to a scientific system—it was diamond cut diamond. At all events they never had the satisfaction of catching notes with either of us.

It would have meant thirteen days punishment for the writers had the notes been found. But Clarke for sixteen years never even kept a pencil on his person. The black lead was buried in the floor of his cell. It would be seen in this extract from Clarke's diary how the ingenuity, the tone of defiance, the feeling of comradeship all have overtones of the account of the much shorter sojourn in the H Blocks

----

given by Joseph Maguire at the outset. But many chapters of the Republican prison saga remained to be turned before Maguire's story begins.

After the executions of 1916, the Irish public's attention switched to the prisoners in English jails—their doings, their tribulations and their outstanding figure, Eamon de Valera, the last commandant to surrender in 1916. Among them was a burly young Corkman called Michael Collins, who was to set the tone for much of the IRA activity of the century and for other revolutionary groups around the world also. No more set-piece temporary takeover of city-centre buildings for him. He was going to blind the State's eyes and ears: its police and detectives. He had had firsthand experience of their deadly effectiveness after the Rising, when he had seen how the detectives specialising in political crime had sufficient information to pick out some of his comrades for the firing squad. His IRA descendants are killing their RUC descendants in Northern Ireland today.

Another prisoner was Gerald Boland, who in Ireland's tragic civil war was to lose a brother and become one of Collins' most inveterate and unforgiving enemies. He was later to become one of the greatest scourges the IRA ever knew in its history, when as Minister for justice in de Valera's World War II cabinet years later, he had the responsibility for carrying out the Cabinet's policy of Olympian implacability against their former comrades. I remember, long after those terrible years had passed, Boland, a man capable of unusual charm and of unusual bitterness who was then in his eighties, telling me something that helped to illustrate his attitudes in Government and those of his colleagues.

> We weren't badly treated really, we had enough to eat, we could get in parcels and there was liberty enough in the compounds. But we made out we were being given a dog's life. Every little thing we blew up for publicity. We'd do anything for a crack at the British. We had the whole country agog with our propaganda.

They certainly had. The tide of sympathy began to swing towards Sinn Féin after the Rising. One of the most effective political posters in Ireland's history showed a man in prison uniform with the slogan under it saying: "Put him in to get him out." The "him" was Joseph McGuinness in Lewes jail, and on May 9, 1917, he became the first felon of the new revolution to win a seat for Sinn Féin, scraping in at South Longford by a margin of only thirty-seven votes—enough however, for the *Manchester Guardian* to declare his win "the equivalent of a serious British defeat in the field." Back in England, uproar in favour of political status for the Irish prisoners continued to be met with varying degrees of success or severity as the conflict wore on, and through it all the Sinn Féiners who had marched to the ships carrying them to jail amidst the boos and insults of the Dublin crowds—many of them women whose husbands were away fighting for the British army—emerged in triumph to top the polls in 1918, obliterate the old Irish Parliamentary Party, and finally force the British to withdraw from most of the country in 1921. But the memory of their own use of prison propaganda and of stories of police brutality, both at that period and later against their former comrades during and after the civil war, remained with Boland and his colleagues, so that they showed themselves monumentally unmoved by similar stories later on when they held power.

The tide of political fortunes had turned. The British were forced to leave a substantial part of Ireland, and the country was divided into a twenty-six county entity ruled by the Irish from Dublin, and a six-county one nominally controlled from London but with a Unionist-controlled devolved government in Belfast. It was not long before it fell to the lot of Irishmen to jail Irishmen.

Bitter civil war followed the signing of the Treaty that concluded the Anglo-Irish war. The Treaty accepted that henceforth Ireland would be partitioned and the South would have dominion status like Canada or Australia; her elected representatives would take an Oath of Allegiance to the Crown which would be formally represented in Dublin by a Governor General. All other signs of centuries of British rule vanished except for those official symbols, but for some it was not enough. They had sworn to achieve a Republic and in the words of Liam Lynch, who until he was killed led the Republican forces, would serve "no other law." However, the bulk of the population would. In the South the people saw that the British were gone. They were war-weary, and they wanted peace.

In the North the Unionist and Protestant element were in a majority and had no intention of seeing the British depart. They felt bitterly aggrieved at seeing them leave the rest of the country, and no Republican was going to be allowed an opportunity of altering those circumstances. There had been terrible bloodshed in Belfast and throughout the Province during the Anglo-Irish war which had also seen millions of pounds of property, mostly Loyalist or governmental, go up in flames. And behind the bitterness engendered by this chaos, there was the memory of pogrom, and of Protestant-versus-Catholic rioting stretching back for centuries. The Protestant slogan during the Home Rule crisis had been "not an inch." After the IRA's victory in the South it became translated as "not a centimetre."

The Protestants outnumbered the Catholics by nearly two to one, had their own militia (the B Specials), a police force (the RUC), and as a makeweight the remnants of the shattered Royal Irish Constabulary (the RIC) which the IRA had driven out of southern Ireland. Along with these there were the remnants of such forces as the Auxiliaries and the remnants of the infamous Black-and-Tans (the "dirty tricks" brigade of its time) and, behind all these there stood, if needed, the regular British army. In the circumstances they were not needed.

The divided IRA couldn't even put a dent in the outer defences of Protestant Unionism let alone its core. An armed campaign in the North was certain not merely to fail but to be unable, bereft of any strong continuous support from the South, even to get off the ground. And in the South, with the IRA divided against itself and once friendly houses closed to members of the organisation, brother fought brother fruitlessly as the people, wearied by violence, supported the government in the draconian measures it took against the Anti-Treaty IRA.

There were seventy-seven executions of Anti-Treaty prisoners, and wholesale jailings, but the country eventually settled down to peace with de Valera miraculously—it seemed at the time—forming a political party (Fianna Fáil) out of the ranks of shattered Republicanism in opposition to the government party, which was called Cumann na nGael and led by W. T. Cosgrave. To the physical force school of Republicans, Cosgrave's administration became as anathematised as had been that of the British. De Valera's Fianna Fáil, though it had strayed off the high road of an All Ireland Republic as aspired to by Rossa, Pearse and Clarke, and entered onto the uncertain by-paths of Constitutionalism, at least contained men beside whom the IRA had fought in the civil war.

In fact such was the interchangeability of membership between the IRA and Fianna Fáil that in the early days of the State Fianna Fáil Cumanns (Branches) by day were often Flying Columns by night. Not that there was all that much to fly at. For although the IRA attracted large numbers of recruits (possibly as many as 20,000), took a pot-shot at an occasional policeman, and raided a barracks or two, the movement lacked the mass appeal of the constitutional parties, particularly de Valera's, for which it campaigned in the election of 1932 that brought him to the power which he was to hold uninterrupted for sixteen years.

One of the most telling slogans of de Valera's campaign had been "release the prisoners," and one of his first acts on taking office was to do just that. One of his principal lieutenants, Frank Aiken, who had succeeded Liam Lynch as the leader of the Republican forces in the civil war, personally drove to Arbour Hill jail to supervise the release of his old comrades. Within the IRA all was euphoria. Their friends were in, their enemies were out, and they were free to move on to an All-Ireland Republic.

However, it was not they, but de Valera who did the moving—with as Republican a form of government as was possible in the circumstances. The Oath of Allegiance was abolished. The

Governor-General went also when de Valera introduced a new constitution. The Land Annuities were retained. These were the sums which the Irish government collected each year from farmers on behalf of the British government, to repay the loans which the British, forced by Michael Davitt's Land League, had raised to buy out the big landlords during the late nineteenth century. By establishing a peasant proprietorship they had settled the great festering sore of the Land issue. However, many people in Ireland felt with a certain historical justification that there wouldn't have been a sore in the first place, had not the landlords come by the land through its being seized by the British in the first place. So de Valera's refusal to pay over the annuities was a highly popular move with the smaller farmers and the nationalist-minded population.

As de Valera tightened his hold on power it would have appeared to an outsider that he had the country before him and the IRA behind him—particularly so on December 29, 1937, when his constitution became law, legislating the Irish Free State out of existence and substituting in its place a new name, Éire, for a very old country. (You could also call it Ireland—depending on which language you spoke, Irish or English.) But always in Ireland appearances were deceptive.

De Valera certainly had the established forces of the country behind him, but the IRA were parted from him. The reason? The old reason of rivalry—as Shakespeare put it: "two stars keep not their motion in the one orb." The immediate cause—as happens with such metronomic regularity in Republican history—was to be found in prison. Seán Glynn, a young Limerick man imprisoned in Arbour Hill jail, Dublin, whence Frank Aiken had freed the IRA prisoners only five years earlier, had become depressed in solitary confinement and taken his own life.

This death had the important but at the time unrealised effect of causing Joseph McGarrity, leader of the American wing of militant Republicanism, Clan na nGael, to break with de Valera, who, from across the Atlantic, in those days of poor communication, he had imagined was somehow still in tandem with the IRA. McGar-

rity then funded Seán Russell, the most extreme IRA leader, to give
the IRA a continuation of the Rossa/Clarke dynamism by transfer-
ring IRA activities away from Ireland, where they were visibly
unprofitable and unwelcome, to a bombing campaign on English
soil. England, being preoccupied with the gathering storm over Germany, would, Russell reckoned, consequently be more amenable to
settling the Irish issue.

However, he reckoned without two factors. Firstly, his campaign
was ill-conceived, ill-planned and badly executed, so that it had the
effect of enraging English public opinion against Ireland rather than
moving it towards a withdrawal from Northern Ireland and an ending
of partition. Secondly, this rage had the effect of increasing British
pressure on de Valera to desist from his policy of neutrality, which he
was maintaining against not alone British opposition but also pressure
from the Americans and Germans. As a consequence de Valera
cracked down hard on the IRA. The shooting of policemen by IRA
men led to the creation of work for Irish firing squads and the English
hangman Pierrepoint, and the reopening of internment camps. In 1938
de Valera had secured the return of the "Treaty ports" from the British
in return for a settlement of the Land Annuities dispute. Regaining
control of these highly strategic naval bases both made it feasible for
Ireland to remain neutral *vis-à-vis* Germany, and very uncomfortable
to do so *vis-à-vis* Britain. Winston Churchill, in particular, was furi-
ous at their loss.

But de Valera's early efforts to curb the IRA were checked for
different reasons. Firstly, Irish public opinion was inflamed against
Britain by the trial and execution of two IRA volunteers, Peter
Barnes and James McCormack, for the Coventry explosion of
August 25, 1939. The explosion had claimed five lives and maimed
many more, but it was accidental, and in any case Barnes and
McCormack had only made the bomb (intended not to take life but
to blow up a power station); they had not planted it. The carrier panicked and left it on the back carrier of a bike in a crowded street.

Secondly, Seán MacBride, himself a former IRA Chief of Staff,
secured bulk releases of IRA men by successfully bringing a Habeas

----

Corpus action to prove that they were held illegally. And thirdly, prison provided a platform, a lonely stage from which a hunger striker successfully defied the Government and de Valera—the first time round. Patrick McGrath, a man who like de Valera had been out in 1916, and still carried a British bullet near his heart as a result, was picked up in a police swoop in September of 1939. But he was released in deference to public opinion on December 9, having been on a hunger strike for forty-three days.

This was one of the high-water marks of success in the history of hunger-striking and the IRA's prison saga—not just the concession of political status, but actual release! However, within a matter of days—two weeks to be exact—the IRA perpetrated one of the most costly triumphs in the movement's history: a raid on the Irish Army's ammunition depot in the Magazine Fort at the Phoenix Park, Dublin, taking nearly all the ammunition which the Irish government had stockpiled to defend the country in the event of an invasion. And in 1939, invasion was anything but a remote possibility.

That was it. The hardline Minister for justice, Gerald Boland, was given whatever powers he needed to crush the IRA, and he set about doing so. Everything that a wartime state needed to wipe out a foe was to hand: military tribunals, changes in the laws of evidence, death sentences, internment and—one of the most efficacious methods of all—censorship. When prisoners rioted in jail or set fire to their huts in the barbed wire enclosures of the Curragh Camp, they were batoned into subjection—and no one outside heard about it until much later. Armed soldiers were to hand at all times, and one prisoner in the Curragh, Barney Casey, was shot dead as a result of the tension. His inquest was closed in seconds after Seán MacBride provocatively asked why he had been shot in the back. Two men died after fifty-five days on hunger strike, Jack MacNeela and Tony d'Arcy. Patrick McGrath was one of those executed for killing a policeman, and public opinion, solidly behind the neutrality policy and supportive of the State, was scarcely moved.

The traditional IRA prison drama was enacted before a smaller and smaller audience. But enacted it was, particularly in

Portlaoise jail, where some of the top IRA prisoners were held and treated as common criminals, without the rights of political status including the right to wear their own clothes. They also objected to having to receive letters with a prison number at the top, and to conforming to normal prison routine. Accordingly they went "on the blanket" and as a consequence stayed locked in their cells all day, naked except for a blanket. They received no letters, since they would not accept any numbered "criminal." They could not go to Mass naked, so this solace was denied them, as were books or conversation. They sat out the war and beyond in solitary confinement with the lights switched on twenty-four hours a day, only being let out once a week for a bath. How they did not go mad was hard to fathom, but finally one of them, Seán McCaughey, embarked on a hunger strike to secure his release. After nineteen days he refused to accept water either and died twelve days later with his body in a horrific condition, on May 11, 1946. That month, however, the Stormont government unconditionally released another prominent IRA man, Davy Flemming, who had been on hunger strike. The contrast was marked and the traditional audience for the Republican prison drama began to swell—particularly when the McCaughey inquest made public the conditions in which the men had been kept for four and a half years, as a result of Seán MacBride's questioning of the prison doctor.

It grew and grew, until finally the Republican Prisoners Release Association, which sought to free all the Republican prisoners held in Britain and the North of Ireland as well as in the South, became a countrywide force. Its cause became a plank in Seán MacBride's Clann na Poblachta Party, which mushroomed up at the end of the war years, and which, to the echo of the cry "Release the prisoners," helped to form a coalition that finally put de Valera out of office in February 1948. The following month the last five Republican prisoners in Portlaoise were released, and that September the bodies of the Republicans who had been executed during the war years were released for burial with traditional Republican rites and ceremonies in their native areas, thereby providing a springboard for renewed

IRA activities as a new generation grew up to take part in the 1950s campaign.

However, along with the springboarding and the reorganisation there was also reappraisal. The IRA took stock of itself after the war.

The road to an All Ireland parliament had led only to jail and to the writing of one of the worst chapters in the IRA's prison history. In Britain Irish prisoners had often been maltreated by warders and by English prisoners—several were hospitalised in this way when the news of the Coventry bombings reached Dartmoor prison. From 1940 Republican prisoners there remained naked in solitary confinement, in an unsuccessful attempt to win political status that began with the setting fire to the prison's D Wing. They were forcibly dressed once a week by the warders and brought before the Governor to receive an additional week in the punishment cells, until the strike eventually petered out unsuccessfully.

Northern Ireland had been the scene of one of the greatest pro-IRA agitations of this whole period—again centring around men in prison, Thomas Williams and five companions. One of them, a young man called Joe Cahill, was sentenced to hang for the murder of a policeman accidentally shot as the IRA group set up a diversion to hide the movement of an arms dump. Three were ultimately reprieved as a result of public and private pressure on the British—Seán MacBride organised the collection of over 200,000 signatories on a petition for clemency—but Williams, the leader of the group, was hanged in Crumlin Road jail on September 2, 1942, as Catholic crowds said the Rosary outside, and Protestant groups sang Orange ballads and shouted obscenities.

In the North, also, there had been some dramatic escapes. Jimmy Steele, Hugh McAteer, Pat Donnelly and Niall Maguire from Crumlin Road jail in Belfast went "over the wall" by means of a twisted sheet rope in January 1943, and the following month twenty-one prisoners tunnelled their way successfully out of Derry jail. But the Southern authorities captured the bulk of the Derry escapees and placed them in the Curragh, and four months after escaping Steele was recaptured.

His escape and that of his friends marked a turning point in relations within the jail between the prisoners and the warders who became progressively less accommodating as the British began to win the war, and the sort of unofficial political status which the prisoners had hitherto enjoyed became denied to them. Prison rules were more severely enforced. In an effort to restore their privileges Steele ordered a "strip strike" wherein prisoners refused to wear prison clothes. This lasted for three months with the prisoners sitting naked in their cells, which were emptied as a punishment compounded by the administration of a diet inferior to that which normally obtained. Steele afterwards wrote of his experience:

> You are in the grip of a mighty machine. What is the use? Others fought against it for years. Some went to an early grave, while others went mad. What was to be your fate? Nevertheless you must not let your comrades down. We are all in this to the end.

But Steele and the others realised that the end would not be successful and called off the strike to enable a prisoner to receive medical treatment.

It was decided after the war to fight that "mighty machine" by other means, which amongst other things included recognising that the South was not a suitable theatre for operations—because the public would not stand for any operations against its police or security forces, but would accept the sort of measures directed against the IRA which the movement had experienced in the forties. Accordingly, Standing Order number 8 became IRA policy in October 1954.

> 1.   Volunteers are strictly forbidden to take any militant action against twenty-six county forces under any circumstances whatsoever. The importance of this Order in present circumstances especially in the Border areas cannot be over-emphasised.

2.   Minimum arms drill shall be used in training in
     the twenty-six county areas. In the event of a raid
     every effort shall be made to get the arms away
     safely. If this fails, the arms shall be rendered use-
     less and abandoned.

3.   Maximum security precautions must be taken
     when training. Scouts must always be posted to
     warn of emergency. Volunteers arrested during
     training or in possession of arms would point out
     that the arms were for use against the British
     Forces of Occupation only. This statement should
     be repeated at all subsequent court proceedings.

4.   At all times Volunteers must make it clear that the
     policy of the Army is to drive the British Forces
     of Occupation out of Ireland.

The only time that this Standing Order was breached deliberately from 1954 to 1980 was once, in a campaign over prison conditions in Portlaoise jail, when a Garda patrol was lured to a
booby-trapped cottage in Mountmellick, Co. Laois on October 16,
1976, by a bogus call and Garda Michael Clerkin was killed. But this
is to anticipate.

As a result of the IRA's new departure, the 1954-62 era saw no
action in the Republic, a very limited amount in Britain and a campaign directed solely against the Six Counties.

However, as this really consisted of a series of raids mounted
and directed against the North from the South, by Southerners, it
soon petered out, and the campaign was long dead before it was officially declared to have laid down in 1962. There was no widespread
popular support for the IRA throughout the North. Virtually no activities took place in Belfast because the movement felt it was too weak
to protect the Catholic population there, and consequently prison
numbers (always an accurate barometer of the physical force
school's strength and activities) were not large, nor did they give rise
to much that was noteworthy in the IRA's history of prison dramas.

Danny Donnelly was the only IRA man of the period to escape from Crumlin Road jail and significantly perhaps Ruairí O Brádaigh and Daithí O'Conaill were two who successfully stepped under the wire of the Curragh Camp which de Valera reopened when he again won power in 1957.

1.   Some cases were recorded in early Indian history also.
2.   *An Irish Felon's Prison Life* by Tom Clarke, Dublin 1922, with an introduction by P. S. O'Hegarty.

CHAPTER 3
Lighting the Fuse

The IRA is not a centralised movement with a head office, pensionable staff and institutional mechanisms that carry it forward from one generation to another like a regular army. It is a wind in the corridors of Irish history, a rustle in the undergrowth of Irish politics, a spark that can, if the wind blows favourably, suddenly ignite with literally napalmesque consequences. Yet it seemed by the mid-1960s that there was no chance of that wind blowing. The movement under its then leader Cathal Goulding had gone over to a policy of non-violent involvement in left-wing activities of all sorts, from strikes to disputes over riparian rights to protest on housing conditions or against multi-national investment. It became markedly Marxist in character and was greatly influenced by a young Trinity College lecturer, computer scientist and Marxist, Roy Johnston.

The movement aimed at uniting Protestant and Catholic workers as a first essential to the establishment of an All Ireland socialist republic. An excellent vehicle for the achievement of such aims appeared to be a Civil Rights Association. The proposal to found such a body came at a meeting of interested parties held at Maghera, Co. Down, in the home of Mr. Kevin Agnew, a leading figure in local Republican affairs in August of 1966—appropriately enough the year of the fiftieth anniversary of the 1916 Rising. Although the IRA backed the new Civil Rights movement wholeheartedly, there was nothing overtly or even covertly revolutionary about either the support or its objectives.

The aim was purely and simply to redress Catholic grievances within the system.

Symbolically and prophetically, the first Civil Rights activity to capture attention was a sit-in at Caledon, Co. Tyrone, led by Austin Currie. He was drawing attention to the fact that, as was customary, a Council house had been allocated to a Protestant over the heads of a long waiting list of Catholics. Some of these had over a dozen children, but the house had gone to the eighteen-year-old unmarried secretary of a prominent local Orangeman.

The injustices suffered by Catholics were such that it is neither unfair nor inaccurate to say that the Catholics in Northern Ireland received the sanctions of the law but not its protections. This is not a history of the period, simply an account of the part played by prisons in the physical force movement generally, with specific reference to explaining the H Block situation. Suffice it, therefore, to say that apart from the fact that the North's very Parliament had a built-in Unionist majority, prejudice against Catholics existed at every level of Northern society. They were discriminated against in jobs and in housing, and in local government where plural voting existed based on a property franchise. Not alone was the allocation of housing unfair; the employment of Protestants in the public service so far outweighed that of Catholics as to be ludicrous. Worse still—the electoral boundaries were so gerrymandered as to guarantee that despite their higher birth rate, the Catholics would stay penned up in areas of electoral weakness. This gerrymandering did not operate for the constituencies returning MPs to Westminster. There, the size of the Protestant majority in the artificially truncated "Province" naturally produced a Unionist landslide every time. The Stormont and local government divisions, however, were scandalously mutilated.

To take but two examples, Fermanagh, where the Catholic electorate outnumbered the Protestant by roughly 29,000 votes to 23,000, was so carved up as to return two Protestant seats to one Catholic. The case of Derry was even worse. A population of 36,000 Catholics and only 17,000 Protestants managed to return a Protestant majority.

But when the Civil Rights Association movement began to

attack these inequities, it was not the IRA which gave the Civil Rights Association its enormous success but a circumstance which no one in political circles anticipated. This was the effect of British education policy which through being extended to Northern Ireland meant that for the first time in the history of the Northern statelet, the Unionist hegemony was being challenged by articulate, politicised opponents who captured the attention of the world's media by marching not to the customary nationalist airs, but to the tune of "We Shall Overcome." Martin Luther King and the American Civil Rights experience seemed for once to exert a greater influence over Northern Ireland Catholic sentiment than that of Terence McSwiney or Tom Clarke.

But it was not to be. Orange atavism reacted with such intensity to the marches and demonstrations that by August 1969 the situation had become dangerously inflamed. It was not a question of securing justice for Catholics but of preventing sectarian warfare engulfing all Ireland. British troops entered the Bogside area of Derry to relieve the beleaguered Catholics, who had been using barricades, stones and petrol bombs to re-enact a modern version of the siege of Derry, only this time in reverse. The Catholics were fighting to keep the Protestants out, in the persona of the hated RUC and B Specials. And in Belfast the troops moved in that month also to end days of rioting and bloodshed that drove hundreds of Catholic families from their homes and in one instance—that of Bombay Street adjoining the Protestant Shankill Road—burned out an entire street of houses.

British public opinion was suitably appalled and every form of commission was set up, politicians were sent over and civil servants were instructed to search out and cure whatever canker it was that was eating into the heart of this nondescript, remote, unfashionable part of the United Kingdom.

An absolute spate of reports ensued (1) analysing, this, as in the case of the Scarman Report into the causes of the August rioting, (2) reforming that as in the case of the MacCrory Commission with Local Government and (3) abolishing the other thing as in the Hunt

Report which administered the coup de grace to the B Specials. On top of all this, emerging out of the Civil Rights struggle, articulate Catholic politicians such as Austin Currie, John Hume, Gerry Fitt, so outclassed their lumbering, not-quite-top-drawer-squire-type Unionist opponents on television and in interviews that if media coverage alone could have worked the oracle the Unionist cause would have sunk without a trace.

But sink it did not. Centuries of religious warfare, of discrimination and Loyalist supremacy against, as they saw it, traitorous, treacherous Fenians who sought only to thrust them under the mantle of the Pope and "the Hells prepared by Rome" (as Catholic majority rule was termed in a celebrated polemical poem by Rudyard Kipling) could not be easily set aside. Kipling's poem was written at the time of the Orangemen's great act of defiance in 1912 when they ran in the guns of Larne that frustrated the Asquith administration's efforts to introduce Home Rule to Ireland and thus end the "Irish issue" once and for all. Certainly had Home Rule been introduced then, on the eve of the Great War, there would not have been a 1916 and the subsequent history of Ireland would have been a different and possibly a happier one.

Like the blacks of America at the same period, the Catholics of Northern Ireland marched faster and in ever increasing numbers demanding "Freedom Now." But so did ancestral Ulster Protestantism, to the stern echo of the old cry of "not an inch." Starting in the mid-sixties, a militant and sometimes lethal Protestant extremism had begun to reassert itself. This was partially in response to the visit of the South's Prime Minister Seán Lemass who officially visited the North's Premier, the liberal Captain Terence O'Neill in 1965. He was the first Southern Prime Minister to do so and had thereby to all intents and purposes conferred a *de jure* status on an administration to which the South at best gave a grudging *de facto* acquiescence. O'Neill reciprocated by coming to Dublin, and hardline Protestants were outraged. In the dark labyrinthine ghetto streets of the Shankill Road and the Sandy Row, Gusty Spence and his cohorts recreated the Ulster Volunteer Force that had once been patronised

by Earls and industrialists in the days of the Home Rule crisis, when
the Tory interest in overthrowing Liberal political power in England
intertwined with that of the bigoted burghers of Belfast. Now the
Organisation was to be a thing of squalid sectarian assassination.

In fact one of Terence O'Neill's first chores, on returning from
the ceremonies commemorating the slaughters of the Somme—in
which North of Ireland Protestants shed a river of blood for the King
of England and that "freedom of religion" that somehow always in
practice seemed to work out denying basic freedoms such as land, a
job, a house to their Catholic fellow-citizens—was to proscribe and
outlaw the UVF. Gusty Spence ultimately found his way into jail for
the murder of a Catholic barman. But the subterranean poison continued to seep through Northern society. A series of explosions blew
Terence O'Neill out of office. (It is noteworthy that along with the
first murder[1] and first explosion[2] of the present wave of violence,
Protestant extremists also had the dubious distinction of killing the
first policeman, Constable Arbuckle, who died after a riot on the
Shankill Road on October 11, 1969.)

But while the subterranean ones went their deadly way, the
public face of ultra-Unionism also turned dark and apocalyptic. The
Reverend Ian Kyle Paisley rose through the ranks of what, for want
of a better term, might be called "Constitutional Protestantism" on
a wave of Bible-thumping Orange oratory that crashed against every
reform, every step aimed at Catholic betterment, every gesture of
reconciliation towards the South, every kind of ecumenism. The
angry Orange tide of Paisleyism drowned the political aspirations
first of O'Neill, then of Major Chichester-Clarke, his cousin, who
succeeded him. Brian Faulkner, who followed as Prime Minister of
Stormont, finally splintered the Unionist monolith to such an extent
that the once solid phalanx of Unionism was split between the Official Unionist Party, the Democratic Unionist Party (Paisley's), and
later the Progressive Unionist Party and the Ulster Democratic Party
besides the Orange Order, the Ulster Defence Association and a
host of other lesser and generally illegal bodies such as the Ulster
Freedom Fighters, the Red Hand Commandos, Tara, and of course

the Ulster Volunteer Force. In a very real sense Paisley has been of immense value in furthering IRA objectives. He has done more damage to Protestant hegemony than they ever hoped to do.

In fact every party involved in the 1969 crisis had a more or less serious split. Whilst the Unionist traumas were the most obvious, the leading Southern political party, Fianna Fáil, also underwent fissures as it became a matter of acting on, rather than just saluting, the party's totem. (Fianna Fáil still observe the annual commemoration of Easter week 1916 and lay wreaths on Wolfe Tone's grave at Bodenstown on his anniversary—but they travel to Bodenstown on the morning of the anniversary, whereas the IRA come in the afternoon.)

In 1970, several leading political figures in Fianna Fáil were prosecuted unsuccessfully on charges of gun-running. One of them, Finance Minister Charles J. Haughey, later became the Taoiseach (Prime Minister). Another, Neil Blaney, was a Euro-Deputy and an independent member of the Dáil. Another minister, Kevin Boland, resigned from the government because he felt that Dublin was not taking a sufficiently strong line to protect the Northern Catholics. Boland, a son of Gerald Boland, the strongman of Fianna Fáil who incurred the opprobrium of crushing the IRA for a time, was not acting illogically *vis-à-vis* his father. The wartime IRA had, as his father saw it, been jeopardising their people's sovereignty and safety by their actions. In 1969 Fianna Fáil was jeopardising the safety of their people, the Catholics of Northern Ireland, by their inactivity. Out of such seeming non sequiturs, an understanding of Ireland's politics was born.

Jack Lynch, then Prime Minister, survived the trauma of the Arms Crisis to go on leading the party for another ten years. Ireland (south), it seemed, wanted tranquillity. Ireland (north), however, wanted redress.

I feel it is worth digressing here for a moment to say that the question of Fianna Fáil's overt appeal to Nationalist sentiment, and the private commitment or lack of it on the part of some of the party's membership to the party's ancestral ideals, raises a very important issue which does have a bearing on the whole Northern question—

and obviously on H Block—what I would term the consciousness of being Irish.

This can all too easily be derided or misinterpreted. For instance, a few weeks after he had become Prime Minister of the Republic (in large part because of the Northern issue) Charles Haughey delivered his keynote address to the Fianna Fáil Ard Fheis (Annual Conference). A week after the speech the *Economist* (on February 23, 1980) quoted an unnamed Whitehall mandarin as dismissing Haughey's statement that "Northern Ireland is a failure as a political entity" with a contemptuous "Well, he would. Wouldn't he?" According to the *Economist*,

> The speech was intended for consumption by members of a party whose primary demand was the unification of Ireland and which caused the former Prime Minister, Jack Lynch, to resign last December because he seemed to have given away too much to Mrs. Thatcher on policing the border.

It further went on to criticise Haughey for the "real disservice" he did to peace in Ulster by disparaging the efforts being made at the Constitutional Conference then taking place under the chairmanship of Humphrey Atkins, the Northern Ireland Secretary. However, even the *Economist* acknowledged that the Conference was not likely to get anywhere (it didn't). Nor did its parallel conference, at which the question of an Irish dimension was raised; it could not be raised at the Conference proper because Paisley would not allow it. But with unconscious and highly significant arrogance the *Economist* pointed out a major benefit which it clearly thought Mr. Haughey should acknowledge: the fact that the setting up of the conference had done what it was designed to do, which was to convince American opinion that something substantive was taking place even though it wasn't.

Said the *Economist*, "the conference and its parallel have already yielded one great benefit: the annihilation of Ireland as an issue in the American Presidential election."

It didn't seem to dawn either on the journalists or on the anonymous Whitehall briefer that not alone was Mr. Haughey being quite
factual in his Ard Fheis speech in which he said that Northern Ireland was *the* political problem facing the country, he was also voic-
ing the genuinely held feeling of the majority of Southern Irish
opinion that after a decade of Northern bloodshed the issue would
just have to be resolved. And that Britain had the primary responsibility for so doing. The said public opinion would be outraged at the
notion that it should subscribe to a cosmetic exercise in tackling the
problem, merely to keep it from being raised by American presidential candidates, and would feel that the more such influences could
be brought to bear, the better for all concerned.

The fact which must be recognised and accepted is that a very
wide spectrum of Irish opinion who would have neither hand, act, nor
part in IRA violence were nonetheless increasingly annoyed that their
entire historical, economic and cultural development should so con-
tinuously and so contemptuously be dismissed by British decision
takers as if it were a mindless, atavistic nationalism. Nationalism may
seem atavistic to the British—who have been expelled from many
parts of the globe because of it—but, most particularly where Ireland
was concerned, it cannot be either derided or shunned as though it
were an ulceration, like Hitler's Wagnerian national-socialism.

To return, however, to the crisis of 1969: I have met people in
Belfast who stood along the Falls Road, during the tense nights of
August waiting to see if the Irish Army were coming. Lynch had
gone on television during the height of the August rioting to say that
the Irish government could not stand by during these momentous
events, and that he was moving field hospitals to the border to cope
with the refugees who might not want to take their injuries to hospitals run under Unionist aegis. The "field hospitals" were taken to
mean combat units by both Protestant and Catholics, and fears and
hopes soared even higher.

But Lynch had literally meant field hospitals. No troops
arrived, and neither did the IRA, to which Cathal Goulding had
appointed his lone intellectual, Roy Johnston, as educational com-

missar. The letters IRA, a constant decoration of walls in the Catholic and nationalist ghettos of Belfast and the other Northern towns— were re-written to read "Irish Ran Away" and long-simmering tensions within the IRA were heightened, leading to a split and the creation of the Provisional IRA.

The split became public knowledge after the IRA Army Council voted secretly in December of 1969 to contest elections, recognising the hitherto anathematised Dublin and Belfast parliaments and accepting partition as a fact of life. In January 1970, however, there was a walkout from the annual Ard Fheis of Sinn Féin, the legal political arm of the IRA, held in the Intercontinental Hotel, Dublin. The dissidents withdrew to the Kevin Barry Hall,[3] Parnell Square. Gaining support from the events of 1969, they formed the Provisional Caretaker Executive of Sinn Féin while the Goulding faction stayed on as "Official" Sinn Féin. Hence the terms Provisionals and Officials were coined. The Provisionals, also known as "Provies," use pins to affix the Easter lily badges commemorating 1916, which both wings sell at Easter, so that the Provisionals were sometimes also known as "pinheads" and the Officials, who use gum, were known as "stickies" or "sticks."

It became evident as the Provisionals began to organise that if the Fifties campaign had been a military flop, still, combined with the resulting prison experience, it had provided the leaders for the next round in the generation to generation cycle of IRA violence. Seán MacStiofáin, with a term in English prisons behind him for a bungled arms raid, emerged as Chief-of-Staff. Of significance to the future would be the fact that some of his prison companions were EOKA guerrillas from the Cyprus campaign. The next campaign would owe more to their harsh tactics and to those of Kenya, Aden and Palestine than it would to the chivalrous years of the 1950s when, for instance, before the Brookeborough ambush of 1956, in which two IRA men were killed and amongst others Daithí O Conaill was wounded, IRA men warned women and children—and *inter alia* their foes—to keep off the streets before the unsuccessful barracks attack.

Other emerging leaders included O Conaill, Ruairí O Brádaigh
and Joe Cahill. But these would have had very little in the way of
public support to emerge to, nor would the Orange and Paisleyite fer-
ment have had anything like the force they had if the British government had continued on its largely even-handed and reformist course,
reigning in its army and impressing Catholic opinion that the barrage
of commissions and investigations it had set up were genuine evidence of a desire for real, lasting change which would not be delayed
or put off by Unionist intransigence.

However, in June of 1970, while the Provisionals were still re-
organising and the fires of Irish nationalism were still only dull red
coals glowing weakly, an event occurred in England which was to
change Irish history drastically. The Labour government fell and the
Conservatives were returned. The Conservative and Unionist Party
was the traditional ally of Ulster Protestantism, "playing the Orange
card" in Ulster whenever it can be of electoral benefit in Westminster.

By 1970 the Conservatives were a very long way from the days
when Randolph Churchill first played the Orange card to frustrate
Gladstone's Home Rule Bill of 1886 by declaring that "Ulster would
fight and Ulster would be right." Later, on the eve of the Great War,
by opposing Home Rule and encouraging Protestant militancy in
Ulster the Tories had won the advantage in the House of Commons
at Asquith's expense. But even in 1970 there was still that interlocking of relationships between North of Ireland and British landed and
commercial interests, of contact between Northern Irish peers with
their English counterparts, of contact in the higher civil service and
in the army, and of course the fact that the Unionist candidates
returned to Westminster (generally winning about ten seats) customarily vote Tory, all adding up to a tendency to see the situation in
Unionist terms.

Accordingly, despite the fact that the resistance to reform and
the major acts of violence were coming from the Protestant side, one
of the Tories' first acts, within two weeks of Mr. Heath taking office,
was to give the army its head, by declaring a curfew of the Catholic
Falls Road area which was sealed off and ransacked for arms. No

searches took place in the Shankill area, although Hansard noted at the time that the Protestants held 107,000 licensed weapons. Yet on the Falls, homes were wrecked, CS gas poured into the streets and houses, affecting young and old alike, three civilians were killed, and fifteen soldiers and sixty civilians injured. A trivial number of arms, held by Republican sympathisers and by people who just wanted protection in case the Orange mobs came back to complete their burnings, were seized. The "Rape of the Falls" as it became known was compounded by two further unfortunate factors. One was the sectarianism of some of the Scottish troops involved in the search, who mocked at holy pictures and in some cases broke statues and crucifixes, further strengthening the local aversion to "their" army, "their" law and "their" order. The following day (the search lasted from July 3 to July 5 during which, apart from a two hour interval, no one was allowed to leave their homes, which in some cases ran out of food) this impression was heightened by the army taking two Unionist ministers through the area in an army vehicle on a triumphalist guided tour.

In savage contrast to all this "official" attention, the RUC had collectively disappeared from the Falls area prior to the burning of August 1969, acting on what was clearly prearrangement. The present army brutality, and the former RUC collusion with the forces which oppressed Catholics for so long, was so offensive to the ghetto people that the effect was exactly as though someone had gone to the IRA spark and thrown a bucket of petrol over it. The dull red coals of nationalism became a conflagration, at least in terms of IRA recruitment in the Belfast area.

The Falls Road curfew never received the attention it should have in the British media, which instead largely concentrated on the "effrontery" of Dr. Paddy Hillery, the South's Minister for Foreign Affairs (later President) for poking his nose into what was not his business by touring the area to see for himself what had happened.

But the strength which the IRA derived from the Falls blunder, which inevitably brought the IRA into more abrasive contact with the army and made the army's retaliatory efforts bear all the more seriously on the civilian population, brought on a second, and even more catastrophic blunder, which *inter alia* led eventually to the appalling impasse of the H Blocks. As the situation deteriorated— though the deterioration should be kept in perspective in relation to what was to occur later in the decade by remembering that the first British soldier to be shot by the IRA, Ensign Curtis, did not die until February of 1971—the Unionist Prime Minister, Brian Faulkner, pressed strongly for the use of a remedy he had used effectively to deal with the 1950s IRA campaign internment.

Incredibly, in view of the Orange opposition to reform and the effects of the Falls Curfew, he got his way and internment was introduced on August 9, 1971. The blow fell solely on Catholics. Not one Protestant was "lifted" and through a combination of IRA preparedness and out-of-date information from the RUC Special Branch, many of those picked up had nothing to do with the IRA at all.

During the days after internment, statements were made to justify its use by security chiefs and by Brian Faulkner, claiming that it had "exposed the gunmen" and that seventy per cent of those sought had been arrested. Said the security chiefs, "a high proportion of the IRA leadership were seized."

In fact, out of the three-hundred-plus internees, only about sixty had any connection with the IRA. No impact was made on the leadership, and the RUC Special Branch intelligence was so faulty that those arrested included the Chairman of the Northern Ireland Civil Rights Association, Mr. Ivan Barr. Over a third of those arrested were quietly set free within a month. But the injustice of the swoops, the methods used during and after them and the Catholic reaction overall meant that nothing else about the issue stayed quiet.

To get rid of the embarrassment, while still trying to benefit from the effects of internment, the British introduced a Detention of Terrorists Order. The Commissioners would hear the cases of detainees, but would sit in private and would not be bound by the Rules of Evidence. Another cosmetic change was to alter the name of the internment camp from Long Kesh camp to the Maze Prison. All these legislative changes were facilitated by the existence in

Northern Ireland of the Special Powers Act, a stricter version of the
South's Offences Against the State Act, which while ostensibly
directed solely against the IRA and terrorism, in effect means—
where the ghetto Catholics were concerned anyhow—martial law in
all but name.

The entire Catholic population of the North felt itself attacked
and responded with every known form of civil disobedience, from
boycotting parliament to not paying rent, rates, gas or electricity
bills. The IRA, far from being crushed, were not even dented and put
on massive attacks to prove it. Joe Cahill, in particular, captured
world attention by staging a press conference in the heart of the Falls
a few days after the supposedly successful swoop.

The British Prime Minister Ted Heath was appalled at what had
happened. The following March, Stormont fell. Internment, however,
remained a feature of Northern life and with it concomitant pieces of
unsavouriness such as the use of torture by the security forces.
Between IRA and Loyalist violence there were a total of 1,382 explosions and an astronomical 10,628 shootings that year.

After the internment blunder the Provisionals—who had previously used bombs or weapons only when attempts were made to
seize their weapons or when troops or civilians clashed—went over
to a new policy of not alone retaliation against the army and the
Unionist government it backed, but to a war aimed at driving out the
British and destroying that government, using youthful working class
recruits for whom British military strategists, early on, developed a
misplaced contempt.

The Provisionals' tactics changed from one plane of deadliness
to another—from attacks on barracks and military posts, they
stepped up their economic warfare. The economic attacks were
aimed simply at destroying the Northern economy. It began with old
buildings near the centre of the city, because they collapsed easily
and made a powerful impression on the population. For instance,
their first car bomb went off on the Queen's Bridge in Belfast, traditionally used by tens of thousands of Protestants going to work each
day. Next on the list came businesses with valuable items such as

cars, television sets, electrical equipment, shops selling inflammable material like paints or plastic materials, and there were occasional "spectaculars" like the destruction of the *Daily Mirror's* million pound plant.

The bombs used were generally carried in duffel bags or holdalls, and held around ten to fifteen pounds of gelignite set off by a battery and clothes-peg fusing system. All too easily set off, in many instances they scored "own goals," prematurely exploding and killing the bombers. Another frequent source of casualty was the youthful volunteers' utter unfamiliarity with firearms. Teenage gunmen sometimes thought that when they had acquired a revolver they were then equipped to take on an armoured car—with often fatal results. Training in fire-power and the use of cover eventually rectified this defect.

As the IRA began attracting more technologically-minded supporters, anti-handling devices were fitted to these and the fusing system was improved. Gelignite became harder to get—the Republic in particular tightened up its gelignite controls—with the result that the IRA started to make its own bombs. The first car bombs—they began to go off towards the end of December 1971—used a mixture of potassium nitrate, sugar and diesel oil; others were made from ammonium nitrate and nitro-benzene, obtainable by blending a fertiliser and a cleansing agent; battery acid, washing soda and even Epsom salts were also used.

The Army response to this was a greatly improved use of computers and a reliance on the theories of Brigadier Frank Kitson, Britain's top counter-insurgency expert, and General Richard Clutterbuck. These two gentlemen set great store on the use of intelligence gathering as a military arm, but along with their psy-war approach the army also used heavyhanded search and arrest procedures, quartering off blocks of houses and arresting all the males in them, with resultant fisticuffs all along the line so that even anti-IRA populations were alienated. However, for the purposes of our story, by 1975–76 these tactics had begun to pay off.

All these operations took place under the aegis of the Special Powers Act whereby failure to answer questions results in one being in grave trouble—even if one had been unjustly beaten in the process. It was and is standard practice for males, particularly young males in the ghettos, to be picked up as a matter of routine, beaten and an effort made to terrorise them.[4] Older Republican suspects even in Castlereagh were generally interrogated by more subtle methods. After a shooting or bombing incident in particular it was standard practice for all the young males in a district to be put up against the wall and beaten or maltreated. Sometimes as a result of such actions they agreed to spy for the army and were thus put at risk by both sides, one blackmailing them into supplying information on the threat of beatings or prison, the other viewing them as traitors punishable by death.

The more physical softening-up process was carried out by interrogators either from the army Special Investigation Branch or the military police, both of whom served two years in the Province and thus had more knowledge than the average four-month stay soldier. These interrogators were assisted by RUC Special Branch men and by the SAS—sometimes at special interrogation centres which the SAS themselves run.

By 1980, not one member of the security forces had ever been imprisoned for either torture, causing loss of life, or any of the abuses of the "conveyor-belt" system, which form the daily coinage of "law and order," North of Ireland style.

1. That of a Catholic barman, John Scullion, who died on June 11, 1966, from wounds received in a stabbing on May 27. Another barman, Peter Ward, was murdered on June 28. Gusty Spence the UVF founder served a life sentence in Long Kesh for the murder.
2. The Silent Valley Reservoir in the Mourne Mountains and an electric installation at Kylemore, Co. Armagh, intended as a link in a joint scheme with the Republic, were blown up on April 29, 1969.
3. Called after a young man executed by the British during the post 1916 Anglo-Irish war.
4. This policy explains the experiences of Seán Carney described in Chapter 8.

CHAPTER 4
Cloak and Dagger

After internment, the IRA's phase of infliction was back with a vengeance. However, the endurance factor came back also with about equal force—prison, as we have seen, was never very far away from IRA considerations. As bombings, killings, sectarian assassinations, knee-cappings and every known form of mayhem multiplied, the IRA leadership gave a Press Conference in Derry on June 14, 1972. Those present included Seán MacStiofáin, Martin McGuinness, Seamus Twomey, and Daithí O Conaill. They invited the Conservative Secretary of State for Northern Ireland, Mr. William Whitelaw, to visit Free Derry, at the time an IRA no-go area for the security forces, and offered a suspension of hostilities to discuss peace proposals. Whitelaw immediately rejected their proposal, apparently without considering it, and Merlyn Rees, who was to succeed Whitelaw when Labour gained power, took fright when he heard of the Press Conference and left Derry precipitously lest it be thought he was involved in negotiations with the paramilitaries. In fact Whitelaw had met Loyalist paramilitaries not long before. Masked UDA men had been discovered arriving at Stormont Castle to meet the Secretary of State, much to Whitelaw's consternation—he would have liked the cloaks and daggers to remain out of sight. He differentiated, however, between talking to the Loyalists and Provisional IRA by saying that he would not talk to anyone who was shooting soldiers.

The IRA were not the only people who were disturbed at his quick rejection. Within the ranks of the SDLP, John Hume felt that the IRA's offer merited more considered examination and he approached the IRA to enquire whether he could explore further. The IRA accepted his overtures and Hume, who couldn't be seen publicly talking to Whitelaw because the SDLP at the time were committed to a policy of no talks whilst internment lasted, contacted Whitelaw privately.

Special Category was Conceded

Whitelaw agreed off the record that he had been too precipitous over the IRA when they offered him a bloodstained olive branch, and said that he would talk to Hume and to Paddy Devlin. Actual face-to-face talks with the IRA were not ruled out but they would have to be held in secret.

The Provisionals agreed to this but stipulated as a precondition for talks that political status for the IRA prisoners then in jail would have to be conceded, and that they wanted Gerry Adams, one of their principal supporters, freed. These demands were matters of extreme delicacy because the IRA prisoners in Crumlin Road jail were at the time on hunger strike in order to gain political status, and the release of a prominent Republican like Gerry Adams was obviously going to infuriate both Unionist and back bench Conservative opinion. The situation with the hunger strikers, moreover, was very grave.

Firstly, Billy McKee and Proinsias MacArt, the leaders of the hunger strikers, were generally reckoned within Republican circles—and the belief was not necessarily confined to Republican circles only—to have been framed. They were sentenced to three years' imprisonment on charges connected with the finding of a revolver in a car close to the scene of their arrest. Both men denied any connection with the revolver, but the judge accepted the evidence of the Scotland Yard detective who had been brought over especially to deal with the arrest and charging.

McKee and MacArt are part of the folk history of Belfast Republicanism, McKee having been badly shot up during the defence of Saint Matthew's Church in 1970 when but for his armed presence and that of a handful of comrades the church would have been burned down.

At the time of the peace feelers a rumour had swept the Catholic ghettos off the Falls Road that McKee was dead or dying, and tension soared. There was a spate of hijacking and stoning and every indication that if the rumour should be borne out then a widespread conflagration would ensue.

The situation was accordingly one of the utmost delicacy. Hume and Devlin flew to London for talks and then came back to Ireland via Dublin to attend a Labour Party function (the SDLP was affiliated to the Irish Labour Party). At the function the redoubtable Dr. Conor Cruise O'Brien, who apparently knew something was in the wind, went to great lengths to find out what was happening and was considerably affronted at being told nothing. On the Friday of that week, Hume conveyed word to the Provisional IRA through Daithí O Conaill that the British had agreed to the Provisionals' terms. O Conaill before accepting asked to be allowed to talk to MacArt in prison on the telephone. McKee was in hospital weakened by the after effects of his wounds and the toll of the strike. O Conaill's request to talk to MacArt was refused but Hume was allowed to speak to him and tell him what was afoot.

A "Special Category" status was conceded to the Republican prisoners and later the benefits were conferred on Loyalists also. What this meant in practice and what the H Block prisoners then wanted restored to them was covered by the following five points:

1. The right to wear their own clothes.

2. The right to abstain from penal labour.

3. The right to free association. (This didn't mean movement from cell to cell but freedom of association within their own prison area.)

4. The right to educational and recreational activities in conjunction with the prison authorities.

5. Remission restored.

The restoration of remission meant that prisoners who had lost their remission through going on the H Block protest would have their sentences treated as though they had been on good behaviour for the duration of the sentence, which could have the effect of cutting their term in prison by fifty per cent, a not inconsiderable consideration. The hunger strike ended. Adams was released and with O Conaill he met Whitelaw and his people to agree to terms for a truce. The terms were as follows:

> Operations were to cease on either side.
> The IRA were to enjoy freedom of movement on the streets, as were the British.
> The IRA were given the right to bear arms.
> An end was agreed to searches of cars or houses and in particular to the P searches (Personal searches by army patrols carried out at random on civilians).

A major element in the Truce was the talks, which were to be held in London between the Provisional IRA and Whitelaw, face to face. This of course was a momentous breakthrough for the Provisional IRA—the first time that the IRA had negotiated with British statesmen since the time of Michael Collins in the Treaty negotiations. There was a division of opinion on the British side, however, as to the wisdom of these talks. The military, and in particular the GOC Northern Ireland, General Harry Tuzo, received the news with outrage, and the demeanour of some of the civil servants with whom the Provisionals had dealings was not exactly welcoming either. However, after negotiations at Cheyne Walk, Chelsea, in a house owned by a junior minister in Whitelaw's cabinet, Paul Channon, a truce was formally agreed to.

Alas, the truce was short-lived. It was a time of sectarian assassination, and of apparent army collusion with the UDA. Whitelaw had talked to the IRA about the sectarian killings and said if necessary he would put a British soldier outside the home of every Catholic in danger. But Major General Ford, known as Commander

Land Forces, (who was less than popular with Catholics since Bloody Sunday when forces under his command shot down unarmed Catholics, killing thirteen of them) met and negotiated with the UDA leader Tommy Herron on July 3, 1972, at Ainsworth Avenue, Belfast, in an army Saracen, after a confrontation between the army and the UDA. The Army behaved with very considerably more circumspection towards the UDA than towards the Catholics demonstrating against internment in Derry on Bloody Sunday.

Not alone did they back down from confronting the UDA; in fact Ford and Herron actually agreed to joint patrols between the army and the UDA. But any effort by the IRA, or even by Catholics unconnected with the IRA, to organise vigilante patrols of their areas to guard against sectarian assassination was prohibited.

It was against this background that the famous Lenadoon incident as it became known blew up. Lenadoon, an area of Andersonstown, had formerly been occupied by Protestants, who, as sectarian passions mounted, had left the Catholic Andersonstown and moved to Protestant districts. There were sixteen houses involved standing empty until the Northern Ireland Housing Executive allocated them to homeless Catholics. The UDA moved into twelve of these to prevent the Catholics getting them. The new lawful tenants then banded together and attempted forcibly to occupy their homes. A confrontation appeared inevitable but the IRA defused it by turning back the tenants. Crowds gathered and the army formed a cordon between the Catholics and the Protestants. Two IRA volunteers were arrested along with a number of Catholic would-be tenants.

The arrest of the volunteers was of course a contravention of the truce terms and Seamus Twomey, then Chief of Staff of the IRA, protested to the British via Seamus Loughran. The protest had no effect and Twomey himself set off to Andersonstown but was stopped by an army patrol and hauled out of his car, thereby putting a further breach in the dyke of the truce. O Conaill got on to the British by telephone and spoke to a senior civil servant, David Steele, who told him that the position from the British side was that the IRA were egging on the crowds to attack the army and that Seamus

Twomey was a "very hot-tempered man who was causing problems." Steele argued that the army were in charge and Twomey had no locus standi in the affair. O Conaill then managed to get through to Whitelaw himself in Cumberland, but Whitelaw's reply was that he was telling him an opposite version of what was happening to the one he was receiving from his own side.

"The army tell me that you were egging the crowds on," he said. Television cameras were at the time filming footage of an army Saracen deliberately ramming lorries piled high with the Catholic furniture. However, Whitelaw said that lie would ring O Conaill within an hour. The call never came and the truce ended.

However, though hostilities resumed outside of the Long Kesh compounds, comparative peace reigned within them through the introduction of Special Category status—conceded not as a matter of natural justice but solely and wholly for a time because British political thinking hoped that it would encourage a truce on the ground outside the jails. It had nothing whatsoever to do either with concern for the prisoners themselves or the merits or demerits of their demands for special treatment but was given as a matter of expediency. It was taken off them for the same reason. The H Block protest was aimed at restoring that status, not at creating a fresh situation or securing an amnesty.

Diplock and the Conveyor Belt

How "Special Category" came to be taken from the IRA in the first place is a question which logically arises here. To understand this it is necessary to understand something of the growth of the IRA-Army struggle and the methods used by both sides. The escalation of this struggle and the many faceted forms it took disposes, I think, of much of the force of the argument that "H Block" was simply a matter of self-inflicted hardship aimed at securing IRA propaganda. The IRA would of course make use of any situation from which it can derive propaganda, but the H Block situation evolved in a more complex way than a mere desire for publicity, and came as unexpectedly and in some ways as embarrassingly to the IRA as it did to the authorities, because the Organisation was just not geared to profit from the issue.

Now at the risk of seeming to point out the obvious I should like at this stage to remind readers that the IRA prisoners were not charged with crimes such as robbing orchards or money boxes. The Provisional IRA numbers among its ranks some of the toughest, most ruthless guerrilla fighters the world has ever seen.

The taking of life, intimidation, bank robbery, kneecappings, bombings were all part of their frequently used tactics. No one knew this better than the British who by the end of 1972 were engaged in a full scale war against the Organisation. One of the factors which they found greatly hampering was that of intimidation, which meant that witnesses in cases involving IRA men were very reluctant to give evidence. Often the reluctance was based on loyalty and the basic Irish horror of being branded an "informer," as much as on fear; to the British the results were still the same. They weren't getting the men they wanted in the quantities they needed to cripple the IRA, consequently, the truce approach and the bait of Special Category having failed, something else was tried. A commission under the Chairmanship of Lord Diplock was set up to investigate

> what arrangements for the administration of justice in
> Northern Ireland could be made in order to deal more
> effectively with terrorist organisations by bringing to
> book, otherwise than by internment by the Executive,
> individuals involved in terrorist activities, particularly
> those who plan and direct, but do not necessarily take
> part in, terrorist acts and to make recommendations.

The Diplock Report, which was presented on December 20, 1972, to Parliament and accepted, said:

> We are thus driven inescapably to the conclusion that
> until the current terrorism by the extremist organisations

of both factions in Northern Ireland can be eradicated, there will continue to be some dangerous terrorists against whom it will not be possible to obtain convictions by any form of criminal trial which we regard as appropriate to a court of law; and these will include many of those who plan and organise terrorist acts by other members of the Organisation in which they take no firsthand part themselves. We are also driven inescapably to the conclusion that so long as these remain at liberty to operate in Northern Ireland, it will not be possible to find witnesses prepared to testify against them in the criminal courts, except those serving in the army or the police, for whom effective protection can be provided. The dilemma is complete.

The only hope of restoring the efficiency of criminal courts of law in Northern Ireland to deal with terrorist crimes is by using an extra-judicial process to deprive of their ability to operate in Northern Ireland, those terrorists whose activities result in the intimidation of witnesses. With an easily penetrable border to the south and west the only way of doing this is to put them in detention by an executive act and to keep them confined, until they can be released without danger to the public safety and to the administration of criminal justice.

Deprivation of liberty as a result of an extra-judicial process we call "detention," following the nomenclature of The Detention of Terrorists (Northern Ireland) Order, 1972. It does not mean imprisonment at the arbitrary Diktat of the Executive Government, which to many people is a common connotation of the term "internment." We use it to describe depriving a man of his liberty as a result of an investigation of the facts which inculpate the detainee by an impartial person or tribunal by making use of a procedure which, however fair to him, is inappropriate to a court of law because it does not comply with Article 6 of the European Convention.

The report recommended that for so long as the "Emergency" lasted, the type of activities engaged in by terrorists—murder, grievous bodily harm, explosives charges, possession of arms etc.—should be known as scheduled offences and that for these type of offences the following rules should apply:

Trials of scheduled offences should be by a Judge of the High Court, or a County Court Judge, sitting alone with no jury, with the usual rights of appeal.

The armed services should be given power to arrest people suspected of having been involved in, or having information about, offences and detain them for up to four hours in order to establish their identity.

Bail in cases involving a scheduled offence should not be granted except by the High Court and then only if stringent requirements were met.

The onus of proof as to the possession of firearms and explosives should be altered so as to require a person found in certain circumstances to prove on the balance of probabilities that he did not know and had no reason to suspect that arms or explosives were where they were found.

A confession made by the accused should be admissible as evidence in cases involving the scheduled offences unless it was obtained by torture or inhuman or degrading treatment.

A signed written statement made to anyone charged with investigating a scheduled offence should be admissible if the person who made it cannot be produced in court for specific reasons, and the statement contains material which would have been admissible if that person had been present in court to give oral evidence.

The result of the implementation of the Diplock Report was to set up what was known in Northern Ireland as the "conveyor-belt" system. Henceforth, the burden of proof was shifted onto the accused and by 1980 it was accepted that around eighty per cent of convictions arising out of the Troubles were on the basis of confessions. As we shall see, the methods by which these confessions were obtained gave rise to very well-substantiated charges of brutality by the security forces. However, for the moment the Diplock approach seemed to offer a better policy than incurring the opprobrium of internment. As the Diplock Courts were also buttressed with the Detention Order, it did appear that whatever about the difficulty of laying hands on the IRA, once held they would stay held.

Ulsterisation, Criminalisation & Normalisation

But the "conveyor-belt" system had two central in-built defects: (1) Its efficiency, if not its justice, meant that prison numbers went up astronomically, as we shall see, increasing the size and weight of prison as a factor in the troubles; and (2) Special Category Status meant that Britain had an embarrassing number of "political" prisoners to account for before the bar of world public opinion and related to this there was the affront to domestic right-wing and Unionist opinion of reading about, and sometimes seeing on television, "terrorists" with in effect Prisoner of War status holding parades and classes, and maintaining their own system of discipline in the barbed-wire enclosed compounds which had been built at Long Kesh to house the internees. A new look at the problem was required.

After a period of years in which an effort to replace Stormont with a power-sharing executive had failed because of Loyalist opposition, and yet another change of government at Westminster which placed Merlyn Rees in charge of Northern Ireland as Secretary of State, by January of 1975 the Whitehall mandarins who effectively control Northern Ireland policy were toying with a new set of formulae.

These became known as Ulsterisation, Criminalisation and Normalisation. Under "Ulsterisation" the security tasks were to be progressively taken over by the RUC and by the Ulster Defence Regiment which replaced the B Specials. "Criminalisation" meant that no vestige of political status would remain attaching to the IRA or their activities. "Normalisation" meant that the Province should be returned to a normal mode of life as soon as was feasible.

And in the pipeline there was the document that was to provide the fuse that finally set off the H Block situation—Son of Diplock, the Gardiner Report, the report of the committee which under the chairmanship of Lord Gardiner (a former Lord Chancellor) considered, "in the context of civil liberties and human rights, measures to deal with terrorism in Northern Ireland." There were at that stage a total of 1,119 Special Category prisoners and a further 535 detainees.

Meanwhile in another part of the forest, as Whitehall prepared to attempt to lift the struggle onto a new plane, and as the Provisionals carried out a savage bombing and assassination campaign in England, independent of all these activities efforts were afoot to secure a second truce. Set up by the Reverend William Arlow and a group of Protestant clergymen in the town of Feakle, County Clare (in the Republic) where the Provisionals met the churchmen face to face on December 10, 1974, the talks bore tangible fruit with the announcement of a ceasefire truce on February 10, 1975, and the opening of a number of "Incident Centres" under the control of Provisional Sinn Féin with a "hot line" to Stormont, the seat now not of a "parliament" but of the Northern Ireland Office, in order to monitor any breaches of the ceasefire. The "elected representatives" of the various constitutional political parties which litter the North of Ireland political scene were outraged, claiming that this innovation both breached the convention whereby there should be no talks with gunmen, only with the "elected representatives." And worse, it accorded to the gunmen a very useful degree of local political status and control, because the centres could be and were used for advice and welfare purposes and for political propaganda.

Special Category Slipping Away; H Blocks Rising

The Gardiner Report, which stated that its terms of reference included the principle that the North would remain part of the UK, said flatly that the creation of Special Category was a mistake. The report, published on January 30, 1975, also said:

> Although recognising the pressures on those responsible at the time, we have come to the conclusion that the introduction of Special Category Status was a serious mistake . . . It should be made absolutely clear that Special Category prisoners can expect no amnesty and would have to serve their sentences. . . we recommend that the earliest practicable opportunity should be taken to end the Special Category.

The Provisionals' representatives who were negotiating with the British at the time told them that any tampering with Special Category would be resisted to the utmost by every means possible, including the shooting of warders, and the talks went on—reaching such a point of significance that the British negotiators managed without actually committing themselves to convince the IRA side that a British troop withdrawal was coming. However, if one was intended it was on the "Ulsterisation" lines only, a distinction and reservation more appreciated by the British side than the IRA because at the same time the British were taking active steps to implement Lord Gardiner's most important and far-reaching report. At the time its importance was very much obscured because the public debate tended to centre on his buck-passing recommendation concerning the use of internment—that a decision to end or retain should be a matter for the government. Internment went later that year, but in name only because Detention remained, as did the "conveyor-belt" system plus an additional refinement which was in effect internment by another name, the use of very lengthy remand periods before prisoners were brought to trial and still longer before sentence.

But Lord Gardiner had made another vitally important recommendation—he advocated the building of the H Blocks. Plans were afoot to build new prison accommodation. He advocated that these be accelerated.

The prison population had risen fourfold from the year after the Civil Rights movement became really active in 1968, when there were only 727 prisoners in Northern Ireland. By the time Gardiner made his investigation there were 2,848. The Gardiner Report gave its reasons why these greatly inflated totals should be incarcerated in a cellular system rather than a compound one and described the North of Ireland prison system as it stood. The description was both accurate and illuminating:

> The prison system in Northern Ireland has a most
> important role to play in the maintenance of law and
> order. We do not believe that it is fulfilling that role ade-
> quately at present and to be blunt, we were appalled at
> certain aspects of the prison situation.
>
> Prior to 1968 Northern Ireland had only one
> prison for men, the Crumlin Road Prison built over
> 100 years ago in the middle of Belfast, and Armagh
> prison for women, of similar age. With detention came
> the emergency building of a temporary prison at Long
> Kesh, now the Maze Prison, with accommodation in
> huts in large compounds rather than in individual
> cells; subsequently a further temporary prison of a
> similar type was built at Magilligan. The result is that
> seventy-one per cent of male prisoners, 1,881 out of a
> total of 2,648, are now in temporary prisons of the

compound type rather than in conventional cellular
accommodation.

Prisons of the compound type, each compound
holding up to ninety prisoners, are thoroughly unsatisfac-
tory from every point of view; their major disadvantage
is that there is virtually a total loss of disciplinary control
by the prison authorities inside the compounds . . . The
layout and construction of the compounds make close
and continued supervision impossible.

In category status this has meant that any convicted criminal sentenced to more than nine months'
imprisonment who claims political motivation and who
is acceptable to a compound leader at the Maze or Magilligan Prisons is accorded special status. They are
allowed to wear their own clothes and are not required
to work. They receive more frequent visits than other
prisoners and are allowed food parcels and can spend
their own money in the prison canteen. They are segregated in compounds according to the paramilitary
Organisation to which they claim allegiance, in the
same way as detainees.

They are more likely to emerge with an increased
commitment to terrorism than as reformed citizens. The
special category prisoners regard themselves in much
the same light as detainees, expecting that an amnesty
will result in their not having to serve in full the sentence imposed on them by the courts, and the paramilitary organisations find it easy to encourage this
misunderstanding in the public mind for propaganda
purposes. The result of this is that the sentences passed
in the courts for murder and other serious crimes have
lost much of their deterrent effect.

Through his report, Lord Gardiner intertwined high-sounding
moral considerations (the need for rehabilitation, preventing young

people from being contaminated by older criminals and so on) with security and political considerations. Wire fences surrounding the compounds could easily be breached, prisoners with Special Category Status would be encouraged to think that no matter what crime they had committed, amnesty was just around the corner.

These arguments, which Lord Gardiner himself may have actually believed, for all we know, are in fact the arguments put forward by the Unionists, the security forces and tidy minded folk who for reasons of administrative convenience like things compartmentalised—not to say cellular! In fact most IRA prisoners generally expect that they won't serve their full sentences anyhow but would be released when whatever campaign has landed them behind bars comes to an end. So it has always been in the history of the movement.

The other argument about the criminalisation effect of the compounds is scoffed at by social workers and chaplains (privately) and by the paramilitary organisations themselves who all say that the degree of normality enjoyed by the compound prisoners makes it far easier for them to adapt to normal life afterwards, and that their rate of return to their paramilitary organisation was tiny by comparison with that of the embittered, institutionalised cell prisoners.

However, despite the fact that the Special Category issue hung over the talks, and that they were increasingly conducted to the sound of building work progressing apace on the new prisons, the British and the IRA kept talking for the better part of that year. The British offered a bait to make the abolition more palatable by offering a fifty per cent remission of sentences for all prisoners whether in a Special Category situation or not. This proposal was also aimed at cutting down the embarrassingly high prison numbers. The fact that it was offering a kind of amnesty didn't seem illogical to the British side. Nor apparently did the IRA see the contradiction in on the one hand talking about troop withdrawals and a British departure while the shadows of a new prison complex—and the "criminalisation" policy—daily grew longer.

The Extent of the British Concessions

Probably the most important part of the entire H Block saga will never fully be known—that relating to the negotiations which took place with the prisoners within the compounds, at the same time that the IRA leadership outside was engaged in Truce talks with Mr. Merlyn Rees' emissaries. However, I have been able to piece a substantial part of the story together, and it certainly throws a most unexpected light on the whole affair. The compound prisoners had at that time of course virtual *de facto* prisoner of war status and the prisoners' leader, David Morley, was able to negotiate with the Northern Ireland office through the prison authorities almost as easily as the IRA delegates outside.

The prisoners had on October 13, 1974, already staged a major protest which had operated from Long Kesh where huts were burned, and spread to the Crumlin Road jail, Magilligan and even to the Armagh jail where the Prison Governor was held prisoner in his own jail for a time. The issue then was the quality of prison food. Now, however, the IRA after a period of calm following the riots, burnings and beatings, launched into a full scale utilisation of the prison system as a part of the overall war effort and succeeded in wresting an almost endless list of concessions from the Northern Ireland Office as a consequence. The major ones included:

1. £10,000 for welfare.
2. Generous compassionate parole (which only lasted as long as the talks).
3. Full recognition of the Republican command structures. (Warders only to speak through OCs and staff officers to the prisoners and to address all men by their rank—Volunteer, OC, Education Officer, etc.)
4. Fifty per cent remission.
5. Extra parcels and a complete range of foods allowed into the prison—from Chinese takeaways to potted shrimps.

6. Electric cookers in each hut and raw food from the prison kitchens delivered daily. (Thus the prisoners could please themselves about when and what they ate.)

7. Billiard tables were allowed at the prisoners' own cost.

8. A TV in each hut, plus a radio and record player. Previously there was one TV per three huts and this was turned on and off (at 9 p.m.) by the prison staff.

9. The right of the OC Republican Prisoners to visit each of the areas under his command (involving compounds) once a week.

10. Full tool kits and work benches for the making of handicrafts for the Green Cross and Irish Republican Prisoners Welfare Committee and the right to ship these handicrafts in bulk—a van load a time—to the outside.

11. Full control of all sports, hurling, Gaelic Football and soccer, along with Inter Compound (Inter Company) football organised and supervised by the prisoners themselves.

12. Weekly consultation in privacy with other factional leaders in the camp—UDA, UVF, etc.

13. The right to vet Prison Staff who came into direct contact with prisoners so that there would be less of a chance of "flashpoint."

Where the compounds were concerned these concessions remained, with the exception of compassionate parole. The H Blocks were however directly under the prison authorities' control and they were very concerned to keep it that way.

There were in addition other gestures to the prisoners, the importance of which would have created bedlam amongst the Unionists and Conservatives had they known what was happening. The

----

prisoners' leader was allowed out of the prison not alone to inspect the H Blocks while they were being built but also to inspect the premises which the Northern Ireland Office was making available to the paramilitaries, in Rosemary Street in downtown Belfast, at a cost of £40,000. In carrying out these manoeuvres, not alone did the British keep the constitutional parties in the dark about what was going on, they also tried to keep one paramilitary group in ignorance of what was being negotiated with the other. For instance in a conversation I had with one UDA leader it became obvious that he was unaware that the IRA had been shown over the new H Block before it was officially opened because he told me proudly, "of course I got concessions the Provos never got. Do you know I was shown over the H Blocks before they were built. . . !"

I thought silently to myself when I heard that, that there's no doubt that the old management maxim for dealing with workers has a very particular validity when applied to the H Block situation: "Keep them in the dark and throw shit at them."

Rosemary Street was intended to serve as a kind of welfare centre for all the major paramilitaries, the UDA, the UVF, the IRA. The Provisionals eventually scuppered the proposals, because they mistrusted the British presence in the welfare scheme; but for a time the proposal certainly held intriguing possibilities. The four paramilitaries entered into a pact that they would not attack any of their rival personnel in the vicinity of Rosemary Street, which thus could have provided a type of mini-Switzerland in Belfast at a time when sectarian assassination was rife in the city. In the compounds the prisoners traditionally get on well together and various gestures of friendship can be instanced, such as Loyalists throwing cigarettes into the IRA compounds when the Provisionals were deprived of cigarettes as a punishment.

The British also agreed to provide an even more imposing premises than the Rosemary Street one, Arnott House, in Royal Avenue as part of the welfare package—a proposal which would certainly have startled the respectable Unionist businessmen who daily use that central thoroughfare in Belfast's commercial heart. A sum of

£10,000 was paid over for prisoners' welfare purposes—providing transport to visit the prison and so on.

But other manoeuvres and concessions to the prisoners were even more startling. For instance, apart from being taken to inspect the new H Blocks, or the premises in downtown Belfast for the welfare project, Morley was frequently allowed out on parole, ostensibly to consult with his comrades on the progress of the negotiations. On one occasion, as part of the general policy of stretching their opponents to the absolute maximum at every hand's turn (during hurling practice for instance the ball would be deliberately driven into the barbed wire entanglements so that a warder would be distracted and have to crawl in after it), the IRA engineered a truly remarkable breach of prison regulations whereby, in direct violation of every known regulation governing the movement of prisoners, the prison authorities were induced to sanction a trip by Morley to the Republic—knowing that of course this meant he was going out of their jurisdiction. He didn't go South in fact, the object of the parole request had only been to see how far the prisoners could push their luck.

On another occasion Morley told the authorities a cock and bull story about being at risk from sectarian assassination and claimed that on an up-coming parole/prison leave, ostensibly to talk to the IRA leadership, he would have to be armed as a safety precaution. He was duly supplied with a revolver and ammunition before he left the prison.

But the most remarkable concession of all was the prisoners' demanding, and getting, an advance copy of a speech Merlyn Rees was about to deliver in the House of Commons on the H Block issue and the IRA generally (on March 25, 1976). The speech was written in the Northern Ireland Office and a copy dispatched to Long Kesh. The authorities explained to Morley that for political reasons Rees would have to come down on the IRA pretty hard and that they were not to be unduly put out by the strength of his language. This was all part of the political game. But Morley actually succeeded in getting some of the terminology altered and some of the stronger epithets taken out.

This must surely be one of the rare occasions in history when a British cabinet minister, or any minister for that matter, had a speech of his vetted in an Irish jail before delivering it in the august confines of the "mother of Parliaments" at Westminster. Eventually, both inside the prison and outside it, the IRA negotiations broke down.

Outside the IRA had apparently been convinced that they were going to get a British declaration of intent to withdraw from Ireland; the only point at issue about this for a time appeared to be a quibble over the IRA demands that they get this *in writing*! Inside, however, the prisoners were concerned with the threat to Special Category, and the fifty per cent remission which they were offered did not allay their fears on this subject.

However, the priorities of the prisoners inside inevitably rated lower than did those of the movement as a whole outside—though the IRA did warn the authorities that if Special Category was tampered with the change would be resisted and warders shot—but the potential significance of the issue to the movement and to Northern Ireland as a whole was not realised at the time. Certainly nothing of the nature and scale of the H Block protest was thought of. Both sides wanted different things from the Truce. The IRA got their incident centres and thought they were getting a withdrawal. The British got a relief from harassment and a valuable respite during the truce which they used to improve their intelligence to a degree which almost wrecked the IRA.

Breakdown

The long drawn out negotiations within the prison on Special Category Status came to an end two days after Merlyn Rees made his IRA screened speech in the House of Commons. The IRA handed over a document to the prison authorities setting out their reasons for breaking off negotiations; it was headed "Policy Statement" and it gave a detailed account of "Provisional IRA prison policy which would only be changed when the British Government reverse their policy on the ending of Special Category (Political Status) for prisoners."

Section one dealt with the Central Office scheme for the resettlement of political prisoners (Rosemary Street etc.).

The Republican Prisoners, the Irish Republican Prisoners Welfare Committee, and Provisional Sinn Féin, will not take part in this scheme and will not avail themselves of the services of that office or any agency connected with that office, (with the exception of the Prison Welfare Unit). This policy will remain in force until further notice. The reasons for withdrawing are as follows:

The scheme was drawn up by prisoners as a means of filling a gap which has always existed and it was meant to deal exclusively with welfare matters. The Northern Ireland Office and the British Government have changed the format of the original scheme and have injected into it a policy which is simply designed to depoliticise the respective military groups and redirect their energies into a situation where the British Government have a measure of control over the various military groups.

Section two dealt with compassionate parole. It said:

In the few weeks since the long awaited agreements on the criteria for compassionate parole there has been a gradual but definite return to the situation as it was before the agreements were reached. These broken agreements only serve to warn those who enter into agreements with the NIO that it can be expected that all will go to the wall when the subject of agreement is no longer politically expedient.

Section three was the most important. It was headed "The proposed ending of Special Category (Political Status)" and it contained the following:

In an address to the House of Commons on Thursday
25 March 1976 the Secretary of State, Merlyn Rees,
declared that one of the main reasons for the decision to
end political status for prisoners was to make it easier
for the RUC to operate in Northern Ireland. This is
probably the clearest declaration of intent ever to
emerge from the lips of the Secretary of State. It is as
we long suspected, certainly within the past few
months, although during that time we were prepared to
listen to the NIO representatives explain their policy on
Special Category, while at the same time we were
putting forward our point of view in the hope that we
could perhaps get the Government to change their
minds and reverse the decision to end political status. It
would appear now that there is no intention to reverse
that decision and the British Government are determined to push this new scheme through regardless of
the consequences.

Those consequences have already been mentioned in a policy statement from Belfast Brigade and
we do not wish to comment on that particular statement, other than to say that whatever Belfast Brigade
decide in the matter will have the full approval of the
prisoners. Already Volunteers of Oglaigh na hEireann
have been instructed that they are not to engage in any
institutional schemes under the control of the prison
administration. They are further instructed that they are
not to wear any clothing provided by the prison administration, even if such clothes are of a civilian type.
They will respond only to the commands and directives
of their superior officers, regardless of the consequences. They are political prisoners and any other
imaginary label tagged on to them by the British Government will make not the slightest difference to that
very basic fact.

We have no doubt that there will now be a hysterical campaign mounted by the NIO which will claim that all prisoners are thugs and criminals. So be it. We are confident that the people to whom that propaganda is directed are capable of recognising just who the real thugs are. The present actions of the British Army in working class areas of the North will be the yardstick by which the people will judge the propaganda of the NIO. The result of that is a foregone conclusion.

It is not the paramilitaries who are in a state of disarray as recently claimed by Merlyn Rees. The only disarray is in the carefully fostered plans of the NIO and the British Government. We are prepared to die for the *right* to retain political status. Those who try to take it away must be fully prepared to pay the same price.

In its own way this document embodies the IRA's "inflict and endure" syndrome. The "consequences" for its enemies referred to as following any removal of Special Category status meant death for the warders. For their own part, the prisoners threatened to die for their aims if necessary—hence their relatives' ever-present fear of hunger strikes.

Nevertheless the British pressed ahead with the removal of Special Category and the installation of the Criminalisation policy.

The British went all out for a military solution. The hot line went cold in the "Incident Centres" and arrests, swoops and the "conveyor-belt" system shot prison totals up even further—for a time in 1975-77 the active service life of the average young IRA volunteer was effectively cut to around three months.

Roy Mason, the hardline Secretary of State for Northern Ireland who succeeded Merlyn Rees in August 1976, was able to talk about "squeezing the IRA like toothpaste" and launched an advertising campaign: "Seven Years Is Enough." The IRA countered this by painting signs on dead walls: "700 years is too much," and followed them up two years later with another: "78 not bate."

In November 1975, a month after the "Incident Centres" closed, Merlyn Rees made the fateful announcement in the House of Commons—after March 1, 1976, Special Category would no longer apply to new prisoners. There would be no further flow of new prisoners to the compounds but existing prisoners would retain this privilege. Rees also announced publicly that even for Special Category prisoners the fifty per cent remission offer already made privately would apply—provided the prisoners were of good behaviour. Otherwise they would have to serve their full sentences.

CHAPTER 5
The Larger Prison

No realistic examination of the H Block situation, or of any part of the Northern problem, is possible without at least a cursory glance at the social and economic situation that produces the IRA—and the type of money that would be needed if they are ever to be eradicated through improving the economy and taking meaningful steps to end partition. The cost, as we shall see, is not slight but it would be money well spent, far better than investing it in building new prisons—Magheraberry Prison complex, which it was envisaged would house 450 male and 70 women prisoners, when it was completed in 1982, was expected to cost £20 million. The cost in 1980 of running the prison service was £25,517m annually. That was a bill for a policy of no policy. You would not rejuvenate Northern Ireland by spending more money on more prisons.

In 1980 alone, the Province, which has one and a half million people, cost British taxpayers net £1000m. This was made up as follows: some £560m to £600m came as grant-in-aid. Three other UK departments then made payments. The Ministry of Justice pays for prisons, courts and the like. The Ministry of Agriculture gives money for subsidies and there was a contribution for national insurance. To this must be added the troop costs.

The economy of Northern Ireland was woefully weak, largely founded on dying industries. Shipbuilding was the most chronic case. Harland and Wolff once employed 25,000 people. Now, like shipyards elsewhere, it faces a lack of orders. In 1980, the workforce was down to 8,000 people (none of them Catholics, incidentally) with more redundancies in prospect. In textiles, Courtaulds, the Province's single largest industrial employer, had been laying off workers because of the recession. Unemployment in Northern Ireland at eleven and a half per cent was almost twice the UK average. It had been estimated that with workers coming off the land and with old industries shedding employees, it would take the creation of 7,000 new jobs each year in order to stand still, but Northern Ireland has no coal and no oil, and no domestic market.

Moreover, the economy was not getting the volume or type of job it needed. The De Lorean Motor Company project was so expensive that the South's IDA, which could have had it, shied away from the undertaking. The project, which was expected to create 2,000 badly needed jobs in West Belfast, received £53m from the British government, which worked out at £26,000 a job although the average was nearer £12,000. The IDA reckoned at the time that it normally spent £5,000–£6,000 per job, although it had gone well over this in preceding years. Job creation in the Republic, however, concentrates on labour intensive technological industries. In 1980, investment in fixed assets was thirty per cent of GNP, far higher than in Britain where it was eighteen per cent, and probably double what it was in Northern Ireland.

Also, the South had some prospect of oil off the West Coast to repay its very high borrowings, and could with reasonable confidence look forward to growth again in the next two to three years, if it could get its balance of payments figures down with a little luck and good management. There was just no prospect of this in Northern Ireland which spent £80m a year in unemployment benefits (1978–9), had the lowest industrial earnings in the United Kingdom, the highest rate of emigration, double the UK prison population per thousand, the poorest housing standards, highest rate of infant mortality and lowest life expectancy, male or female, in the UK. On top of this was the fact that the hardest hit areas were the Catholic ones.

The whole creaking economy, based on the assumption that it should be an adjunct of the UK and thus protected from world recession, rather than linked with the Republic in cross-border co-operation which would enable it to make its own way in the world, recession or no recession, had one further lowering statistic. There were so many people involved in security in the Province that the total population rating to security personnel in 1980 was 1:38 as compared to 1:2078 in the case of doctors. Not including administrative, catering or maintenance staff, the total employment in security, both part-time and full-time, was 25,664.

Commenting on these facts to me one day, a knowledgeable social worker involved with prison welfare work, Sean MacDonald, said to me "you needn't be surprised at the numbers in prison—they're queuing up to get into the H Blocks. It's an escape from the larger prison into the smaller prison." And along with "them," i.e. the IRA men and women volunteers, there were the ever swelling totals of the people who actually staff the prison service. There were 224 of these in 1969. Ten years later there were 2,594—ill fares the land where jobs decay and prison warders multiply. Despite the IRA's attacks on them from the time the H Blocks protest started people still came forward to replace the dead warders in the absence of any other work.

They also came forward to join the ranks of the people who killed them—the IRA. The social conditions saw to that. The pressure of the resultant IRA recruitment on the security forces meant a retaliatory pressure from the army, action and reaction interconnect, and so the grim, futile struggle continued inside and outside H Block.

And that struggle certainly was grim.

If the H Block system was seen by the Catholics contaminated by it as an injustice within an injustice, a prison within the larger prison of the unemployment ridden ghettoes of Northern Ireland, any detailed examination of the problem began to make one wonder whether or not injustice was a self-perpetuating growth feeding on itself like cancer.

Pat McGeown, then twenty-two years of age and on the blanket, came to his position via the familiar Castlereagh-Diplock-"conveyor-belt" system. He had got as far as the compounds via a fifteen-year sentence for attempting to blow up the Europa Hotel. When he attempted to escape he was caught and sentenced to an additional six months for the attempt. But the significance of his case lay in its implications for the other prisoners in the compounds who had political status but whom, it was feared by many, it was planned to criminalise. For McGeown was not placed back in the compounds there to serve his additional six months but transferred to the cells of H Block where he lost his Special Category status and went on the blanket on March 31, 1978. He would remain there unless the situation was resolved until the entire fifteen years was served. In 1980, how long this might take—his child then aged four, was five months old when he went in—was anyone's guess.

His wife Pauline, then a bright low-sized girl of twenty-one who had joined the charismatic movement and was studying French with Father Wilson's classes, had already found the child throwing stones with two other boys aged five and six—at British soldiers. "They saw the big boys at it and there they were sitting on the side of the pavement with little piles of stones at each toddler's feet."

Her husband Pat was thirteen when he became a vigilante, patrolling the streets at night, keeping watch for sectarian assassins. He had been interned when he was sixteen. As the troubles continue it seems reasonable to suppose that his little boy may become involved in "the movement" or "a movement," but certainly something that would have him en route to H Block considerably earlier— that was if he were not killed first.

Pauline McGeown was more politicised than most. She attributed this to Pat's influence. They were married when the couple were each seventeen. Pauline was pretty, pale, and it was only when you had been in her company for a while and watched her closely that you realised that she smoked incessantly and spoke with a too deliberate calmness. To the casual observer she seemed calm and unaffected by her tribulations.

> He was always interested in politics and he used to talk
> to me about what he read. The trouble is he was too
> bright. When they sweep the areas, they lift the brains.
> They know he has got a political mind, that he reads a

lot and could see ahead, therefore he is a threat. Talking is not enough to change the system. You must take action. What type, though, is another matter. I wonder does it have to be violence but you can't walk away from it. We are all in a prison here. If you try to run away you are only running away from yourself. You don't leave H Block behind you. I worry about Pat's mental condition. I think he is deteriorating but I know he will stick it out. I am afraid hunger striking is only around the corner. They can't give up the protest. It is part of them. They would lose their spirit, lose their soul. By failing to resist and admitting the criminal status, they would admit that the whole cause is criminal. It goes back to the moment you are born. Pat was ten when he was on the barricades.

When you have seen your father kicked out of jobs, you don't blame them for taking up a gun. You know yourself you would do it very easily. Our family had a shop in the Oldpark district. But we were put out. "They" just advised people not to buy anything in the shop so that was it. That gives you an insight into things.

Then you see them letting the "hoods" run riot. They are a kind of support for the authorities. They help to make things so bad that the authorities hope they are going to get people so fed up that they will let the RUC back in. And then of course, they also use them as informers, when they pull them in. They tell them they won't release them unless they promise to get them information when they get out. Then when they do start giving them information they make them go on giving it by threatening to let the Provos know that they are informers. The British get a lot of intelligence that way. I am cynical about institutional forms of authority. I don't think the politicians are playing anything like the proper role by a long shot—nor the clergy. If it wasn't

for the Charismatics I don't quite know what I would be
now, but they helped me a lot. I mean a year ago I
would certainly have agreed with violence as a solution
and you know it's hard not to even now.

For instance, if you could do a bit of research and
get a hundred or so "statements," the actual "statements"
themselves made by a hundred or so different people
who are now in the Blocks or compounds or waiting to
go up for sentence, and read them, you would see what I
mean about the system being unjust. The minds of the
people who drafted them come through and they are not
the minds of the men who are getting the sentences. They
have got the same approach, the same ideas, the same
phrases and sentences, even misspelled, which would
soon show you that they are done by the same small
group of people but that's what they call "law." Anyone
from the Falls can tell that the phrases in the "statements"
are written in language that Falls people don't use.

They are only now moving onto French in the
Blocks for instance. They've become fluent in Gaelic
and some bright spark decided that French was the basis
of revolution so they are taking up French. That's the
kind they are. I am afraid that the hunger strike is only
around the corner unless the Church or someone does
something. There is nothing that dazzling about life
here, as you can see, [meaning Belfast and the ghettoes]
and there is even less in the prisons. They don't think
about death the way other people do. It's only my own
idea of myself as a person that keeps me from suicide,
and I am on the outside. The way the Provisionals see it
there is no way for them to put pressure on the British
except in death, or dying themselves, or doing something that they will really take note of like the tubes in
London for instance. I mean what else are you going to
face them with if everything else has been tried?

They would ease up on the warders I know if there was an ease up in H Block. They know, we all know that the young soldiers and the warders are only pawns.

Pauline stood up to go. "My sister-in-law would be worrying about me," she said. "They know I have been down to the hospital with my son. I live on my own but I am very lucky. I have a very good family both my own and my in-laws. They would want to hear about how my son was getting on." He had a cyst removed earlier that day, and as far as Pauline knew, he was all right—for the time being.

PART TWO
Anatomy of Defiance

CHAPTER 6

How it Started

So much for the historical, political and economic background to the H Block saga, but how and with whom did the protest emerge in prison history? The protest took the form it did almost by accident, being begun by Ciaran Nugent, a man who looks you very straight in the eye. In 1980, he was an obviously tough but likeable customer of twenty-two. About five foot nine, he tended to fat, a stylish trim for his red hair and beard—and mistrust for everyone and everything save his belief that the IRA would win eventually.

Being the first prisoner to go on the blanket he is something of a celebrity in Republican circles. He is vehement that he never intended to go on the dirt protest at first but simply to follow the general IRA policy of protesting by refusing to wear the prison uniform when the removal of Special Category status became applicable as it did with him on September 14, 1976. He had been sentenced for hijacking a van and vowed "that they would have to nail the clothes to my back" if an attempt was made to criminalise him after sentence was handed down.

He was quite clear in his mind even at that age that the removal of Special Category status was part of the Ulsterisation, Criminalisation and Normalisation policy. Both personally, and as a matter of conforming to IRA policy, he violently disagreed with being branded as a criminal instead of a prisoner of war as he saw himself. He refused to wear the prison clothes and embarked on the now familiar routine of surviving on a concrete floor from 7:30 a.m. to 8:30 p.m.

each day with no mattress, bed or reading material. His Bible was removed after a period and the diet deteriorated from the commencement of the protest. The only furniture in his cell was a chamber pot. With the benefit of hindsight it is obvious how symbolically and psychologically this article of furniture would take on a significance of its own as matters progressed.

Nugent also made a point which the other prisoners corroborated—as have visitors to the prison—that the initial slopping of faeces and urine in the cells was done not by the prisoners but by the warders. The routine was that a trolley came around with the food for the prisoners' meals, followed by another one for their slops. The routine was food in, slops out. But the prisoners claimed that what happened was that the warders started returning the blanket men's pots half full, sometimes kicking them over the floors. So this, say the protesters, is why it became necessary to throw the faeces out of the window in the first place. Later it was daubed on the walls to get it off the floors where the men slept: "We had to put it somewhere so it was better on the walls than the floors."

The thing escalated from there with complaints subsequently coming from both prisoners and warders that sometimes pots of urine and faeces were hurled at and by one another.

Though slow to speak until he had thought out his answer Nugent had obviously become politicised and hardened by his experiences. He regarded the use of force as a matter of inevitable necessity. "We would have been murdered in our cells only that the IRA started shooting the screws outside," was one of his comments. Nugent's experiences do not differ all that much from those of other prisoners, but it is worth looking a little at his attitudes and experiences because of the importance of the effect that this uncompromising young man has had on the minds of the over 400 men and women who, in 1980, were still on the blanket in the H Block and in Armagh jail.

Nugent has tested his theories and his answers against the questioning of top American television interviewers and print journalists, and before I met him he had concluded a successful propaganda tour of the States from which British Foreign Office pressure subsequently succeeded in excluding him by means of a State Department ban.

He said, "We have to be very hard. I remember the head warder coming around and I told him to get out of my cell. He said, 'This is my cell, I stand where I like in this prison.' We stood looking at each other and then we both laughed, but you have to remember the scalding baths, the icy baths, the head shaving, the mirror searches, the table searches and all the rest of it.

"If a prisoner wants a doctor they make him wear the prison uniform to go and see him. You can die if you don't, for all they care. Then if your mother or father dies you get the aul soft talk, the aul easy talk: 'I am sorry but if you'll sign here (a declaration that the prisoner intends to come off the H Block protest) you would get parole.' Otherwise it's back to the cell."

Nugent gave a chilling insight into the prisoners' attitude to the killing of warders. "I remember Governor Myles. He said, 'we are going to break you.' He stood there shouting at me. Gave me a slap in the face and then he stood back and watched the other warders beat me up. When he was shot on December 20, 1978, that was a great morale booster."

Nugent's view of this shooting was but one more graphic example of how differently the prisoners, and the IRA (and to an increasing degree the prisoners' relatives and friends as the protest progressed) viewed the killing of warders as compared with the shock and revulsion of the general public. Governor Myles had been on television a short while earlier and had expressed a humane and professional attitude towards the prisoners which won him widespread respect. Even to the battle scarred psyche of Northern Ireland, his death came as a sickener.

However, Nugent provided a different perspective: "When I was leaving, the screws used to say to me, clear my name. I am alright. Tell the boys I am getting married. Bastards! They have got supermarkets, pubs, shops in the camp, dances, all the drink they want. They drink very heavily. You have a fellow telling you 'I love my wife, my kids,' so you'll speak for him when you are getting out, but the same man would come back after lunch with a feed of drink on him and 'bang'." Nugent made a gesture of smashing his fist into his open palm. "There was always beating except when the priest comes. If he was not due you can hear the man next door or down the corridor getting it; that's if you were not getting it yourself.

I was a kind of figurehead because I was the first prisoner and if anything happened to me the media used to know about it. I used to play on this. I remember getting a black eye after a thumping by the screws and the Governor said to me, "you have a lovely eye. That'll look good in the newspapers." Normally I wouldn't retaliate or get into fights but once a screw was giving it to me like. I just lost control and bang! I hit him. He went back against the door and cut his arm falling and then I was on him, and they just left us to it. The other screw just locked the door and ran for help. I wasn't treated too bad after. I was supposed to get about a quarter of an orange and he gave me half an orange after and grinned at me to make up like.

Nugent became very hard. He wouldn't take a visit after beginning the protest for approximately eight months. "It would have upset them and me at first, but you get used to being beaten up and the diet, even the baton sometimes. I remember Ciaran Doherty, he was in for GBH (Grievous Bodily Harm) getting into a fight. He was a big lad and the warders just got him by the arms and legs and one of them squeezed his testicles until he went unconscious."

Possibly even more disturbing in its implications for the future was Nugent's attitude towards the UVF. "I hate the UVF," he said. "I remember they put a man's head in a vice in the compound and squeezed it until he was dead." But there were other reasons for Nugent's attitudes. I noticed that he coughed and he told me why.

When he was fifteen, he and another lad of the same age, Bernard MacErlean, were fired on by a Loyalist assassination squad.

He was shot six times. He remembers a car pulling up alongside of himself and the other boy and someone shouting his name and "I turned around and there was this fellow with a short arm and another with a sub. I ran but I got hit in the leg and fell and the fellow with the sub came up to me and stood over me. He stopped to put in a new mag and I got up and ran. He fired a second burst at me. I got into my own house. I remember I was all burning up and I remember the ambulance coming and someone saying 'It's no good, this one's dead. Take him instead.' So they took me."

In 1974 he was caught in possession of arms and held on remand in Crumlin Road jail for five months but was released. Subsequently, however, the security forces made a swoop on Divis Flats. The flats were a high-rise building on the Falls Road that have been a breeding ground of hardened Republicans since the troubles began, of not alone the Provisional IRA and the Official IRA but also the Officials' offshoot, the Irish Republican Socialist Party, and its military wing the Irish National Liberation Army, which killed Airey Neave. For a time the Irish Republican Socialist Party (IRSP)[1] was so active in the flats that they earned the name Planet of the IRPS. On the night in question, as the soldiers searched the flats, Nugent, fearing arrest, jumped out of a second storey window and broke both legs and both ankles. He was picked up by a friend and driven to Dublin where his legs were reset so that he walked without a limp.

Nugent comes from a family of ten brothers and sisters. He hadn't slept at home since being released after his three and half years on the blanket. He had no chance of picking up a trade due to his activities and was banned from America and England, which probably in effect meant Australia and any other likely point of emigration. But he planned to get married in 1980. One wondered what his children would be like by the time they are twenty-two, if the North of Ireland problem is not ended by then.

1. The IRSP had about forty members in prison, some of whom were on the blanket. Their protest was often overlooked, as attention centred on the IRA.

CHAPTER 7

Family Life

As the battle of the bowels went on, some of those most affected were the ones who waited at home suffering for a cause by association, hoping that the protest would end and that their sons and husbands would gain at least their prison objectives if not their liberty.

In 1980, Mrs. Margaret McMullen was fifty-two. Her son Jimmy was doing fifteen years for possession of arms and IRA membership. Rosemary MacAuley was twenty-four. Her husband Jim received a comparable sentence. Neither woman believed in violence and would vote for peace if the H Block situation was resolved. However, in general they supported their men folk in their protest, though occasionally, when they felt their health was at a low ebb, they might try to argue that they give it up. Both of them said: "Sure they've known nothing but trouble since 1969," but as Mrs. McMullen put it, "we feel we don't belong anywhere. Who cares? They don't want to know about us in the South and if we go out on a march they say we're Provie-lovers. The young lads always end up throwing stones anyway."

In a real sense the starting point for both women's ordeal was 1969. For like many families in the Falls Road, Margaret McMullen had a Republican connection—her father was a Republican of the Forties period though he had gone entirely dormant. But when the Protestant mobs invaded the Clonard area of the Falls Road in August 1969 a powder train was lit which blew her son and Rosemary McAuley's husband into jail. On a wall in the rebuilt Bombay Street—the Orange mobs gutted the old Coronation-Street-type row

----

of houses—there was a plaque to Gerard MacAuley, Rosemary's brother-in-law. Waterville Street leading to Bombay Street has been renamed Sráid Gearóid MacAmlaigh (Gerard MacAuley Street) and the plaque on the new Bombay Street wall read as follows:

> Gerard MacAuley, Sinn Féin Cumann, in proud memory of Fian Gerard MacAuley who died defending the people of Bombay Street on August 15th 1969.

On other gable walls round about one could see slogans such as "smash H Block" and odd looking inscriptions which turned out on enquiry to be the nicknames of men "on the blanket" from the district—"Okey, Slane, Fra, Brackey, Teapot."

Those white painted nicknames were as pointed and as prominent in the minds of the area's residents as the plaque to Gerard MacAuley who was shot while throwing stones at the petrol bombers and gunmen who without his presence and that of scores of names like his and the nicknames would certainly have burnt down the whole area.

"Teapot" was the nickname given to Mrs. McMullen's son, and to avoid confusion between him and Jim MacAuley I will refer to him by this name henceforth.

Rosemary, button bright, with a merry little face, slender to the point of thinness, laughed at her size for a moment. "Gearóid used to call me Twiggy." Mrs. McMullen, low sized, plump, neat and well preserved was naturally greyer but, like Rosemary, only betrayed her anxiety in direct comment, not in tremblings or Valium taking. Both women found religion a great solace to them.

As Rosemary put it, she went to God for help before anyone else. Margaret sometimes sat in a church, not praying, just willing herself to peace. She was saying the Rosary when "Teapot" was lifted. "I often say to myself, Our Lady got him lifted for some reason but got him away from something worse."

> I would love to bring him in a big meal. But I am not
> allowed to bring him even a crumb. You know it's funny

the things you think of. He has got no nail cutter. They
rub their nails on the concrete. I am afraid they will never
grow up. They will come out the same as they went in.
Jimmy (Teapot) never had a clue about money. Now he is
sitting in a tiny cell, looking at nothing, learning nothing.
He is safe at night I know but sometimes it gets too much
for me. If it wasn't for Father Reid, we would have nothing. I go and see him when it gets too much for me, and I
keep on at my other sons not to join the IRA. We are in
the thick of it round here. I am afraid I will be dead
before he comes out, that's what I worry about.

Rosemary was obviously full of life but hated going out because
people in the ghetto would talk if she was seen with another man.

The other day I was out with my in-laws in the car and I
kept thinking, "what if somebody sees me?" They will
say I am carrying on. There are a lot of them that are,
but I would never leave him. We have been going
around since he was sixteen. I worry though about getting older. I am twenty-four now, but I would love to
have more children—about four. Will I be too old when
he comes out? I see the child sitting there and she has
no one. Sometimes she gives me trouble and I smack
her and I get sorry. I cannot leave her alone upstairs
because she is deaf and she screams for me. She can't
occupy herself. A cry helps, or I go to Father Reid, or
some of the other Clonard people, they are great. A cry
helps. Then I get a pen and I write to Jim but sure then I
think, does he get the letters?
    Sometimes I get letters from him and he asks
questions. Stupid little niggling things that annoy me.
He would blow up at something I said. But we have to
wait for a month to sort it out, a weekly visit would
help—he says to me, give us a kiss but I couldn't with

----

the warders looking. I'm funny that way. When I think
of them going to the toilet in front of each other. . .

Both women would love their men to come off the strike.
"They chew our heads off us when we say anything to them. We support the Relatives Action Committee and go on marches but there
always seems to be trouble after them. Wee fellows throwing stones,"
says Margaret.

Neither of the women knew what their men were doing when
they were arrested, though Margaret had heard about an IRA group
arrested on the radio and she instinctively guessed that her son was
one of them. Rosemary was "sickened" that Jim, who was just out of
hospital, should get himself picked up again. "I was sickened; I
couldn't go up for a week. You meet a woman who couldn't recognise her husband with the blood all over him after interrogation. I
didn't know what to expect. When I read in the newspaper that he
had gastro-enteritis I nearly died. I thought he would come off then,
but he went right on the blanket."

Both men were nearly killed before eventually being picked up
on a charge (possession of arms) that led them to H Block. "Teapot"
was shot during the ceasefire because he hadn't heard a "halt" warning as he drove by an army patrol. Margaret said, "the British opened
up; one bullet just missed his spine and another came off his skull. A
surgeon told me that another one-eighth of an inch and it would have
been in his throat, and he would be dead."

Jim MacAuley was shot at twice but didn't tell Rosemary at the
time, because she was expecting. He initially got a two year suspended sentence having spent seven months on remand, during which
time he fell ill with jaundice—she thinks—and she remembers going
to see him in the hospital and being appalled at his appearance.

He is 6' 2" and he weighed only eight stone. I remember
the big long hands of him. He would scare the life out
of you with the big aul drip out of him. He was in hospital for a week before they told us, and back in jail

before we knew it. He would never tell you if he got a
hiding or anything but you keep thinking of that sort of
thing all the time. I find it kills me when I hear that
another girl's husband was getting out. But then you
hear that so and so got three days parole for something
and instead of spending time with his wife he goes out
with his mates. That makes you think. Sometimes you
can't control yourself. I remember rearing up on this
woman in the office. Her husband was getting out. She
came round to me afterwards and said "Oh God help
you." I was sorry then.

There are times when I could throw furniture
through the window. I wonder what he will do when he
gets out. What will it be like living together? I don't
have to wash a cup if I don't want to or do housework. I
worry about what it will do to Lisa [her child]."

Both women had one abiding fear—that the men would go on
hunger strike. "That would be the end," said Rosemary. "They are
too weak. How can they eat stuff on the floor like pigs? Sometimes
you get terribly depressed. Then you get a bit of hope."

Both women thought that "it's the worst thing that has happened." Rosemary said everyone was tired. "It has gone on so long.
You were just waiting now for someone to die. Sometimes I feel like
strangling people who write to the papers about H Block. They don't
know anything about H Block. I heard a man on the train talking
once and I couldn't help myself. I burst out and attacked him. I said
you don't know what you are talking about. He got very sorry then
and apologised to me. I was sorry too, but things like that irritate
you.

"There was this woman who was dead patriotic. All talk about
the 'struggle.' We were letting down the lads—by criticising the
protest—while her husband was on remand, but then he didn't go on
the blanket when he was sentenced. Now she says they were all
intimidated. That maddens me."

The two women agreed on this point. Said Margaret: "Jimmy said to me, 'What do you mean, Ma, the 'RA's making us do it. Sure we are the 'RA.' You know in some ways they have great peace of mind. They don't have to call anyone sir. In some ways I think it keeps them going, the blanket, I mean. They hope everyone would get political status, loyalists and all if they win."

Both women watched television but Rosemary could not content herself to read. She would find herself agitated in a room by herself. She would start thinking about things like her husband and his comrades going to the toilet in front of each other. Margaret did read a little—books by Catherine Cookson mainly.

Both women agreed with the Pope's appeal for peace at Drogheda during his visit to Ireland in 1979. Said Margaret: "The IRA could have proved to Paisley that they listened to their leader. You don't know what would have come out of it." While both women were obviously deeply religious and attribute their continuing grip on sanity to individual priests such as in particular Father Alex Reid, they don't think the clergy were sufficiently supportive of the people in the ghetto areas. They think the clergy have antagonised many people though neither of them would ever allow the priests "to put them away from their religion." Both agreed "we would always go to church."

Both for instance felt that the clergy should have condemned the Protestant violence and shown more interest in prisoners, and they particularly criticised the failure of the clerical authorities not to allow the Delaney remains into a church. Kevin Delaney died when a bomb he was transporting blew up on a train at Portadown. But his case was lifted out of the commonplace of such tragedies by virtue of the fact that the Roman Catholic authorities decided to make the case the one in which the sanctions of the Church would for the first time be invoked against a dead IRA man. His widow was refused permission to have him buried from a Church in the normal way, with Mass and prayers at the Church.

Other women differed in degree in their experiences through having men on the blanket, but not in kind. It was a matter of intensity.

For all of them the foreseeable future contact with their men folk would consist of a half an hour visit sitting at one side of a table, their men on the other, four warders standing closely around them, and trying not to notice that the object of their affection was smelly, emaciated, yellowing, and half naked. Trying to banish the thought that one or other of the parties to the visit might be dead before either the H Block protest was ended or the prisoner set at liberty. They tried not to show their feelings at visits. In their own way they tried to buck the system too. "We don't want to upset them, and we keep cracking jokes with them," said Rosemary. "I couldn't kiss Jim in front of the warders but I sent him a Valentine."

Mrs. McKenna lived in Cullingtree Road, "off the Grosvenor," which, as any Falls Road dweller tells you, means that if you were going towards Belfast you turn off the Falls Road when you come to Grosvenor Road and then go left and left again through a warren of little streets that would be confusing to find your way in, in daylight and in peace. At night and at war the place was unbelievably eerie and chilling.

There are a few street lamps left on the Grosvenor Road, less than on the Falls itself but still enough to see by. Once one gets off the road however, and into the warren of streets, the darkness is total, stygianly menacing. Here and there your car headlights throw up a figure on a street corner or a patrol of scared soldiers momentarily show up in the glare and you brake and switch your lights out, heart pounding in your throat as a couple of the young Scotsmen drop to one knee and take aim at the driver—you. This is one of the day to day hazards of Belfast life. The soldiers are terrified of being illuminated for a sniper; the drivers of being picked off.

The lights were off in Cullingher Road because it was stated that the army wanted them off. Not because the Provisionals prevented the maintenance being done by the corporation as the authorities claimed. The locals say that the corporation simply wouldn't come there and put them back on, just to hassle the Catholics a little further so as to make them disinclined to shelter the IRA.

Mrs. McKenna had to walk home every night through those

darkened streets and the kind of tension indicated above—but there were other tensions too. Apart from "the hoods," young gangsters who infest these streets in the absence of policing and go in for crimes like burglary, rape, bag-snatching and so on, there was still the aftermath of the feud between two wings of the IRA, the Officials and the Provisionals.

Mrs. McKenna lived alongside a drinking club run by the Provisionals but she had to traverse the Leeson Street area, an Official stronghold to get there. The club had a huge, ugly, concrete porch-like structure built around its front door taking up most of the footpath to prevent bombs being thrown in. But there was nothing outside Mrs. McKenna's next door home to prevent her house being attacked either by mistake or as a point of entry to the club.

Mrs. McKenna, a pleasant grey-haired woman in her fifties, smoked a lot and her lips trembled, particularly when she talked about her son Peter Paul McKenna, then aged twenty-five, serving a life sentence on the blanket. He was found guilty before a Diplock Court on a number of charges which included the deaths of two soldiers, the wounding of three more, bomb making and giving "gun lectures." He was first arrested in 1972 when he was seventeen. 1972 was one of the worst years—if not the worst year—in the Northern decade of agony to 1980. Stormont fell and sectarian assassination was rampant. Peter had been in and out of trouble ever since. His story is a familiar enough one. But the cultural background which obviously awakened in him, as the drama unfolded and he became ensnared in the tumult, was instructive as a pointer to why someone with a record like his should literally feel enraged to his very bowels at not being acknowledged as a prisoner of war rather than a common criminal.

Mrs. McKenna added little, significant brush strokes to the picture as she talked. Her father was in prison, too, for Republican activities. She remembered when, during the war years, it was unsafe for British soldiers to come home on leave. Times like the rioting of the Thirties, particularly 1932 and 1935 when possibly only one Catholic man out of twenty worked. As the Phil Coulter song has it in "The

Town that I Loved so Well," *The Men on the Dole Played a Woman's Role.* The women worked as seamstresses in upholstery factories, or in domestic service. The men stayed at home and minded the children. As a girl, Mrs. McKenna remembered the tunnelling—the system whereby in Catholic districts exposed to sniper fire from Protestant areas during times of civil unrest, the walls separating the kitchen house gardens were tunnelled through so that people could go about their daily lives, shopping, going to school, and visiting their families without being fired on. In some cases the actual houses were tunnelled through.

Those tunnels run through the folk memories and the minds of families on the Falls Road today.

The Protestants were never fired on by the soldiers and none of them were ever brought up for shooting either, but if the Catholics fired back, then they got hammered. I remember when the troubles started, my husband was standing behind the counter of the shop and in came X [a famous RUC Special Branch interrogator whose name was much linked with malpractice at the Castlereagh interrogation centre]. He told my husband, "you are first on the assassination list." Warning him like. Trying to put the wind up him that the UVF were going to kill him. But they are all the same, UVF and RUC.

My husband knew, so he just quietly took off his white coat and said, "Is that so, X?" and he drove to where the Branchman's son was coming home from school and he came up to him and he just said, "excuse me, son, could you tell me the way to Royal Avenue?" X had followed him and he came out of his car and rushed over to my husband and said, "you leave that boy alone. Get away from him." My husband just looked at him and said, "you see how easy it is. . .," and there was no more talk of assassinations.

There wasn't much Mrs. McKenna could do for her boy, but she did go on the marches.

> The hills are bad and sometimes the marches go on for
> ten miles but you try to keep up. You would be ready to
> drop but there is this man who comes along and wears
> nothing but a blanket and he marches in his bare feet,
> no matter what the weather is like. I don't know who he
> is but when you see that, you have to keep going.

Mrs. Mary Connolly has seven children. One, the second eldest, John, at twenty-two was entering his second year on the blanket. He was hurt when an IRA bomb went off prematurely. He was taken from the Royal Victoria Hospital on the Falls Road to Musgrave Military Hospital in a Saracen armoured car hours later for an operation. He was arrested on February 13 before Special Category status ended but because of his youth and the intercession of Fathers Faul and Brady he was moved out of the military wing of the hospital. He escaped out of a hospital window but was picked up in the Beechmount area of the Falls Road later, and the residents testify that "terrible screams" were heard as he was taken into the Saracen. The army later said he received his injuries resisting arrest. His sentence would have been ended in April of 1979 but because of the protest he had lost his remission and would not be released until 1981. Mrs. Connolly sighed philosophically, however, "at least he is alive." John was then taking "advanced Irish." His mother said: "He asked me what was I doing for Lent. I said praying for you. He told me to go to confession."

I met Mrs. Connolly and Mrs. Lillie MacCordy, a mother of eight children, on the same occasion. Both ladies had by mistake gone to a hotel some miles away while I waited for them in another part of Belfast. I was able to occupy my time by talking to other prisoners' relations, but they waited patiently and, then, learning of my true whereabouts, came down to see me. "Anything that might help the boys," said Mrs. MacCordy, even though their other children were waiting at home for their meals.

Her son Liam, who got five years for hijacking, was in fact on his way to act as an IRA policeman in curbing the activities of "hoods" who had been reported causing a nuisance.

The saga of the IRA's attempts to introduce community policing to fill the vacuum left by the RUC exclusion, and the British and Unionist efforts to prevent the Organisation thus legitimising itself, was one of those long and tangled dramas that runs parallel not alone to the H Block activities but to the entire North of Ireland struggle. What was required was an unarmed police force acceptable to the local community though not necessarily drawn from it. For instance, to avoid graft through family or neighbourhood pressures, it might be necessary to have the ghettoes patrolled by police recruited from Armagh or Derry and vice versa. But each community would have the easement of knowing that the police would probably be at least nominally their co-religionists, whether or not they were practising Catholics, and that the Catholic members of the community were not automatically regarded as disloyal, potential or actual criminals because of their religion. The Unionists, who resist this development, for their part would have the recompense of the ghettoes becoming ordinary housing areas—instead of launching pads for attacks on them and their institutions.

Community policing—the replacement of the hated RUC by an unarmed force acceptable to the ghetto communities—remains a fundamental issue which must be resolved, so that the ghettoes can one day return to their normal law-abiding state. At the moment those ghettoes were squalid, back street abscesses poisoning the life of not alone Belfast but many parts of Ireland with every type of crime, ranging from armed robbery to sexual assault. Bank robbery, a thing unheard of in Ireland before the "troubles," was now a commonplace as both paramilitaries and freelance criminals employ the techniques learned in the North towards easy self-enrichment.

Liam MacCordy, a member of the Clonard Men's confraternity and of the Green Scapular Sodality, lost his job in 1969, and continued his education in jail where he was regarded by the other prisoners as one of the jokers of the place.

"He keeps them all going," his mother said. "I told him there was a man writing a book and he said—good, tell him to put me in it. But he was shaking very badly and looked terrible. I know there was something wrong but he wouldn't say anything, but your instinct tells you. I would say that he got a hiding before the visit." The women nodded in unison as one stated and the other repeated or amplified their attitude to the struggle and their sons' ordeal. "We like everything Irish but the thirty-two county Republic is a kind of dream. We would love to see it. But we don't know whether we will or not. We would die if the lads didn't get the Status. We are on the street for everyone, Civil Rights protesting, the Green Cross [a Republican Welfare Fund]. We think we are doing something. They ask us how the marches are going. We tell them there were thousands. We never thought we could hate, the way we hate the screws. We don't hate the British, it's just the Army we don't like."

Mrs. Connolly remarked: "John says: 'I couldn't do this for a criminal offence but only for something we believe in. The 'RA are not using us. We are the 'RA.' They keep sending out word that they want to go on hunger strike but the 'RA are stopping them. I dread the thoughts of the hunger strike. There is no way they would give up but they would die like flies."

After talking to me the two ladies shook hands and apologised for having to run off but "the children are waiting at home. Please God it will be alright one day," said Mrs. MacCordy. Meantime she, Mrs. Connolly and the other women go on trying to put their sons' predicament out of their minds, seeing their faces before them last thing every night and first thing in the morning, physically only seeing them for one half-hour visit every month and hoping that something, anything would turn up before a catastrophe like a hunger strike arises to worsen the situation.

Michael Fitzsimons, whose career as an employee in a pork factory was cut short by the troubles, received fourteen years for "possession with intent" when he was eighteen years of age. In 1980, at twenty-one, he was in his third year "on the blanket." His father Liam, a tough, rather agitated man, then in his forties, balding, blackhaired, of powerful physique and forceful views, had a natural sense of humour that tried to contend with his anxiety over his son's predicament. In a normal society he was the sort of man you would expect to find active in a residents' association or the local youth club.

"I keep fit by jogging with a set of other geriatrics," he laughed. He was off the drink and cigarettes as a kind of gesture of solidarity with his son: "If they can do it so can we. I wouldn't have the courage to do what he is doing." He wasn't Republican in any way prior to 1969. Since then he felt that "they," the British and Unionist element, "want to see every Catholic in jail and every Protestant guarding them. I remember when the troubles started I was thinking that it was a good job we had moved from the Falls Road. I didn't want the lad caught up in rioting and that sort of thing but there was just no way. It was inevitable. I remember when I first saw him after we were let visit him when he had been 'on the blanket' for five months. He was so thin, my wife and I walked right by him. We didn't recognise him." For a moment recollection was too much for the speaker; he got agitated and said to me:

Why is the book only being written now? My son has been on the blanket for years. I have seen children cheer when they heard a warder was shot. What do they care in the South? What do they care in your newspaper about things like that? People will just have to help us. Do you know what it's like to see your son beaten up? The mere fact that they live up here means they get beaten up by the soldiers. They stop them on the streets and abuse them. It makes you hard in your heart. The soldiers are only a number. It's different with something like Neave or Mountbatten. Why are the British here anyway? They have been put out of every country except this.

They talk about law and order. One day I was in the Suffolk Inn [a well known pub in the Anderson-

----

stown area which was later bought on behalf of the Provisionals] and someone ran in to tell me that the soldiers had my son outside with another young fellow. I ran out and they were lined up and two young soldiers had guns on them. They were up against a wall. They were roughing them up. I shoved the soldiers away and I brought the two lads into the inn. After a while they followed us in. One started shooting through the ceiling. They panicked. You could see they were shaking with fear. I was frightened myself. One of them stood in front of me and at point blank range shot me in the chest with a rubber bullet. A bullet seems to have ricocheted off the ceiling and got my son on the ankle. I went down—he went down.

There was a fellow there who was on the run and was connected. (I wasn't connected with anything.) And he got my son's shoe. It was all blood and he smeared it all over his face and got himself led out and away with him. Good luck to him. But my son was taken off to St. Patrick's.[1] I was taken to Lisburn Military Barracks. Of course I got a hammering. I got this big fellow down when they came at me. He had big boots. I remember thinking I'd have to keep them away from me but they got me down on the floor. Then just before it got really bad in came a military policeman and he said 'that's my prisoner' and took them off me. He was a real big fellow, so I didn't do too badly. But I got brought up on a charge of attacking the soldiers and so did my son. I got six months suspended. Let off for good behaviour. He just did one day in St. Pat's but the point was that convictions meant that we couldn't sue for wrongful arrest or injuries or over the shooting, anything like that. It was a frame-up. That's law and order for you.

At first I didn't like going to see these plays[2] they put on, and I didn't want my wife to see it, but then I thought we should see it and help us to understand what we are going through. People should know about these things. It was the same with them getting engaged. He had this girlfriend and she came with us on the visits. She was monopolising the visits, really. A nice girl, studying to be a nurse but after a while she wanted to get engaged. That's no life for you. You can't have children. You can't live like that with him inside. I thought it was just emotionalism like, but then after, I told them, think it over for a while, you go ahead with your studies. If you still want to marry after some years then go ahead get engaged after two years. They did get engaged. They were a great help to each other but you can imagine it, getting engaged after two years on the blanket and eleven more to go."

Mr. Fitzsimons paused for a moment, then he shook his head resignedly and said: "Sure there were others worse than him. Just think about it, nineteen-year-olds with life sentences on the blanket with no remission. Yes, I'm behind my son—sure I couldn't be in front of him," and he laughed nervously.

Mairéad Farrell was twenty-two in 1980, with four years served out of the fourteen to which she was sentenced on charges arising out of the bombing of the Conway Hotel, one of the many Belfast hotels destroyed in the IRA's economic war. She was also the leader (OC) of the women prisoners in Armagh jail, and the only girl out of a family of six. None of the five boys were in the Provisionals—though one brother Niall regularly broadcast from East Berlin, having being attracted to Communism via the Connolly Clubs movement set up by the British Communist Party to attract Irish nationalists.

Mairéad's grandfather was a Republican but neither of her parents took any part in politics and concentrated all their energies on building up their business interests in Belfast. They owned two shops, one managed by Mairéad's mother and the other by her father. Mairéad attended a convent of the Sacred Heart, did very well in her school exams, and seemed set for a university career until she got caught up in the troubles. Mrs. Farrell, then a grey-haired smartly turned out lady of fifty-nine, with an air of calm concern about her said: "Mairéad is never out of my mind. My husband is sixty-five. We feel we will never see her home. My husband idolised her. It's a horrible thing to be sitting at home with a son or a daughter on the blanket thinking about them all the time and you helpless." In defence of Mairéad, however, she argued that "there is no more just cause than the freedom of one's country," but she dreaded the thought that one day her child would tread the fatal hunger-striking road of Frank Stagg. This ever present bogey was common to all relations of H Block prisoners, and more frightening for the relatives of the Armagh prisoners who were of course all women.

Mrs. Farrell was critical of the official attitude of the Church and individual clergy and nuns who never inquired after or visited Mairéad though they were in frequent contact with the family before she got into trouble. She thought the attitude of the Church to the Delaney funeral was very wrong—as did all the prisoners' relations, whether of H Block or Armagh prisoners, that I spoke to.

But she was intensely religious herself. Without prayer she couldn't get through her ordeal. She had a Mass said every week that she would have the grace and strength to continue. She recalled her father saying on his deathbed to her, "Don't let any of them [her children] get involved." "Now I know what he meant." She found the ordeal of her daughter and of the H Block protesters so unreal and grotesque that she believed, perhaps unfoundedly, that if the public at large had been aware of their plight then it would speedily have been ended. "I am listening to Afghanistan on the BBC in every news bulletin. I can't stand it. Why don't they show H Block or Armagh? Mairéad says: 'I don't care if the Russians come. Send them to Armagh first; we will worry about them afterwards.'"

As a woman, the thought of her daughter enduring the particularly feminine discomforts of being on the blanket clearly disturbed and upset Mrs. Farrell greatly, and though one part of her mind was obviously revolted she did what she could in little ways to keep

Mairéad's morale up. For instance, she got the well known disc jockey, Pascal Mooney, to play a record for her. There was a big cheer in the prison when Mairéad's name—though not her location—was read out. This was a device used to encourage the H Block men also. Requests were played for them on Downtown Radio, at the behest of people who simply gave the men's names and the name of the record.

While Mairéad was in jail her father was arrested and brought to Castlereagh for interrogation, even though the security forces—with their undoubtedly accurate sources of information—must have known that he was entirely unconnected with the movement. The harassment was just one of the side effects of Mairéad's imprisonment, along with the worry as to her health and the possibility of a hunger strike, and was one of the many shadows which the troubles have thrown over the lives of not alone the Farrells but thousands of other families in Northern Ireland.

1. St. Patrick's College on the Glen Road, run by the De La Salle Brothers, was a corrective institute for young offenders.
2. A mime play about H Block, *Thoughts of a Man on the Blanket*, was presented by sympathisers.

CHAPTER 8

"Too Long a Sacrifice..."

By now readers will have had a fair insight into what it felt like to be a mother with a son "on the blanket." It was a tormenting experience. But cruel as that ordeal was, "the troubles," that euphemism for the poisoned net of tangled tragedies which has fallen over Northern Ireland since 1969, sometimes deals even more cruel cards to the victims of those events. Can one imagine for instance the mind of a mother visiting one son in H Block each month where he was supporting the Provisionals' protest—and who has had another boy shot dead by the Provisionals, killed deliberately as an informer?

Mrs. Kathleen Carney was such a mother; grey-haired, hazel-eyed, this widow and mother of four was born in Glasgow of Irish parents, but despite all that has happened she would like to be considered wholly Irish. She had about her that ineffable air of kindly efficiency that suggests both a Scottish housewife and an Irish hospital worker.

Her house in Lenadoon, the celebrated district in which occurred the demise of the Truce between the IRA and the British army, bore no sign of the agonies which the failure of that Truce cost Andersonstown in general and Mrs. Carney in particular. The paper on the walls was fresh. The paint work sparkled, the carpets were new, plentiful, and the furniture comfortable and well chosen. Being Andersontown, there was inevitably a Long Kesh plaque on the wall.[1] Being Catholic there was also a large picture of the Sacred Heart.

Not for the first time during my research for this book, I felt as though I were in some way participating in a Sean O'Casey drama as Mrs. Carney sighed and pointing out the Sacred Heart picture to me said:

> Michael kissed that Holy picture going out every night
> and morning. I didn't want him to get involved but one
> day he came back after he was supposed to be at school
> and you could see the mark of the beret on his forehead.
> I knew he was out on a Fianna march. He said he was-
> n't but I went down and saw the Brother. He told me he
> wasn't at school that afternoon and I kept him in for a
> fortnight even though he tortured me to let him out. I let
> him out eventually. I had to. The trouble started getting
> worse. I had this wee feeling—from the fellows that
> were calling for him and that. At that time the IRA was
> running classes in houses all over Andersonstown. I
> asked him was he in the IRA. He said he wasn't. I asked
> him would he kiss the picture and tell me that he wasn't
> in the 'RA, on his word. He wouldn't kiss it and then as
> he went out he turned to me and said, 'Mother what do
> you want me to do with them lads on the blanket.' So
> then I knew.
>   Then he got himself kneecapped. Seán, his twin,
> got into a row with this fellow in a pub and Michael
> came over and started fighting with him. We heard
> afterwards that he was something important in the IRA
> and anyway they kneecapped Michael. But he was still
> in the 'RA. Then he was lifted and brought to
> Castlereagh. They tortured him and they told him they
> would shoot him. They warned him that if he went
> away they would shoot his next of kin. So he gave away
> a dump and some other volunteers. When he got out he
> told the 'RA what he had done. The 'RA took him away
> for two weeks to interrogate him. Then Anne, my
> daughter, was lifted by the Army. They told her that the
> Provisionals had Michael. They said he was an informer

and that they would shoot him. He would be found with
a bullet.

Anne told me. I was all worried but she said why
should I be worrying? Didn't he go to the 'RA himself?
A lot of young lads broke in Castlereagh and they
would go to the Provisionals and tell them what happened. The Provies would move the dumps and tell the
lads that were mentioned to get away but that's all they
would do, because so many were being lifted and talking. Whoever had talked couldn't work as a volunteer
because he was known, but he could do political work
or help with the Sinn Féin or something. I remember I
was going to Knock that weekend—I've a great devotion to Our Lady of Knock—but on July 12, 1979, they
found Michael at Newtownbutler near the border. He
had been shot four times in the head."[2]

Tears came into Mrs. Carney's eyes. They often welled up
while she was talking though she fought them back and didn't actually cry.

"We used to be five, now we are three," she said. Seán,
Michael's twin, at that time still lived at home with her in Andersonstown, as did Anne, who was the eldest. "Seamus, the second eldest,
is 'on the blanket.' When I went to tell him what happened, he said I
was to forget it. It was just one of those things that happened. I can't
forget it. They took my son. After kneecapping him and all. You
know, poor Michael, he used to say the Provisionals done him a good
turn by kneecapping him because when they would be interrogating
him he used to point to his knee and say: 'Me in the Provos, after they
had done that! No way'." Mrs. Carney's husband Seamus, after whom
the boy in H Block was called, was a brass moulder in the shipyards
when he died; one of the very few Catholics to hold such employment. "He was a good man, very religious. He had great devotion to
the Sacred Heart and he died on June 2, the feast of the Sacred
Heart—a brain haemorrhage."

How did a family with such a religious background become involved in deeds of such ferocity? Again the answer that tells all and solves nothing: "the troubles."

"We used to live in East Belfast," explains Mrs. Carney, "but we had to move out when the boys were little. At first we lived in 'Brian Faulkner's bungalows' on the Glen Road." (These were a set of hutments which Faulkner obtained from the Shelter Organisation when "the troubles" first broke out, and they were put up as temporary dwellings to house the refugees. The area was subsequently taken over by itinerants.) "When we came here it was different then. The 'RA were running Irish classes and history classes in the houses, indoctrinating the young fellows, and the soldiers were stopping everyone. The boys got stopped and arrested that often, I can't tell you. I remember coming home one day and I saw them with Michael up against the wall with the point of a gun and I went over to them and told Michael to come on home. The soldiers said you are not taking him away. I said I am. I am his mother and he is coming home with me, and they let me take him."

Seán, Michael's then twenty-one-year-old twin, tall, well-built, with black hair, working in a leisure centre and studying fitness, recalled their childhood. "The house was always being raided. They always said they would shoot Seamus when they caught him. Then they took him in a jeep and let him out in a Protestant estate. They shouted 'there's a Provo bastard.' They did that to me and Michael one day too. They brought me up the Shankill Road and then let us out. If we hadn't run we would have been dead. They hung me up by the feet in Fort Mona [an Army post in Andersonstown] and beat me. A couple of the Paras had been shot around the estate that day. But that was nothing. Another time Seán and Patsy [names supplied] were taken to a quarry somewhere up the hills. They were beaten to a jelly and then they reversed the jeep over their hands. That was the Commandos. You know Commandos are wild. They tell you there's not enough aggro. They like having riots with the people. Everyone got it when they were around. They would jump out of the jeeps, put you up against a wall and tell you, 'you are going over to the quarry.'

I remember an officer [name supplied] in the Parachute Regiment putting me up against a wall telling me I was lucky it wasn't dark or I'd go over the edge of the quarry, but that there were too many people around. Then he brought down the rifle butt on my toes. After them, they would bring in a softer regiment, then a hard one again. The Black Watch was the worst of all. I remember JF we used to call him. He was an Intelligence Officer. Always wore a shortarm and had long curly fair hair. He said to me one day: 'I am going to blow your head off when I get you into Fort Mona.' They want to get rid of us all—Catholic people."

The mother interjected—"You see the boys were very tall, that was why they always got stopped." Despite this litany of harassment Seán did not follow his elder brother into the IRA, but Michael did after Seamus was "lifted." "You know they would say to us, 'you were just Paddy bastards, Irish bastards. We don't like our job. We would make it hard for you.' They want to soften us up. They do the opposite, for people hate them." Seamus was picked up in 1976 and got fourteen years for conspiracy to murder. His orders had been to shoot an off-duty UDR man who worked in a factory. The first day that the UDR man came out of the factory at the appointed hour, Seamus could not bring himself to pull the trigger, but he was ordered back the next day to carry out his task. However, there were concealed cameras set about the factory and he and the driver of the car were arrested on the second occasion.

He was taken to Castlereagh and subjected to "deep interrogation" treatment there. Then after almost a year on remand, he was sentenced and went on the blanket. He warned Michael not to join, but history and harassment led his brother to disregard his advice and take the road that led to Newtownbutler. Mrs. Carney's eyes well up again: "When I think of watching Michael growing up for them ones to come and take him away. He was my son, they took him over. I couldn't stand it for a long time but I pray. Father Reid helps me. I take the dog and I go for a walk up the hills. I talk to God and I cry. They won't let me do it at home. They see me opening his drawer with his medals and pictures. Anne says to me, why are you crying, our Michael's in Heaven. I don't bother with anyone or talk to anyone. I just try to make the home as comfortable as I can for those that are left."

Mrs. Carney got up at this point and got me a "parcel" which she had made up for Seamus. It contained four refills of hard pencil lead, four biro refills, cigarette paper, a blade from a pencil sharpener, six flints, a half ounce of tobacco. All were enclosed in a Polythene wrapper and made a compact cigar shape which would fit up Seamus's rectum without discomfort. "But they caught me trying to hand it over to him and he did time on the boards. Before Michael's death I used to go on the marches to support the Provos. Now I don't go on them. I feel for some. I wish it was over but I would not ask them to give up. They would make them scrub floors and call the warders sir. You do get a decent warder sometimes. One let me give Seamus some chewing gum and I wanted to give him a Rosary beads and he went and asked a prison officer for permission to allow him to have them. That was a comfort. But when I hear of warders being shot or soldiers, it doesn't have any effect on me."

I thought of Yeats' lines "too long a sacrifice can make a stone of the heart"[3] but Mrs. Carney had the last word: "I would love to have grandchildren but I don't know now that I will be alive to see them."

1.   It shows a bird, an eagle or a phoenix, symbolising freedom, rising above a background of the tricolour and the flag of the Fianna intertwined and flying over a map of Ireland.

2.   Obviously it was very difficult to make meaningful enquiries into the background of an incident like the shooting of Michael Carney. All I could learn was that the fact that he was in custody in Newtownbutler may have had something to do with it. Belfast IRA circles customarily treat cases of men cracking in Castlereagh in a different fashion. It was known that senior IRA decision takers in Belfast were away at the time of the Carney shooting. Obviously I am only giving the family version of what happened, but I did encounter a reluctance to place any other version on the record.

3.   Quote from "Easter 1916" by W. B. Yeats.

CHAPTER 9

The Pettigrews

In 1980, John and Katrina Pettigrew lived in Ballymurphy in a three bedroomed bungalow made of aluminium. They had ten children, the youngest of whom was ten. They lived largely on the "berew."[1] £52 a week for John, and the Children's Allowances, £4 a week, for those up to sixteen.

A number of the children were no longer eligible for this benefit, including John who was interned, went on hunger strike and was later released, and who got fed up with unemployment in Ballymurphy and went to England with his wife and two children in search of a job and a home. He had just gone a few days when I had talked to the Pettigrews and they were worried about not hearing from him. "I suppose he was all right," sighed Katrina, then fifty-one. "We would have heard if there was anything wrong. Bad news travels fast, but you know the way it is with the Special Powers and all, they can pick you up and put you away and the family never hear of it. Look at what happened to Giuseppe Conlon."

(Giuseppe Conlon died of a bronchial complaint in Hammersmith Hospital, London, on January 23, 1980. An elderly man in poor health, Mr. Conlon was himself quite unconnected with the IRA, but his son was among those arrested in connection with the Guildford bombings of 1974. On hearing the news, he travelled to England where he was arrested and subjected to some highly suspect forensic "tests," which have since been discredited, but which then purported to show that he had been handling explosives. He was sentenced to prison, and died protesting his innocence, the efforts of Cardinal Hume and others to secure his release having proved unavailing until it was too late. The medical evidence of experts like Dr. Joseph Hendron, who actually treated Mr. Conlon before he set off for London and who knew him to be a very sick man, was also overlooked.)

There were three other Pettigrew children for whom benefit was not applicable either. One was Brian, the second eldest, twenty-five in 1980, who was serving ten years for unarmed robbery. Two out of the three years he had been in custody had been spent on the blanket.

Another for whom no benefit could be granted was Ann Marie who was blown up in a premature explosion—an incendiary device fried her alive. Her memory is commemorated in a plaque on the Pettigrew wall—"Staff Captain A. M. Pettigrew and Volunteer Francis Wall." An "own goal" the British army call such deaths.

The third was Katrina, serving eight years in Armagh jail, for being found in possession of incendiary devices. When I spoke to her family she had completed a year on the former "limited" protest and was then on the dirty protest. "She is starting to smell," said her father John, then a slim, well preserved man of forty-eight who had been unemployed for ten years. "I would work night and day if I could get it. But the only kind of jobs you can get here are with McAlpines and Wimpeys. Now they don't give our sort a job at Gloucester House [the labour exchange] if you live above Castle Street."

It's probably fair to say that the Pettigrew mother Katrina was the more Republican of the two. She supported her family and thought of the struggle in terms of winning freedom. John would like a better house, a chance to work—"our kind would never get into the shipyard," he says. "This house is all right. It's thirty years old. The walls are beginning to rust a bit. We pay £5.46 a week for it. We would like some place better."

The Pettigrews kept the house well, remarkably so for a home that had reared such a large family, but the paint was dull, the lights were dim, the ceilings were low and Ballymurphy is a ghetto of ghettoes.

By 1980, the troubles had claimed approximately sixty lives from the district, and the legal "conveyor-belt" system has shuttled literally hundreds from the neighbourhood through interrogation, courts, camps and jails. For Ballymurphy was a natural breeding ground for the IRA. Statisticians differ only as to the extent of the male unemployment there. In 1980, I had never seen a lower statistic than thirty-three and a third, and I had known estimates to go as high as forty-eight per cent, with sixty per cent for male unemployment. What the accuracy of any such statistic from the area is one didn't know. Any enumerator going about the district would have to have either a degree of trust amongst the inhabitants and the IRA that is very hard to imagine, or he would have to be accompanied by a heavily armed guard. I don't know how one would set about evaluating the information thus collected.

Women can get some types of work—cleaning and so on—but if they do, it is deducted from their husband's "berew" and the result is not worth it. The Pettigrews were obviously what in other circumstances in Northern Ireland would be called "well-doing" people. John cultivated his garden—"They call me farmer Brown, the kids, I mean." Katrina had learned crochet at Father Wilson's social services centre.

The value of Fr. Wilson's educational efforts cannot be overvalued in a place like Ballymurphy, with its mediocre design, its absence of green spaces, its torn-up paving stones, its slogan-bedaubed council houses and gimcrack council flats.

Another Pettigrew boy was then eighteen. I met him and his fiancée, also eighteen, in the Pettigrew home. They were taking their turn at minding yet another daughter's baby so that she and her husband could go out for the evening. The child was obviously adored by its grandparents and youthful aunts and uncles and was handed from one to the other and played with, receiving that casually expert affection that one finds in large families.

The eighteen-year-old told me about his plans for setting up a home of his own. "We are going to move in with her aunt. She lives on her own. You will have to get me a suit for that day, Ma!" he grinned at his mother. The mother sighed and said, "We will get it some place. It's amazing the way the money comes." The boy was a pleasant, courteous lad, obviously of good basic intelligence but he had no job and was, he said, studying to be a Roman Artist. "Roamin' the streets and drawing the berew." He didn't go to the country much, or to the sea, "just sitting around the house all day." He didn't see himself leaving Belfast. "I like this old place." His fiancée agreed. He didn't think that people in the "State" wanted to know people from the North. He was only in Dublin once, significantly en route to Bodenstown. But the soldiers, and fear of sectarian assassination, ensured that he rarely left Ballymurphy. Amusements such as going to a cinema didn't arise. One wonders what sort of outlook and background would the experience of this youthful bridegroom confer on his children?

Already his younger brother, then aged ten, who had literally known nothing but "the troubles," would find it very difficult to find his way around the centre of the city, a distance in good times of ten to fifteen minutes on a bus. His parents hadn't been to a cinema, once their favourite pastime, since "The Sound of Music" was seen in Belfast.

To Brian, on the blanket, the IRA seemed to offer the only possibility of changing the system. So long as he stayed on it, his example and the conditions of Ballymurphy would go to ensure that others were going to follow in his footsteps. According to his parents, Brian had told them that he felt he was a second-class citizen. "That we all were. He wanted freedom," said his mother. As so often happens, a desire for freedom and troubled times cause happenings which where the IRA is concerned lead one to paraphrase Madame Roland: "Oh liberty, what blunders are committed in thy name."

In Brian Pettigrew's case the peculiar charge of unarmed robbery arose out of a rent, rates and facility strike which the Catholic population embarked upon in Northern Ireland, as a result of internment. Very large arrears built up for rent and for gas and electricity supplies in particular and a decision was taken by the authorities either to reclaim these or cut off supplies. The IRA decided to resist this attempt, and Brian Pettigrew was one of the Volunteers deputed to warn off the gasmen when they entered Ballymurphy.

According to his parents, he and his companions simply ordered the man and his helper out, but in court it was claimed that he had robbed £700 worth of takings from the gasmen. "Sure there was no money in the gas meters for anyone either to collect or to rob," said his mother scornfully. He was also charged with the attempted murder of a soldier on another occasion but this charge at least was dropped when the judge called for maps of the area and pointed out that the soldier who claimed that Pettigrew had attempted to murder him from point A while he stood at point B was actually out of sight. Neither B nor A could be seen from either point. However, membership of the IRA, and the attempted intimidation of the gasmen, resulted in the ten year sentence and three days in deep interrogation. Pettigrew still carried the marks of the bruises of this on his face and body when he was brought to court. His parents said they were just keeping going until the gates opened and they all got out.

"I hope it's over soon, believe you me," said his mother. But by "it," they didn't only mean the blanket protest, or even Katrina in Armagh jail. What John meant, for instance, was that he wanted to be able to get a job and keep it. There was work in certain districts if one could avail of it. He got started in a Protestant district, rebuilding a public house in which the publican had been killed carrying out a bomb. But two of his fellow workers got chatting with him during the morning tea-break on the day he started, and when they found out where he was from they immediately advised him that he was "very foolish," and he just went back to the Labour Exchange and told them why. He was never called again.

John said: "I am not anti-Protestant. There is good and bad everywhere. Everyone is entitled to live. Those men that warned me weren't being nasty or anything, they were just telling me what the dangers were."

It was obvious talking to people like the Pettigrews that they were more frightened of Protestant extremism than bigoted against Protestants in general. They had lurid fears and theories about figures like Paisley, for instance. "I was talking to a man that said Paisley had a big picture in his church of him sitting on a throne and the Pope kissing his feet," was one example. But their conversation also contained two verifiable examples of actual killings by Protestant extremists.

Michael for instance talked wonderingly of the details of the "Shankill Butchers" case. "Imagine they offered him a cup of tea [a victim who was being hacked to death at the time] and another fellow dressed up as a priest to give him the last rites." This remark sparked off other recollections: "The young one that was beaten to death with a brick over a day by them three women and her little daughter crying outside the door," contributed the mother. Whilst outside the Catholic ghettoes people talk in similar terms about IRA atrocities, these are the fears and preoccupations of the unemployed Catholic working class in the ghettoes like Twinbrook, Ballymurphy, Turf Lodge, Andersonstown and so on. The situation so engulfs them that outside distraction is almost non-existent. A colour television, the only luxury item in the house, provided a window on the world. And Katrina read light romances and James Bond books. John liked cowboy stories but preferred the garden to television. Obviously in such a situation the plight of their children bulked large. The father in particular could be heard mentioning Katrina intermittently during the conversation. "She looked bad, very jiggy, I thought," and other aspects of her incarceration perturbed them also. For instance, they didn't like the idea of her being imprisoned with the Protestant women sentenced for the killing of the young woman. "They beat her to death with a brick. I hear they are taking sleeping pills. So well they might," said Katrina.

To put the brick murder case in perspective it should, I think, be noted that the Protestant women involved in that horrific murder were just as much a product of and victims of the North's history, as was their victim, or the Pettigrews' daughter.

The two, Henrietta Cowan, known in the prison as "Ettie," and Christina Smith, known as "Chris," were sentenced in February of 1975, when they were then eighteen and seventeen respectively, for the murder of an unmarried mother, thirty-one-year-old Ann Ogilby in a UDA "Romper Room," as the torture centre in the Sandy Row area was called.

Her crime was that she had been visiting a married UDA man in Long Kesh, taking him parcels. Her killers—and there were at least ten other people implicated in the killing, one of whom, Lily Douglas, an older woman, has since died in the Prison hospital— were only seventeen and sixteen at the time of the murder, and came from a particularly low stratum of Belfast society. Smith's brother was shot dead by the Provos. Drink may have played a part in the actual beating. Certainly the allegations and innuendo which formed the background to the killing were all conducted in a public house. Ogilby's six-year-old daughter was sent out to buy sweets while her mother was hooded and bound, but was then left standing, weeping, outside the locked Romper Room while her mother screamed her last inside. Both Smith and Cowan were later described by visitors to the prison as "just ordinary, decent poor divils." Both were detained for life at the pleasure of the Secretary of State.[2]

The harsh milieu which formed and deformed Cowan and Smith is one moreover which is imbued with a form of debased Protestant sectarianism which sees itself as superior to the "Scarlet Whore of Babylon's Romish supporters" (i.e. the Catholics, their clergy and the IRA which at least earlier in the troubles were portrayed as interchangeable). So it is understandable that the fear and loathing so generated should have resulted in some really unspeakable fates being visited on Catholics who fell into the clutches of those who ran the "Romper Rooms." Poor Ann Ogilby was "one of their own" after all. The tortures reserved for one of "the others" are better imagined than described, but they played a very real part in the fears of families like the Pettigrews.

The pub, the traditional refuge of the Irish working class, didn't play much part in the Pettigrew lives. "We can't afford it," said John. Religion and their sense of identity, of nationality, were obviously important to them. In giving me a cup of tea, Mrs. Pettigrew pressed me to have something to eat as well, saying, "that's a real English cup of tea—nothing with it." Mrs. Pettigrew obviously found that apart from the therapeutic effects of prayer itself, the Church's teaching on issues such as divorce and contraception was beneficial to society. "Large families were more united. They tend to stick it better. Sometimes I say I am away, I have had enough, but I am back in a few minutes to see if they are all right. I think you would be better off if divorce wasn't introduced in the Republic, there are a lot of young people splitting up here. You have got the strain of the young men being locked up, the young women going out to the clubs. They taste the freedom and then the husband is forgotten about. It's no good."

Many things about Ballymurphy and allied districts are "no good." It is no accident that it was the strong deadly spark of Republicanism that was potent enough to get young Michael out of Ballymurphy and down to the South on his one visit to Dublin—en route to Bodenstown. Unfortunately that same spark had laid invisible signposts in many a mind in Ballymurphy and places like it, pointing out of the ghettoes, certainly, but leading very often only to the grave or the H Blocks.

1.   A Northernism originally derived from "Social Welfare Bureau."
2.   See Chapter 16.

CHAPTER 10

Women on the Dirty Protest

The "dirty protest" is bad enough to contemplate when men are on it, but it becomes even worse when it is embarked on by women, who apart from the psychological and hygienic pressures which this type of protest generates, also have the effects of the menstrual cycle to contend with. But the "dirty protest" with all its implications spread to Armagh jail in February 1980. The Republican women prisoners there had previously been restrained from outside the prison by the IRA, which felt it had enough on its plate with the men.

However, prison life has a dynamism of its own, and despite the objections of the people outside, the women in Armagh, some thirty in all, under the leadership of their OC, Mairéad Farrell, had gradually built up a campaign of "limited protest" by refusing to work, which had led to some restrictions being placed on them as a result. But the prisoners were still allowed to exercise for an hour and a half in the mornings and for some three hours in the evenings. Although the atmosphere in the prison was not good, at least a full scale H Block confrontation had been avoided, despite the fact that there had been trouble at the prison in May 1978 when, after disturbances broke out amongst remand prisoners, a squad of male prison officers in riot gear locked the women in their cells for several weeks. It was particularly hot during that period and this proved to be a severe punishment and left a legacy of bitterness.

In fact, from the time that the former Governor, Hugh Cunningham ("a very fair man," I was told) was transferred to Magilligan camp—which had remained significantly quiet following his arrival there—the atmosphere in Armagh was alleged to have hardened. His successor, Mr. George Scott, was described to me as a stickler for discipline. Allegations were made to me that as the situation worsened, insensitivities causing complaints became common. For instance, I was told that women suffering from diarrhoea were left in the cells for over half an hour after ringing their cell bells to be allowed to go to the toilets, and if a woman had had her period on, say, the third of a month then she got her sanitary towels on the third of the following month, even though the period might have arrived earlier. There were also complaints that sometimes the supply of sanitary towels was inadequate. I cannot honestly say, having spoken to Mr. Scott that I found him either inhumane or insensitive. He seemed to me a basically decent man caught in an impossible situation.

The flashpoint arrived with the Delaney funeral issue. As Delaney had three sisters serving sentences in Armagh, the Republican women prisoners decided to hold a commemorative ceremony for him. They did this wearing the quasi-military black skirt uniform of Cumann na mBan. A week later, on February 7, really serious trouble broke out in B Wing, a three storied building with cat-walks.

The food at the prison had not been particularly appetising for some time, probably because of the protest, and the women did not as a rule show much interest in their meals. However, on this occasion it was announced that there was to be chicken and apple pie for lunch. All the women left their cells and lined up at the hot plate from which the midday meal was served. As they lined up, a prison official announced that their cells were to be searched—it transpired later for the black skirts—but the women paid little heed, being engrossed in the unusually good food. But apparently the reason that the food was so good that day was to get them to line up on the ground floor and out of their cells, because immediately following the official announcement, the women were surrounded by some sixty male and female warders, some of the former drafted in from Long Kesh. Panic broke out. Plates were thrown and the women were kicked and punched until order was restored, largely by their own leaders, and they were all locked up in the wing's two association cells. Their own cells were searched, and according to the women's version, "wrecked."

The women were returned to their cells after an individual body search but were then informed they were to be brought to the guard-room for "Adjudications"—the allocation of punishments for those involved in the fracas. Men in riot gear, armed with batons, appeared in the cells again. The women were beaten and carried down the stairs to the guard room to receive their punishments. The toilets were locked and they were confined to their cells for twenty-four hours, on a diet that fell far below chicken and apple pie.

Inevitably the women's pots filled up with urine and excrement (as the lavatories were locked) and the women began pouring them out the spy holes of their cells. Beatings continued. The following was an account given by Anne Marie Quinn to her parents:

At approximately 12:20 yesterday [Thursday, February 7, 1980], a squad of 30–40 male officers came into B Wing, Armagh Prison. We were all at the hot plate get-ting our dinner and they lined in front of us. Our leader asked what was going on and the officer mumbled about cell searches. I turned to lift my dinner and turned back to see two male officers trail Shirley Devlin into a doorway so I ran toward them. Before I got near them a male officer put his arms around my head and throat and started manhandling me. He tripped me judo style and landed me on my back with full force. I must have blacked out for a minute or so for someone helped me up and stood me at the hot plate. I was still dizzy and had to stay there for a while. Anne Bateson asked me was I all right. She had a black eye and badly swollen face. Everyone got thrown into two Association cells where we were locked till after three o'clock. Then we were body searched and brought back to our cells one at a time. My cellmate Eilís O'Connor came in and tried fixing the cell up. It was wrecked. Then Mairéad Farrell

shouted in that they wanted Eilís and three other women
down to the Governor as they were on report earlier in
the week. Mairéad got to B2 going towards her own cell
when twelve female officers grabbed her. They took
turns at trailing her. We could see this from our spyhole.
Next we heard the screams from Anne Bateson, Eileen
Morgan and Mairéad as they were beaten and trailed
from their cells to the prison authorities. Then the male
officers ran up the two flights of stairs and called "Eilís
O'Connor." Before we knew what was happening three
men in riot gear and more behind them charged into the
cell. I was banged against the wall with a riot shield and
two men jumped me—one jumped and dug his knees
into my chest. I yelled with pain. The other one twisted
my anus. I called them names and they laughed in my
face. I didn't even notice Eilís being dragged from the
cell but I heard her screams from downstairs. I shouted
"Are ye all right" and then I had to keep my mouth shut
for the next five minutes while they held me, because if
I'd opened my mouth, I'd have screamed and that's
what they wanted because they kept twisting my wrists
till I thought they were broken or would break. Then
they jumped up and twisted my wrists till they got out
of the door. Then I heard Rosie Callaghan and Margaret
Nugent next door as the male officers were trailing
Rosie out to the Governor. A few hours later a nurse
came into me and took note of the bruises and scratches
on my wrists, arms and below my left eye. My shoulders, back and ankles were also hurt but showed no
marks. I am five foot one inch and weigh eight stone ten
pounds. The three officers who attacked me were all at
least five foot ten inches and looked heavy men.[1]

The spyholes were nailed shut; the women started throwing the
excrement out of their cell windows, but these were boarded up.

Armagh jail opens directly onto the street. By February 12, a full scale dirt protest was in operation with the women smearing their excrement on the cell walls and refusing all clothing except what they stood up in. They were locked in their cells twenty-three hours a day—they refused to accept what was known as "closed" association, that was a few prisoners using the association cells at a time. Initially the women compounded the dirt protest by using tissues instead of sanitary towels, but these were issued to them and the practice discontinued.

The real trouble about the Armagh protest is that it began virtually by accident. I have given the stated *casus belli*, but misunderstandings and poor communication played at least as great a part in allowing events to take the turn they did. The IRA had been restraining the women from going on the Dirty Protest for at least six months beforehand, having enough on the organisation's plate in trying to cope with the H Block protest's effects. When word of the intended protest following the events of February 7 leaked out, the IRA tried to get a message via Fr. Reid to Cardinal O Fiaich to get him to intervene in the situation, but the message was blocked en route. To compound this position, Father Murray, then chaplain at Armagh, who was held in high respect by the women, was temporarily excluded from the prison in the aftermath of February 7, and precious time was lost when negotiations were being conducted to have him readmitted, but by the time this was done the avalanche was moving downhill. The women had embarked on the protest and did not come off it. The part which happenstance plays in ordaining the course of events in the super-charged emotional atmosphere of prison cannot be overstressed.

A visitor to the prison described it to me as "being quite extraordinary. There's a sickly sweet 'hum.' The lights are on in their cells—because the cells are blocked up—and the women won't even use clean sheets when the old ones are due for replacement. They won't wash and they've no change of underwear. They have the excrement all round their cells. The only things spared are holy pictures. You see here and there pictures of the Blessed Virgin on the walls framed in shit. The Loyalist members of the prison visitors committee think that's dreadful."

When word of the February 7 events got out, the Westminster MP for Fermanagh, Frank Maguire, wrote to the Secretary of State calling for a public enquiry into the beating of the women. He was replied to by Michael Alison, the Minister responsible for the prisons as follows:

25 February, 1980.

I am replying to your letter of 9 February to the Secretary of State.

A full investigation of recent events at Armagh Prison has already been carried out by the Governor of the Prison. I am satisfied that there is no question of any prisoners having been attacked by staff, or having been denied access to toilets. I can see no justification for holding any form of Public Enquiry.

This is of course the sort of reply one expects from officialdom in such cases, but one of the questions one would like to have answered is why, given the highly volatile nature of the prison situation in Northern Ireland, the male officers were imported into Armagh on February 7 for the chicken-baited search. The women's cells could easily have been searched when they were at Mass or on recreation. But there seems to have been some planning put into the choice of methods of heavy-handedness. All the prisoners in the other wings were locked in just before 12:00 that day and all social workers and ministers of religion sent off the premises.

On Wednesday February 20, 1980, before it was known outside the jail what was going on inside it, Michael Alison had already been precipitated into letter writing, this time by an article in the *Irish Independent* by Bernadette Cahill, in which she described a protest which was being planned because of conditions in the prison. Alison immediately replied—too immediately, because apart from the fact that conditions then and subsequently were far worse than Miss Cahill had described he also made the following statement.

Ms. Cahill refers to the prisoners being "detained for political offences." All those to whom she refers have been sentenced to periods of imprisonment, having been found guilty in a court of law—after due trial—of serious criminal offences including murder, attempted murder, arson and explosives and firearms offences. There are no political prisoners in Northern Ireland.

Mr. Alison was using a narrow definition of the term "political" prisoner. In fact, apart from the prisoners in Long Kesh who were acknowledged as "political" by their Special Category status, two of the most celebrated "political" prisoners of the decade were actually in Armagh jail itself—Dolours and Marian Price who had been convicted of causing explosions in London on March 12, 1973. They were transferred to Armagh in June 1974 after being on a hunger strike, during which they were forcibly fed for 206 days. During their struggle to be allowed to serve their sentence in an Irish jail, where their relatives could visit them, they had brought injunctions against the authorities in an attempt to prevent themselves being force-fed. After their transfer, to silence both medical and legal critics of the force-feeding policy, as well as Unionist and Conservative critics of the decision to concede on the transfer of the sisters, the then Home Secretary Roy Jenkins announced that henceforth in any case of hunger striking prisoners, force-feeding would not be used.

This decision was to have very far reaching effects because behind the Parliamentary language what it meant in effect was that henceforth any prisoner going on hunger strike would be allowed to die. One prisoner, Michael Gaughan, had in fact died in Parkhurst prison on the Isle of Wight (on June 3, 1974) by the time of the Jenkins statement in July of that year, and another, Frank Stagg, would die two years later in Wakefield Prison (on February 12, 1976). But the effects of the Jenkins policy, and of the possible outcome of such a protest being embarked on, had led the IRA outside to use its influence all through the H Block protest to prevent the IRA inside from trying to emulate the Price women's success.

In fact both women paid very dearly for this triumph, contracting anorexia nervosa as a result. Marian also suffered psychological damage to such an extent that she would have died in prison, had she not been released on the intervention of Cardinal O Fiaich on May 1, 1980, to be treated in a hospital in the South.

The following was an account of a day in the life of Armagh prison, smuggled out by one of the protesters:

> I hear the key turning in the lock; the screw sticks her head in. "Out for breakfast" she says. I can see by her face that the stench in the cell must be pretty bad because even through the mask her face is in a grimace. I pull on my jeans and the duffel; lift the two plastic cups and head out. I glance at my watch and see it's 8:10 a.m. We're early this morning. Yesterday we were among the last at 9:40 a.m. So maybe this is our lucky day. My cellmate hasn't moved. We take turns each morning to collect the food and I know what she's thinking and hoping. She doesn't have to say a word to convey her thoughts as in each cell the same thoughts are running through everyone's head. "Please God let it be cornflakes." As I approach the table I notice the silence, not a word is spoken. There are six female screws; no one else except me and them on the wing. I put down the mugs for the tea. I am afraid to look. But I know deep down in my heart, I know it's porridge. Well that's what it is supposed to be—we call it gruel. I like porridge and I'm not a fussy eater. You couldn't afford to be in this place. But nobody could stomach that porridge. It's nothing but hard lumps. I have nothing in my stomach but were I to even attempt to eat that stuff I'd be physically sick. It has happened before. Cornflakes are seldom on except for Sunday as half of us get our breakfast before Mass, the other half after Mass. So we can always rely on cornflakes for Sunday. But this happens to be Tuesday.

I glance down and my worst fears are con-
firmed—it's porridge. The screw has poured tea into the
cups. I lift them immediately. She won't touch the mugs
even though she has gloves on; they don't like to touch
anything belonging to us. Still the silence. I turn round
and head back to the cell. As I do the three screws
behind me start to laugh. The three up at my door just
watch. It used to annoy me the sniggering but not any
more. Sometimes I felt like throwing the tea around
them but why waste the tea. They'd just love a good
enough reason to get stuck into me. They can laugh.
But the false laughter fades when they open our doors,
and the smell on the wing isn't so pleasant either. I'm
used to it, having no other choice. But I doubt if they'll
ever get used to it. I return to the cell, the door bangs
locked. Sineád looks up. I just shrug my shoulders. I've
said it all before. Why repeat myself, the look on my
face should be sufficient. "Here drink your tea before it
gets cold" I say and the next minute I hear the wall
banging. Eilís is banging from the cell next door. I lean
down to the pipe that runs through all the cells. She
shouts through "Go on, tell me it's bacon and eggs! " I
laugh. It's the only way as I shout back "How did you
guess?," "It figures" is the only reply. Again it's not
necessary to elaborate, just routine. Sitting back on the
bed I drink my tea. Our walls are covered in excrement.
There was nothing else to do with it. You can't pile it
up in the corner—that would be unbearable. This way
it's not half as bad. It dries and the smell isn't so bad
after an hour or so. The urine is the worst smell. You'll
probably find that hard to believe. But the stench of it
just seems to cling to the air. It's dark in the cell. I for-
got to turn the light on before I came in—the switch is
outside the door. It's kept on most of the time as it's
always dark with the boarding on the window. I look up

at the window. I can't see out but I think it's raining. I can hear it beating down outside. There's not even a crack I can see through. I must give it to the male screws—they do a thorough job. Sineád breaks into my thoughts "maybe we'll be among the first for dinner." "Maybe," I reply, but I'm not very hopeful as being early for breakfast usually means late for dinner and then the dinner is freezing. Some bright spark on up shouts from behind a window "Good morning campers! "And then starts into the theme of the cornflakes advert "Good morning, the best to you each morning. Sunshine breakfast. Kelloggs cornflakes crisp and full of sun." A groan is also heard as the bright spark gets a whack from her cellmate. From the other side of the wing we can hear one of the women shouting over to the remand prisoners on "B" wing to let us know what was on the news. Armagh Jail comes to life as women get up, dress and make their beds for another day on the "no-wash" protest.

It's six weeks now since it all started. From the day the male screws rushed onto the wing. The thought of it still makes me shiver. I was sure we all were goners that day. Male screws surrounding us and then the beatings. But we survived it and we'll survive this too. Our comrades in H Block lie with only a blanket. At least we have our clothes. A sudden movement on the floor grabs my attention. That spider again. It has been here since we moved to "A" wing. It is huge. It doesn't appear too often. It disappears and then comes back again after a week or so just to prove that it can't find a way out of here either. You know the superstition that goes with killing spiders—bad luck—joke, what would be bad luck—porridge tomorrow! I laugh to myself as Sineád says "I must take my cards down." Again I look at the floor. It was her birthday yesterday

on St Patrick's Day. She's 22. We put the cards up on
the floor—nowhere else for them. The floor is filthy but
the cards certainly add some glamour to the place. Our
mail hasn't been restricted yet but in this place nothing
lasts too long. We start discussing the cards. She'll
probably have more today and decides to keep them up
for another while—cheers the joint up a bit. St Patrick's
Day cards were also left in. Some we received. Some
we didn't. The ones we got had St Patrick on the front.
The others it seems had a leprechaun holding a sham-
rock in one hand and a tricolour in the other—because
of the tricolour the cards weren't allowed in—pettiness.
If it had been the stars and stripes or any other flag
there'd have been no bother.

The rest of the morning we just talked amongst
ourselves or into next door. It's pointless trying to shout
out the doors to others as the screws make too much
noise. All our games we keep until night time when the
screws go off and only the night guard is left. She never
bothers us. At 11:45 a.m. we hear the dinner arrive. It'll
be another fifteen minutes before they start to distribute
it. Whoever's out first knows they're for early exercise
after dinner. The rest have exercise after tea. We listen
intently. They've started opening doors at the other end
of the wing so we're among the last. A voice shouts
"what's for dinner?" The woman replies, "stew, and rice
for dessert." Not bad, the stew isn't up to much and
we'll not have ours for another hour as it's only one
woman out at a time, a very slow process, but the rice is
filling and it doesn't matter if it's cold—we eat it anyway. As we lie patiently awaiting our turn we can hear
the screw screaming at one of the women who's out.
They always do that. They don't bother in the mornings.
Too early to use their vocal chords, but by dinner time
they're well in tune—a deafening noise. Eileen comes

to our door. She's on her way to collect her dinner. She takes the chain off our spy and pulls the shutter back. They chained them shut so we couldn't open them. There's also a steel plate around the spy but with holes in it for the screw to look in. Eileen looks in "how goes it." "Sound" is our reply. "I'll not see you in the yard today cause you're among the last half." With that, the screw is up behind Eileen telling her to move on. Eileen ignores her. She continues the conversation with the screw shouting in her ear "come on, no more will get out if you don't move on." Eileen says "see you" and we can hear her singing her way down for her dinner. The screw is raging. She bangs the shutter over the spy and replaces the chain.

Our turn for dinner over an hour later. The stew's freezing. Really cold, not even lukewarm but we eat it. Too hungry to refuse. The rice is also cold but add a drop of milk and it's even enjoyable. I feel a lot better after. The first sixteen are out for exercise. I sit down and write a few letters home. I had my visit last week. Just the family. Had to put their minds at ease. Conditions are bad and it's worse for the ones at home who hear it all. My next visit is three weeks off. Only the one a month. We lose all privileges for refusing to work—for refusing to accept the label criminal. Britain's latest whim—class us as criminals to disguise the war situation here in Ireland. But it isn't working. It failed from the start as all Britain's policies on Ireland have. I look round the cell at the way I'm forced to live. I know who the real criminals are! I've written my letters and already it's nearly tea-time. If you're beginning to think our day centres round our meals nobody here will argue. We're one of the first to be opened. I go and get the cups filled. Sinéad will collect the food. A salad, could be worse. At least there's no problem with it get-

----

ting cold. So the women coming after won't mind.
Somebody calls me. It's hard to figure where it's coming from. Through which door. I trace the voice.
Dolores is saying something about a letter. I can't hear
with the screws whining in my ear. They're always
harping at us. Some cocky screws push and shove. Then
the rest join in. The next you know it you're being
trailed back to the cell with no food. Back with the
cups. Sineád's out for the food. It's very little but with
bread you can make a couple of sandwiches and it fills
the emptiness you're feeling.

    Now exercise. On with the coats. Bring the cham-
ber full of urine and throw it on the wing or else it'll be
kicked round the cell when you return. You see they
search our cells when we're out and lift furniture and
dishes or whatever else they can find. It's very cold out.
Raining too. The only drop of water that touches our
hair and bodies so we don't mind it. A whole hour to
mix with some others and catch up on some news from
home. Scandal is flying all directions. Too soon it's
over. Back to the cells as the screws call out your name
in rota from her list—one at a time. The screws come
round asking do we want association. We refuse as it's
not the same free association we used to have but just
moved from this cell to another larger one to be locked
into. This we won't accept. The evening passes swiftly.
The singing has started. Different ones called for a
song. The supper arrives. A pancake each. Big deal.
We're locked in for the night. We listen to the male prisoners cleaning the wing. Soon they'll be off and all will
be quiet. Then our entertainment begins. Every night at
9:00 p.m. we have the Rosary in Irish. One shouts it out
the door and the rest respond. Afterwards we have our
Irish class shouted out the doors. Our voices are good
and strong now from persistent shouting. Then perhaps

bingo from our own made cards. It's good crack. Anne-
Marie next door persists in cheating but is always found
out. Then at eleven the ghost story is continued from
the night before as most lie in their beds under the cov-
ers to keep warm—as they listen to the story. At mid-
night all noise ceases—an order lain down by our own
staff. I get into my bed under the blanket—no sheets or
pillowcases. Those too were taken by screws[2] and think
another day over as Sineád voices my thoughts "perhaps it'll be cornflakes tomorrow." Yes maybe tomorrow will be our lucky day.

While the "Dirty Protest" was difficult enough for a healthy
woman to sustain, it became vastly more so when any of the prisoners were suffering from ill-health, as the case of Pauline McLoughlin from Derry illustrates.

Charged in October 1976, she spent sixteen months on remand,
during which time she displayed a tendency to get sick after eating.
In February 1978 she was sentenced and joined her comrades in
Armagh jail on B Wing, where the women were on protest for political status. At this stage it was not certain whether Pauline would be
moved to the Special Category status wing as the offences she was
sentenced for occurred before March 1, 1976, and the withdrawal of
political status. Therefore Pauline remained on Protest wing with her
comrades. Her privileges were not refused pending a reply from the
North of Ireland Office. During this time Pauline's father became
seriously ill, and since there was no direction from the Northern Ireland Office she was permitted to visit her father in hospital under
escort. However, in March 1978, the Northern Ireland Office ruled
that she was not entitled to Special Category status. Pauline immediately joined her comrades on the protest and her privileges were
removed.

Shortly after this her father died and she was refused parole to
attend the funeral because she was on protest. Her stomach complaint
became more serious. Having lost all privileges she could no longer

----

receive food parcels and after each meal nothing of the prison diet remained in her stomach.

By February 1980 Pauline had at various times been declared unfit for punishment, thus enabling her to receive a food parcel weekly and a visit so that her condition improved to the point where she was deemed fit for punishment again. Declared unfit again and removed from the prison hospital to Craigavon hospital, there she received treatment that did nothing to halt the weight loss and vomiting. The "Dirty Protest" meant that Pauline lay in her filthy cell amidst her own vomit in addition to the rest of her bodily secretions.

Ordinary activity such as stair climbing, walking in the yard and so on became too much for her and she began to faint at intervals. On Monday March 18, she was brought to the prison doctor who warned her that under the present conditions on A Wing she was going to die and reminded her that nobody, no matter how ill they were, would be released from prison. In the view of the Northern Ireland Office, who had made this rule, her condition was similar to that of a person on hunger strike, and there was to be no force feeding. It was her decision to die. The doctor told her she was inflicting the conditions on herself and she would continue to deteriorate. He said that he was a strong man but could not endure the conditions on A Wing. The prisoners say that he recorded the conversation in case any question of a law suit against him arose. Despite her condition Pauline remained defiantly mute throughout the interview. She was weighed and recorded as being six stone one pound at that time.

Finally, her companions persuaded her to come off the dirty protest.

1.   Source: *Black February Armagh Prison—Beating Women in Prison*, compiled by Fr. Denis Faul, February 1980.
2.   The prison staff said the women refused sheets and pillowcases as part of the protest.

CHAPTER 11
Torture, Politics and Censorship

In dealing with any aspect of the vicious struggle between the IRA and the security forces, one has to keep before one's mind at all times the fact that one was down in a pit of sectarianism, "official versions," propaganda, dirty tricks on both sides, lies, injustice, murders—and torture. Torture, "ill-treatment," "cruel and degrading treatment," "interrogation"; choose any description one wishes; this had been an integral part of the Northern scene since at least 1971. For the crackdown on the Catholic population of the North did not cease with internment.

Apart from newspaper accounts, particularly in the *Sunday-Times*, the *Guardian*, the *Irish Press* and the *Irish Times*, there have been a number of major official reports dealing with the use of torture or "ill-treatment" against IRA suspects in Northern Ireland since internment. These are

(i)   the Report of the European Court of Human Rights issued in Strasbourg on January 18, 1978.

(ii) a report by Lord Parker of Waddington, adopted on January 31, 1972.

(iii) a report in November of 1971 by Sir Edmund Compton on an enquiry under his chairmanship into the reports of security force brutality towards detainees during and subsequent to the internment swoop of August 1971.

(iv) a report of an Amnesty International mission to Northern Ireland published in June 1978.

(v)   a report on an investigation into police interrogation procedures in Northern Ireland under judge H. G. Bennett published in March 1979.[1]

Compton found that the principal allegations against the security forces were correct. These included, in the words of the report itself:

(a) *Hooding.* Head hooded in a navy or black coloured bag of tightly woven or hessian cloth at all times other than interrogation interviews.

(b) *Noise.* Held in a room where there was a continuous noise variously described as loud and deafening like the escaping of compressed air, the roar of steam, the whirring of helicopter blades, or a drill. Returned to the room with this noise between periods of interrogation.

(c) *Enforced posture on wall.* Facing wall, hands high above head on wall: legs spread apart; forced with batons to maintain posture; so kept till collapsed, when lifted up again; treatment continued for two or three days.

(d) *Sleep.* Variously complained that they had none for two or three days or very little.

(e) *Food.* Variously complained that deprived of food for two or three days, or that diet severely restricted to occasional administration of dry bread and a cup of water until the last day or so. One man (Mr. Shivers) said he had nothing to drink for the first four to five days.[2]

However, the report glossed over or discounted reports that some detainees had been savaged by Alsatian dogs, very badly beaten, forced to run over obstacle courses which included broken glass in bare feet and threatened with being dropped from helicopters, which they were bundled into and out of. The helicopter episode, said Compton, constituted a measure of ill-treatment and the obstacle course incident may have brought to the men concerned "some measure of unintended hardship"! Overall, however, Sir Edmund found:

> Our investigations have not led us to conclude that any
> of the grouped or individual complainants suffered
> physical brutality as we understand the term.

Sir Edmund's "understanding" was not that of the Catholic population of Northern Ireland who regarded the report as a white-wash job, and "telling a Compton" became common usage in the same way that "telling a Hammer" came to describe Sir Hamar Greenwood's House of Commons denials of security force excesses during the Anglo-Irish war earlier in the century. Nor was Sir Edmund's view of what constituted brutality shared by the North of Ireland courts, which subsequently awarded sizeable sums of money to some of the victims (including Mr. Shivers) of the interrogation procedures. Nor was it that of Southern public opinion.

On December 16, 1971, the Irish Government, to the great annoyance of the British, submitted to the European Commission of Human Rights in Strasbourg an application against the United Kingdom seeking guarantees for the minority in the North of Ireland that the rights guaranteed by the Convention of Human Rights would be guaranteed to all, and alleging certain breaches of the Convention Articles in the application of internment and certain techniques and practices used by the security forces as a result.

After winding its way through the lengthy labyrinth of the European Commission and Court judicial process, the verdict on the "torture case," as it was generally known in Ireland, was delivered by the Court of Human Rights at Strasbourg on January 18, 1978. It found that the use of "the five techniques" as they were known constituted "inhuman and degrading treatment" which was in breach of Article 3 of the Convention on Human Rights, but that these practices did not constitute torture within the meaning of Article 3.

The "five techniques" largely those described by Compton, though given now in more detail—were as follows:

(a) *wall-standing:* forcing the detainees to remain for periods of some hours in a "stress position," described by those who underwent it as being "spread-eagled against the wall, with their fingers put high above the head against the wall, the legs spread apart and the feet back, causing them to stand on their toes with the weight of the body mainly on the fingers";

(b) *hooding:* putting a black or navy coloured bag over the detainees' heads and, at least initially, keeping it there all the time except during interrogation;

(c) *subjection to noise:* pending their interrogation, holding the detainees in a room where there was a continuous loud and hissing noise;

(d) *deprivation of sleep:* pending their interrogations, depriving the detainees of sleep;

(e) *deprivation of food and drink:* subjecting the detainees to a reduced diet during their stay at the centre and pending interrogation.

Even though these findings were not delivered for several years, the case was a considerable embarrassment to the British government which, in an effort to defuse the situation, had set up the Compton Committee. As we saw, his report was derided, and less than a fortnight after adopting it the British were forced to set up another committee, this time chaired by Lord Parker of Waddington to consider

whether, and if so in what respects, the procedures currently authorised for interrogation of persons suspected of terrorism and for their custody while subject to interrogation require amendment.

The Parker Report, which was duly adopted on January 31, 1972, and contained a majority and a minority opinion, considered the methods then in use as being illegal under UK domestic law, though the majority report, subject to certain safeguards against excessive use, did not find them immoral. The minority report, however, by Lord Gardiner did not accept that these methods were morally justifiable even in terrorist conditions.

Accordingly on March 2, 1972, the United Kingdom Prime Minister Ted Heath, stated in Parliament:

> The Government, having reviewed the whole matter
> with great care and with reference to any future opera-
> tions, have decided that the techniques . . . will not be
> used in future as an aid to interrogation.

Somewhat belatedly the same assurance was given to the European Court on February 8, 1977; the United Kingdom Attorney-General made the following declaration:

> The Government of the United Kingdom have consid-
> ered the question of the use of the "five techniques" with
> very great care and with particular regard to Article 3 of
> the Convention. They now give this unqualified under-
> taking, that the "five techniques" will not in any circum-
> stances be reintroduced as an aid to interrogation.

At this stage I would ask readers to cast their minds back to the Diplock Report. In the introduction to the report it was stated that Lord Diplock's firsthand experience of conditions in Northern Ireland during the compilation of the report consisted of "two visits to Northern Ireland, each lasting two days, during which he met *members of the security forces on the ground*" [my italics]. The rest of the seven weeks of the report's compilation were spent in London. So on the basis of what many journalists would consider a firsthand experience barely adequate to the preparation of a series of articles, Lord

Diplock introduced to Northern Ireland a system of courts which by 1977 had produced the following results:

> Researches undertaken by the Law Department of Queen's University, Belfast, showed that ninety-four per cent of the cases brought before the Diplock Courts resulted in conviction. Between seventy per cent and ninety per cent of the convictions are based wholly or mainly on admissions of guilt (self-incriminating statements) made to the police during interrogation. Only in a minority of cases is other evidence—forensic evidence, intelligence evidence, or testimony of witnesses—produced in court to secure a conviction. Forensic evidence is rare, and in the current situation in Northern Ireland the use of witnesses is restricted by the fear of intimidation and reprisal. Intelligence evidence can, by its nature, hardly ever be used in court. (*This report was first published in the* Sunday Times *of October 23, 1977*).

Lord Diplock in his report did not show himself unmindful of the sort of temptation to procure confessions which his recommendation would entail for the police. He said:

> We would not condone practices such as those which are described in the Compton Report (Cmnd. 4823) and the Parker Report (Cmnd. 4901) as having been used in the crisis resulting from the simultaneous internment of hundreds of suspects in August 1971. The use of any methods of this kind has been prohibited for many months past. As already mentioned they are, in any event, now regarded as counter-productive. Certainly, the official instructions to the RUC and the army are strict. So are the precautions taken to see that they are strictly observed. There is stationed on permanent call at the

centre where suspects are questioned by the police an army medical officer who is not attached to any of the operational units stationed in Northern Ireland, but is sent out on a rota from England for a period of four to six weeks. He conducts a thorough medical examination of each suspect on arrival in the absence of the police and a similar examination at the conclusion of the questioning. He informs the suspect that if he wishes he will be allowed to see the doctor at any time while he is at the centre. The possibility of ill-treatment which injures the suspect physically or mentally going undetected by the doctor is remote.

The only point I would make about that observation is that it has as much relevance to what actually goes on at army and RUC interrogation centres as have the proceedings at Disneyland. By the time of the Bennett Report's findings being made public in March 1979 it was generally accepted as a fact of life that torture was an integral part of the "conveyor-belt" system. The most notorious centres were at Castlereagh Barracks near Belfast, run by the RUC, at other police stations throughout the North and at army controlled centres such as Palace, Girdwood and Fort Mona. Apart from complaints by church leaders and by representatives of the minority community, individual civil rights workers such as, in particular, three Catholic priests, Father Denis Faul, Father Brian Brady and Father Raymond Murray, had compiled dossiers of the procedures used. Both the Amnesty and the Bennett Reports were published against a backdrop which saw both the solicitors involved in the bulk of the "scheduled offence" cases and the police doctors concerned, publicly condemn the system, which by then was not solely directed against Catholics—in October of 1977 the Ulster Defence Association announced that it had a "thick file," a dossier of maltreatment of Loyalists. The following month the thirty solicitors who most commonly work in the Diplock Courts wrote to the Secretary of State Mr. Mason stating that

ill-treatment of suspects by police officers, with the
object of obtaining confessions, is now common practice, and that this most often, but not always, takes
place at Castlereagh RUC station and other police stations throughout Northern Ireland.

A factor affecting the solicitors' work, which the Amnesty
Report corroborated, was the fact that it was virtually impossible
under the Special Powers Act for a person to see a solicitor while in
police custody. It was also common practice to interrogate minors
without the presence of parents or a guardian. The practices most
commonly referred to were beating, threats, e.g. of rape to a woman
suspect, or to one's family, psychological or sleep deprivation techniques. In addition men often complained of having their testicles
kicked, beaten or squeezed.

At the risk of stating the obvious I would point out here that
none, or at least only a tiny part, of the foregoing was a matter of
random brutality. These procedures were engaged in to arrive at
specific results, either a confession of actual guilt, or an agreement
to a statement already prepared by the police. All I can say on this
last point is that several times in the course of my research I was
assured that young people in particular are presented with a list of
crimes to which they are induced to plead guilty, whether they committed them or not, so as to keep up the police statistics. Naturally,
the young people choose the lesser crimes on the list—arson rather
than murder and so on. But sometimes charges involving huge sentences are involved in this practice. It is, I stress, very difficult to
know where the truth lies in such cases, but one can certainly
accept without doubt that the climate and the practices engendered
by the "conveyor-belt" system do produce a massive feeling of
injustice against the system, amongst both prisoners and their families, to such a degree that one would never expect to find either
ever expressing any regret or guilt for anything they have done. In
their eyes, the system justifies any sort of protest, including the
H Block one.

The Amnesty Report said categorically:

maltreatment of suspected terrorists by the RUC has
taken place with sufficient frequency to warrant the
establishment of a public inquiry to investigate it.

Amnesty also recommended that fresh rules governing arrest
and detention, interrogations and the admissibility of statements
should be considered, and that suspects should be granted access to
lawyers at an early stage in the interrogation.

The Bennett Commission set up as a result made a number of
recommendations for improving supervision of police methods, and
improving prisoners' access to solicitors after forty-eight hours in
custody, but for the purposes of this work one recommendation is
central:

Our own examination of medical evidence reveals
cases in which injuries, whatever their precise cause,
were not self-inflicted and were sustained in police
custody.

The RUC had been arguing that prisoners had been injuring
themselves either to damage the force or win compensation.

Southern Politics

The effect of a good deal of the foregoing disclosures was blunted by
happenings in Southern Ireland which have a marked bearing on our
story and which ultimately could have, or at least should have, by force
of example, a beneficial effect on Northern Ireland, and in particular
on the H Block situation. It is necessary therefore at this stage to take
up the thread of the story as it winds through Southern paths.

On March 2, 1973, power changed hands in Dublin as the result
of a General Election in the Republic. A coalition of Labour and Fine
Gael, led by Liam Cosgrave, took over from Fianna Fáil. This gov-

ernment was to show itself obsessed with the need for putting down the IRA during its tenure of office which lasted until 1977. Although abroad the Coalition stoutly pursued the Strasbourg case against Britain, domestically it seemed that Irish political attitudes were British attitudes.

The early part of the Cosgrave regime saw a hopeful initiative, the signing of the Sunningdale Pact at Sunningdale, England, in December 1973, involving the Southern and Northern political leadership and the British government. Under the terms of this agreement there was to be an executive in Northern Ireland based on power-sharing (between Catholic and Protestant); a move towards a North-South coming together in the form of a Council of Ireland; and cross-border co-operation on security.

However, the British did not keep their share of the bargain. Power changed hands in England too. The Tories, including the principal architect of the Agreement, William Whitelaw, were ousted and when in the following May (1974) the Loyalist paramilitary organisations staged a strike against the power-sharing executive and in particular the Council of Ireland, the new Labour Government vacillated in the face of Loyalist intransigence and its own army's unwillingness to crush the strike, until a point was reached where the delighted dissidents realised they had the ball at their feet and were able to influence the power workers into coming out in sympathy with them, paralysing the Province, causing the collapse of the power-sharing executive and the demise of the Council of Ireland. However, despite this, the Southern government maintained a "hot pursuit" type of policy towards the IRA and persons suspected of giving aid and comfort to that Organisation, in the spirit envisaged in paragraph 10 of the Sunningdale Agreement:

It was agreed by all parties that persons committing crimes of violence, however motivated, in any part of Ireland should be brought to trial, irrespective of the part of Ireland in which they were located.

The desire that the IRA should be "brought to trial" resulted in a gradual build-up of public reaction against three aspects in particular of the Coalition's policy: (1) reports of police brutality towards IRA suspects; (2) the conditions of IRA prisoners in Portlaoise jail; (3) efforts to control the media.

Under (1) above it should be noted that by a number of amendments to the Offences against the State Act (the South's version of the Special Powers Act), by the formal declaration of a State of Emergency and by the setting up of Special Criminal Courts the South had gone so far in the direction of order over law to counter the IRA as to be nearly back at the position of World War II. All that was missing was the death penalty and some people, on both the government and the IRA side, were at a stage of bitterness where that could be arranged, too.

Suspects could be held for interrogation for seven days before being charged. The onus of proof of persons charged with IRA membership had been shifted to the accused; unless they could prove otherwise they could be sentenced to seven years on the word of a police superintendent. As IRA members generally do not recognise the courts—as they do not recognise the legitimacy of the State which set them up—heavy sentences became the order of the day, to a degree which became self-defeating, as the IRA subsequently did recognise the courts, contest the police evidence, and often got off. However, enough went down before the Special Criminal Courts (the South's version of Diplock, also designed to beat the IRA's custom of intimidating jurors by sitting without juries) to swell greatly the numbers in Portlaoise.

Eventually all three factors interacted with the economic situation to produce a landslide result against the Coalition and in favour of Fianna Fáil, in the subsequent election of 1977, which gave the incoming Government the largest majority, 84 seats out of 144, in the history of the Irish State. In that massive majority, prison conditions had certainly played a part, and the overall Northern policy of the Coalition plus the three factors mentioned above had combined to create the old Clann na Poblachta vote of almost thirty years earlier.

Republicans who never voted in any elections as a matter of principle cast their votes for Fianna Fáil on the grounds of the old slogan "Put them in to put them out".

Amongst those "put out" were the two principal spokesmen on the North and on law and order policies generally, Dr. Conor Cruise O'Brien, who had been Minister for Posts & Telegraphs, and the Minister for Justice, Mr. Patrick Cooney. The ex-Prime Minister Mr. Liam Cosgrave subsequently resigned the leadership of the Fine Gael party.

Media Control

The background to this electoral broadside was as follows. In his report which was to have such a far-reaching effect on Irish affairs Lord Gardiner gave public utterance to the official British attitude about what media coverage of the "troubles" and IRA activity should be:

> The view has been expressed to us that the news media
> must bear a degree of responsibility for the encourage
> ment of terrorist activity in Northern Ireland. Interviews
> with terrorist leaders on television and radio and the
> practice of some newspapers in accepting advertise
> ments from paramilitary groups may provide propa
> ganda platforms for those whose aim is the violent
> overthrow of lawful government. There is a tendency,
> which exists elsewhere, towards sensational reporting of
> shootings and bombing incidents which lends a spur
> ious glamour both to the activities themselves and to the
> perpetrators. In addition there are ill-founded and false
> allegations against the security forces.
>
> There can be no question of introducing censor
> ship in a free society in time of peace. But this does not
> mean that nothing can be done. We recommend that it
> be made a summary offence for editors, printers and
> publishers of newspapers to publish anything which

purports to be an advertisement for or on behalf of an illegal organisation or part of it.

The authority of the Press Council extends to all newspapers and magazines within the United Kingdom, including Northern Ireland. Although it possesses only the powers to censure a publication, newspapers are, in fact, highly sensitive to such action by their peers. It also has the authority to consider general policies about publication with the public interest in mind; it has, for instance, issued a general caveat against newspapers printing and paying for the memoirs of criminals. In the present situation, we suggest that the Press Council should closely examine the reconciliation of the reporting of terrorist activities with the public interest.

Finally, the Governors of the British Broadcasting Corporation and the Independent Broadcasting Authority should re-examine the guidance they give to programme controllers or companies about contact with terrorist organisations and the reporting of their views and activities.

The Coalition in Dublin vigorously espoused a similar policy; during the first half of its term in office, every one of the four major newspaper groups in the country—and the weekly journal *Hibernia*—were prosecuted for contempt of court, on charges connected with the treatment of IRA prisoners. The *Irish Press* was the only paper to win its case. But the most celebrated controversy concerning press freedom arose out of an attempt to extend the kind of control maintained by the state over the national television and radio service, Radio Telefís Éireann, into the newspapers.

Dr. Conor Cruise O'Brien, who implemented the broadcasting policy, led the charge. Bernard Levin noted approvingly of O'Brien in *The Times* (September 23, 1977) that he was the one Irishman for whom if Ireland were being towed out to sea and sunk, the British government would "send a helicopter to take Senator O'Brien off at the last moment". It had become known in Dublin in October of the previous year, that Dr. O'Brien was contemplating a situation where the forces of the law would descend upon uncooperative newspaper editors like myself at the *Irish Press*, when in the course of an interview with Bernard Nossiter of the *Washington Post*, he revealed that the purpose of a section of the anti-IRA legislation then being brought before the Dáil was aimed at inhibiting the freedom of people to write letters to the Editor of the *Irish Press* (about, for instance, conditions in Portlaoise and related matters) by bringing sanctions against the Editor.

However, I conducted a vigorous campaign against the legislation, and the offending portion of it was dropped, but not before the publicity worried the President, Cearbhall O Dálaigh, sufficiently to send the resultant legislative package to the Supreme Court to be tested for repugnancy to the Constitution, before he affixed his signature to it, thereby allowing it to become law. He was later criticised for doing this by a Coalition minister, Mr. Patrick Donegan, the Minister for Defence. The President resigned, drawing the inference, correctly as it happens, that Mr. Donegan's open criticism reflected the cabinet's secret thoughts. This episode damaged the government's credibility greatly, and the effects of the Portlaoise situation and of reports of police brutality were to make a bad situation worse.

For just two days after the Irish papers reported that the Court of Human Rights had decided to pronounce on the torture allegations, despite British objections (February 12, 1977), to most people's minds, telegraphing the fact that they were going to find in favour of the Irish—the *Irish Times* began a series of articles reporting that something similar was happening in Southern Ireland. Most damningly it was revealed that there was in existence a police "heavy gang" which went around the country conducting investigations of Republicans by heavy-handed means. This shocked public opinion for its own sake and caused great annoyance that the publicity impact of the Strasbourg findings should be lessened in this way.

And lessened it certainly was. Fleet Street turned the heat off the news from Strasbourg and onto that from Dublin. So did the electronic media. For instance I took part in a full length pre-recorded edition of "Panorama" which dealt with the background to the Strasbourg case and the entire Northern issue in depth; a most useful and illuminating programme, I thought. However, it was scrapped because of the *Irish Times* disclosures, and instead on the evening of the first article (February 14) another "Panorama" went out with only one item from Ireland, a snippet in which the only Parliamentarian from the Coalition with the courage to appear, Senator Mary Robinson, battled gamely uphill to try to establish the distinction between what was happening North and South.

The Portlaoise Solution

Finally there was the Portlaoise issue. A combination of the traditional Republican defiance, coupled with the Coalition's almost theological aversion to the IRA—"we did it before and we'll do it again" (a reference to the executions and crushing of the IRA during the Civil War struggle, during which of course Liam Cosgrave's father, William, led the victorious side) was an attitude commonly met with in cabinet circles of the time—had produced appalling conditions in Portlaoise.

To describe the entire saga would occupy a chapter in this book in its own right. Suffice it to say that the place was a fortification outside, with armed soldiers everywhere, and a cauldron within, with members of the Gardaí augmenting the normal prison staff, a total loss of privileges for the prisoners, and fights, beatings, intimate searches, and an ugly brooding air prevailing over all. The issue, of course, being the familiar one of some sort of recognition of the prisoners' political, or as they would say themselves, prisoner of war status.

The years prior to the Coalition's fall saw hunger strikes, riots, attempts on the life of the prison governor, a curtailment of visiting, baton charges outside the prison, and the first deliberate breach of Standing Order Number 8 since it was introduced—the deliberate murder by booby-trap of Garda Clerkin on October 16, 1976. (Another Garda, Thomas Peters, was permanently blinded in the explosion).

Obviously something had to be done, and it was, but in a very Irish way. When Fianna Fáil took over, the "heavy gang" was quickly put out of business, and when on September 23 of that year (1977) Amnesty issued a report criticising the Special Criminal Courts for their readiness to accept statements from the police (against the Heavy Gang background outlined earlier) the Government set up a Commission under justice Barra O Briain to enquire into police activities and to make recommendations necessary for the preservation of public confidence and the good name of the force. Its report was not implemented publicly, but privately a good deal of the heat went out of the situation, and Portlaoise was defused—to the extent, that is, that the Republicans' aspirations and a duly elected Government's rule can ever be brought into harmony.

After Fianna Fáil took over, the Republicans let it be known that they would co-operate with the new regime and gradually normality was restored to the prison. The prisoners were not formally allowed any particular status, but they were allowed to wear their own clothes, to associate freely, to resume handicrafts, normal visiting routines and parcel receiving, and in everything but name got themselves a *de facto* Special Category status. From that time to 1980 at least it proved possible to be able to hold the prisoners and maintain a workable peace within the prison—an invaluable headline for ending the H Block situation, one would have thought.

Censorship by Pressure

However, this was not to be—not yet, at any rate. To revert now to the Northern situation. The fact that since Strasbourg the British had stopped putting in the boot in one way and were now effectively putting it in in another, was largely overlooked. This was partly because of the events in the South which I have outlined, but also because of the British policy of actively muzzling the media along the lines advocated by Gardiner, and unsuccessfully attempted by the Coalition government in Southern Ireland, which does not have the D-Notice system to assist it.

A "This Week" programme on the Amnesty Report was banned by the Independent Broadcasting Authority, already under pressure because of another "This Week" programme on "Life behind the Wire"—an examination of the Special Category issue which went out in September of 1977 showing prisoners drilling openly in paramilitary uniform unchecked by staff at Long Kesh.

Unionist politicians in the North, and in Britain Conservatives like Airey Neave, had attacked this portrayal of the "Sandhurst of terror". Neave had called for an immediate stop to be put to the "flow of Irish terrorist propaganda through the British news media". To make matters worse, a prison officer who had spoken impressively on the programme, Desmond Irvine, was shot dead ten days later and the programme was blamed.

This shooting completely overshadowed the programme's examination of the issues involved in "special category". A similar fate had befallen an attempt by Keith Kyle to highlight the proceedings at Castlereagh Interrogation Centre on the BBC on March 2 on the "Tonight" programme. He interviewed an Enniskillen school teacher, Bernard O'Connor, who was totally unconnected with the IRA but who was methodically tortured at the centre for a period of days. When an RUC man was shot by the IRA nine days after this programme, the Chairman of the Ulster Police Federation commented:

> There can be little doubt in anybody's mind that the
> BBC had returned a guilty verdict against the Royal
> Ulster Constabulary. The sentence—a cowardly bullet
> in the back—has now been carried out by the IRA.

One can imagine what this sort of thing does to the attitudes of decision-taking people in the higher reaches of the media, when it comes to the reporting of Northern Ireland especially as, quite apart from the shootings which followed the two programmes mentioned, the general climate concerning such reporting was so inauspicious. In the words of Peter Taylor of Thames Television, writing in *Index on Censorship* (volume 7, no. 6, London 1978):

When it comes to Northern Ireland the pressure is constant. It consists of not just the standard letters of
protest from government and opposition to the IRA and
the offending contracting company, but personal meet-
ings between the Chairman of the Authority and the
Secretary of State and Chief Constable of the RUC.
These discussions are confidential, but their results
gradually filter down through the broadcasting structures suggesting that more "responsible" coverage
would be welcome. [There is little talk of censorship.
Government and broadcasting authorities are usually far
too adept and experienced to fall into that trap.]

For "broadcasting structures" one might well substitute "newspaper structures" in a great number of cases. At all events, while
using "special" approaches in the world of media, and "special"
approaches in the arena of the courts, the British Government and the
Northern Ireland Office continued to deny "special" status to the
prisoners in the H Blocks. Some extremely "special" steps, bluffs
and prevarications were used to land them there, despite the alarm of
people whose views should have been noted such as the police doctors employed by the RUC. And the doctors had good reason for
becoming alarmed, as we shall see.

1.   I exclude the Widgery Tribunal findings on the Bloody Sunday shootings
     of January 1971, although some would very reasonably argue that shoot-
     ing thirteen people dead in cold blood during a peaceful protest might be
     called brutality. Widgery, however, has a continuing milestone effect on
     Catholic opinion. The list of tribunals mentioned, together with that of Lord
     Scarman into the August 1969 rioting by its subject matter alone gives a
     graphic insight into the continuing drift of events in Northern Ireland.
2.   *Report of the enquiry into allegations against the security forces of phys-
     ical brutality in Northern Ireland arising out of the events on August 9,
     1971.* Sir Edmund Compton, GCB, KBE.

CHAPTER 12

The Deadly Campaign

Having lit, as it were, the fuse of the Special Category issue, Merlyn Rees departed the Province, to be replaced on August 10, 1976, by Roy Mason, whose tenure in office as Secretary of State was to be characterised by a dogged pursuit of the "Ulsterisation, Criminalisation, and Normalisation" policy, and a marked acceleration of the "conveyor-belt" process. Between July 1, 1976, and July 1, 1978, Belfast saw 2,293 people charged with "scheduled" offences. The bulk of evidence in these cases was obtained by "confessions."

By November 10 one police doctor at least, Dr. Robert Irwin, was so concerned about the methods used to obtain these confessions that he wrote to the Secretary of the Police Authority about what was happening. He got nowhere, and ultimately in January of 1979 he decided to go on the ITV programme "Weekend World" to express his concern publicly. A particularly nasty tactic was used against him as a result—the Northern Ireland Office and the RUC leaked the fact that his wife had been raped, possibly by a soldier, in such a way as to try to make it appear that his revelations were motivated by anger over the rape rather than based on fact.

However, other police doctors, Drs. Elliot and Alexander, also complained about what was happening not alone at Castlereagh, but also at places like Gough Barracks in Armagh. The SDLP took up the issue of torture also. A statement from the Party as early as October 6, 1977, accused the police of "illegal, inhuman and obscene behaviour" towards suspects. But nothing was done to check these practices until Amnesty International reported (on May 2, 1978) and the Bennett Committee was appointed as a result on June 8 of that year.

Throughout all this time Mason held a weekly meeting with the Chief Constable of the RUC, Sir Kenneth Newman, but concentrated not on controlling police excesses but on getting more convictions. Newman was in fact allowed to issue a statement (on June 24, 1977) on the allegations of police brutality in which he said that prisoners were injuring themselves as part of an IRA propaganda campaign against the police. Said Newman: "People who recklessly engage in purveying serious and unproven allegations against the RUC are playing a dangerous game with policemen's lives."

The attitude revealed in this statement remained official policy until Bennett reported a year later, despite the fact that literally hundreds of documented cases of torture were brought to the attention of the authorities in the meantime. I am not at all sanguine about believing that Bennett has eradicated the type of behaviour outlined, but for the purposes of our story this outline of what went on under the "conveyor-belt" system would suffice to indicate why the prisoners in H Block would have had a sense of injustice over and above the ordinary when they arrived there—quite apart from the removal of Special Category Status. In the circumstances it was inevitable that some form of protest should have been embarked on, though the form it was to take could hardly have been foreseen.

However, for our purposes the significant thing to note about all this was that thus arranged, the confrontation between the Army "conveyor-belt" and the IRA had reached a stage of attrition whereby a new form of organisation was forced on the IRA in order to remain operational. Throughout the latter part of 1977 and during 1978 the Provisionals reverted to the old Irish Republican brotherhood "cell" system of Michael Collins' day whereby the old Command Structure of Brigades, Battalions and Companies gave way to the virtually impenetrable cells of the nineteenth-century continental models.

Indeed, before the new cell system had got under way, the low profile maintained by the IRA had conveyed the mistaken impression—notably to Mr. Roy Mason—that the Organisation had been beaten into the ground. The cell system works by putting unknown men and new recruits into an operational cell which ideally consists of four people. The total membership and size of each cell was known only to its leader, and to his leaders with whom he in turn may not be fully familiar. The practical result of this, from the interrogator's point of view, was that you can capture and "break" three out of four members of a cell without necessarily learning anything at all, because your captive simply does not have the information himself. These cells operate mainly in urban areas, and tie in with the old Brigade and Battalion structures in a radically new way. They were controlled by the Brigade's operations officer. Each cell was financed through the cell leader, and specialised in particular activities such as sniping, bombing, robbery, "executions," intelligence, and so on. The cells did not even control their own weapons or explosives, except when they were given them immediately prior to an "operation" or when they dumped them overnight. Moreover, the members normally employed disguises and operated outside their own areas, so as to confuse British intelligence.

This streamlining has its own disadvantages. It may be useful for decreasing the chances of detection and extracting information, but it does make it extremely cumbersome to set up a specific attack—all the more so when the target is not strictly a military one, as in the case of warders. That is why the new system brought such a marked change in the public profile of the IRA, with less of an immediate impact on the civilian population. Operations became fewer and far more selective; shooting army, police, and warders, with an occasional splurge of bombings. The new system was and is deadly efficient. But with the new streamlining and economy of numbers, concentrating on such things as spiriting a gun to and from the scene of a shooting which would be planned by one person and carried out by another, there came an inability to deal with the sort of large-scale political propaganda exercise which the IRA had mounted in earlier parts of the decade. Taking part in H Block marches under the eyes of the SAS and "Oscar Papas"[1] was not on.

Inside the H Blocks, however, the striking prisoners pressed for propaganda marches, demonstrations and so on. Outside their relatives pressed for action to publicise their plight, and within the ranks of the IRA itself the more traditionally minded argued that marches on the Falls Road and in other parts of the country were a waste of time. What was needed was direct physical action—i.e. the shooting of warders.

By 1980, eighteen warders had died at the hands of the IRA, when the Loyalists began to follow the IRA's lead. Early that year there was a lull in the Provisional attacks, but if the H Block protest were to deteriorate any further, there was the horrifying prospect of a huge upsurge in the death toll. In this connection it is worth remembering that although the "dirty protest" was then the largest political factor pressing the IRA towards shooting prison officers, in fact the campaign of death had started several months before Ciaran Nugent went on the blanket in September 1976. The issue originally was the removal of Special Category, not the blanket protest itself. And the toll of prison officers was grimly tangible evidence of the Provisionals' commitment to the stubborn protest by their imprisoned comrades.

But like the marches, the shooting of warders takes organisation, particularly under the cell system. Every attack on a warder—and there have been far more unsuccessful attempts than successful ones—meant time and planning diverted from targets more prized by the IRA. Moreover the actual "Dirty Protest" campaign itself was slow to win public support. Its bizarre and repellent nature, the fact that the marches almost inevitably ended in stone throwing and violence, and the public view that the whole thing was only a Provisional propaganda stunt, all militated against widespread public support.

True, there were good attendances at a propagandist mime play on the H Block inmates, "The Thoughts of a Man on the Blanket" by Michael MacGillacuddy, which was shown to audiences in the Catholic ghettoes of the North. And there was a certain amount of public sympathy throughout the country at the sight of women relatives of the prisoners taking part in protests "on the blanket" themselves in inclement weather. But the marches did not attract large crowds because of their Provisional association. Most people in the

Republic at least remained mystified by the significance of the signs "Smash H Block" which one saw frequently on dead walls. And the IRA, far from seeing the H Block situation as a Heaven-sent propaganda bonus, found it an embarrassing reminder of an unsuccessful period of negotiations which nearly wrecked the movement, as well as a strain on military tactics. They would be heartily glad to see the chalice pass rather than have the issue protracted.

In fact it was demonstrably in the interests of all the parties concerned—IRA, British Government, warders, and especially prisoners—to see the H Block issue resolved without further loss of life. This could have been achieved with a minimum of flexibility and negotiating skill, on principles basically acceptable to each of the hostile parties. But as the spiral of bitterness and death cut deeper on all sides, attitudes were locked into intransigence and the way towards a solution was blocked by an obduracy bordering on hopelessness.

1.   The name given to the OPs or concealed observation posts, manned by soldiers with radios, as opposed to the fixed fortified positions, which can be seen at strategic points in cities. These were known as "Sangurs."

PART THREE
Reactions and Repercussions

CHAPTER 13
Telling the World

The official reaction to the embarrassment of the H Block issue varied amongst religious and political leaders affected by it according to their backgrounds. The British tried to minimise the situation using diplomatic niceties to cloak the situation. Pointing to the degree of self-infliction in the prisoners' plight, they avoided questions about torture and the "conveyor-belt" system. The Irish government, uneasily looking over its shoulder at Portlaoise where, as one government spokesman explained it pithily for me, "You never know when some fellow is going to start taking off his shirt," had the difficult task of both soft-pedalling the issue, and raising it officially but privately. Where the church leaders were concerned, Cardinal Tomas O Fiaich visited the prison and condemned it openly and unambiguously, but the Protestant reaction tended to be that the Cardinal was giving aid and comfort to an enemy.

The Archbishop's Statement

After trying and failing to get anywhere with private entreaties to Roy Mason, Archbishop O Fiaich of Armagh, the Roman Catholic Primate of All Ireland, who has frequently condemned the IRA, visited the prison and afterwards issued a statement on August 1, 1978, deploring what he saw. Both as a description and as an analysis I think the statement was accurate and important. It said:

There are nearly 3000 prisoners in Northern Ireland today. This must be a cause of grave anxiety to any spiritual leader. Nearly 200 from the Archdiocese of Armagh are among the total of almost 1800 prisoners in the Maze Prison at Long Kesh. This is the equivalent of all the young men of similar age groups in a typical parish of this diocese.

Last Sunday I met as many as possible of these Armagh prisoners as the bishop appointed to minister to themselves and their families, conscious of Christ's exhortation about visiting those in prison. I am grateful for the facilities afforded me by the authorities.

On this my second visit as archbishop to Long Kesh, I was also aware of the grave concern of the Holy See at the situation which has arisen in the prison, and I wanted to be able to provide the Holy See with a factual account of the present position of all prisoners there, something which I shall do without delay.

Having spent the whole of Sunday in the prison I was shocked by the inhuman conditions prevailing in H Blocks 3, 4 and 5, where over 300 prisoners are incarcerated. One would hardly allow an animal to remain in such conditions, let alone a human being. The nearest approach to it that I have seen was the spectacle of hundreds of homeless people living in sewer-pipes in the slums of Calcutta. The stench and filth in some of the cells, with the remains of rotten food and human excreta scattered around the walls, was almost unbearable. In two of them I was unable to speak for fear of vomiting. The prisoners' cells are without beds, chairs or tables. They sleep on mattresses on the floor and in some cases I noticed that these were quite wet. They have no covering except a towel or blanket, no books, newspapers or reading material except the Bible (even religious magazines have been banned since my last visit), no pens or writing materials, no TV or radio, no hobbies or handicrafts, no exercise or recreation. They are locked in their cells for almost the whole of every day and some of them have been in this condition for more than a year and a half.

The fact that a man refuses to wear prison uniform or to do prison work should not entail the loss of physical exercise, association with his fellow prisoners or contact with the outside world. These are basic human needs for physical and mental health, not privileges to be granted or withheld as rewards or punishments. To deprive anyone of them over a long period—irrespective of what led to the deprivation in the first place—is surely a grave injustice and cannot be justified in any circumstances. The human dignity of every prisoner must be respected regardless of his creed, colour or political viewpoint, and regardless of what crimes he has been charged with. I would make the same plea on behalf of Loyalist prisoners, but since I was not permitted to speak to any of them, despite a request to do so, I cannot say for certain what their present condition is.

Several prisoners complained to me of beatings, of verbal abuse, of additional punishments (in cold cells without even a mattress) for making complaints, and of degrading searches carried out on the most intimate parts of their naked bodies. Of course, I have no way of verifying these allegations, but they were numerous.

In the circumstances I was surprised that the morale of the prisoners was high. From talking to them it is evident that they intend to continue their protest indefinitely and it seems they prefer to face death rather than submit to being classed as criminals. Anyone with the least knowledge of Irish history knows how deeply rooted this attitude is in our country's past. In isolation and perpetual boredom they maintain their sanity by studying Irish. It was an indication of the triumph of the human spirit over adverse material surroundings to notice Irish words, phrases and songs being shouted from cell to cell and then written on each cell wall with the remnants of toothpaste tubes.

The authorities refuse to admit that these prisoners are in a different category from the ordinary, yet everything about their trials and family background indicates that they are different. They were sentenced by special courts without juries. The vast majority were convicted on allegedly voluntary confessions obtained in circumstances which are now placed under grave suspicion by the recent report of Amnesty International. Many are very youthful and come from families which had never been in trouble with the law, though they lived in areas which suffered discrimination in housing and jobs. How can one explain the jump in the prison population of Northern Ireland from 500 to 3000 unless a new type of prisoner has emerged?

The problem of these prisoners is one of the great obstacles to peace in our community. As long as it continues it will be a potent cause of resentment in the prisoners themselves, breeding frustration among their relatives and friends and leading to bitterness between the prisoners and the prison staff. It is only sowing the seeds of future conflict.

Pending the full resolution of the deadlock, I feel it essential to urge that everything required by the normal man to maintain his physical and mental health and to live a life which is tolerably human should be restored to these prisoners without delay.

The statement elicited a barrage of criticism from all sorts of quarters including the unlikely one of the English Catholic publication, *The Tablet*: "We hope the leaders of Irish opinion ... disassociate themselves from a statement which can do no good to the cause of peace in

Northern Ireland." However in a subsequent Radio Éireann interview (on August 2) the Archbishop remained unbowed. As he put it, "The refusal to submit to criminal status was nothing new. It had been going on for more than a century. O'Donovan Rossa and the Land League; William O'Brien spent a year wearing a newspaper in Tullamore jail because he would not wear prison garb. In 1972, Mr. Whitelaw found a way round it and with a bit of flexibility the authorities could now find a way round a horrible situation.

"When I went into the first cell my breath was taken away. I was unable to speak for a couple of minutes with the stench, dirt and filth all round me. I really could not believe it. It is hard to believe people could exist in those conditions for a long period."

Northern Ireland Office: "These criminals"

To all of this, as Anne McHardy wrote in *The Guardian* on August 2, 1978, "the Northern Ireland Office reacted like a wounded bull" and issued a long statement which, while it hardly deals adequately with the legal process by which the H Block men were sentenced, nor with the continuous reports of beatings and ill-treatment inside the prison, nevertheless contained the official view of the time. Therefore it too deserves to be given in full.

> These criminals are totally responsible for the situation in which they find themselves. It is they who have been smearing excreta on the walls and pouring urine through cell doors. It is they who by their actions are denying themselves the excellent modern facilities of the prison. It is they and they alone who are creating bad conditions out of very good conditions.
>
> Each and every prisoner has been tried under the judicial system established in Northern Ireland by Parliament. Those found guilty, after the due process of law, if they are sent to prison by the courts, serve their sentence for what they are—convicted criminals.

They are not political prisoners: more than eighty
have been convicted of murder or attempted murder and
more than eighty of explosive offences. They are members of organisations responsible for the deaths of hundreds of innocent people, the maiming of thousands
more and the torture, by kneecapping, of more than 600
of their own people.

All prisoners, including those who are protesting, are entitled to monthly visits, normal meals, to
use the toilets, medical facilities and daily exercise.
Simply by observing the rules—an essential require-
ment if good prison administration is to be maintained—these protesting prisoners would immediately
have all furniture, books and magazines returned to the
cells (indeed they were only removed because they
were being broken or fouled by the prisoners themselves) and be able to watch television, listen to the
radio and continue with their hobbies, handicrafts and
recreation.

These facilities are better than those available in
most prisons in the rest of the United Kingdom.

The medical and public health aspects have been
closely watched. All prisoners in Blocks H 3, 4 and 5
have been moved during the last two months so that
their dirty cells could be thoroughly cleaned and reno-
vated. Most prisoners have dirtied their cells again, once
they were returned to them. But in the interest of prisoners, this cleaning programme will continue.

The Northern Ireland Office receives daily reports
from the doctors at the prison. Every protester who
reports sick is seen by a doctor without delay, and to
date no prisoner has been found to be suffering from
any form of illness, physical or mental, major or minor,
attributable to the protest.

This protest action is the basis of a propaganda

campaign which has been mounted by the IRA. It has been roundly condemned north and south of the border.

Not surprisingly, there have been allegations made to the Archbishop about ill-treatment of prisoners by prison staff. There is no truth in these allegations, and prison officers know that any such complaints by prisoners are thoroughly and promptly investigated and, if substantiated, lead to disciplinary action.

Indeed, only recently the work of the prison governor and his staff, in the difficult conditions in these three cell blocks, was commended by the prison's independent board of visitors, the members of which are drawn from all sides of the community. The Board has access to all parts of the prison and the chairman pays frequent visits to the protesters' cell blocks.

It is not the government's wish that the protesting prisoners should continue to put up with their present conditions. But the prisoners and those who influence them should realise that the government will stand firm on its policy on special category status.

No one who is convicted of a crime carried out after March 1, 1976—and that includes those involved in the "dirty" protest—will be given any form of special status.

As soon as this decision is understood and accepted, conditions in the cell blocks can return to normal.

Protestant Churchmen's Reactions to the Protest

The *Church of Ireland Gazette* waited until its January review of the year to observe that the Archbishop, after his visit to H Block "left the rest of us in little doubt about where his loyalties lay" and went on:

A statement which castigated conditions in the prison
without really questioning why the men were there in
the first place, did little to reassure middleground
Protestant and not a few Roman Catholics.[1]

The Governing Committee of the Presbyterian Church in Ireland met after the Archbishop's statement on August 4 and sharply
rebuked him; they drew attention to "the clear reaffirmation of the
General Assembly in 1976 supporting the United Kingdom Government in their ending of special category status for convicted prisoners" and continued in a statement:

> The deplorable, degrading and inhuman conditions to
> which certain prisoners at the Maze have now reduced
> themselves in some of the most modern prison accom-
> modation in all Ireland is naturally a cause of great dis-
> tress to their relatives and friends: though the alternative
> of enforced hygiene might be considered even more
> degrading and provocative.
>
> Nor is it only for the prisoners but for the prison
> staff in their thankless and dangerous service that con-
> cern should be expressed.
>
> The recent statement of Archbishop O Fiaich,
> however, seems to show grave moral confusion in
> obscuring the primary responsibility of the prisoners
> themselves for the situation. They have freely chosen so
> to act as part of a campaign which, out of prison, has
> been waged by them and their associates with bomb and
> bullet and terrorising punishments, which have befouled
> life and conditions for so many.
>
> Excuses offered give an appearance as if not only
> the ultimate aims but even the immediate tactics of the
> IRA are being blessed.
>
> The Churches' ministry to those in prison should
> unequivocally encourage their repudiation of those

deeds and policies which the Churches themselves, separately and together, have so often publicly denounced.
To fail in this destroys the credibility of what the
Churches have been saying and means a painful erosion
of the hard won measure of co-operation and common
commitment to a peaceful solution of our differences
and of the personal confidence on which many had
hoped these might develop.

Dr. Victor Lynas, a former moderator of the Presbyterian
Church and convenor of the committee, speaking on RTE Radio on
August 6, continued this criticism, saying that Presbyterians inter-
preted the Archbishop's remarks as blessing the IRA campaign, and
that he showed no regard for the victims of the crimes of those in the
Maze prison, for which those men had been convicted. Asked
whether it was unrealistic to say that Dr. O Fiaich supported murders, bombings and kneecappings, Dr. Lynas replied: "One can only
take the logic of his statement that, in a negative way, he refused to
ask them to repudiate what had been done; he must be supporting
them in what they are doing." Dr. Lynas said that the Presbyterians
could not say the Archbishop was supporting the IRA campaign,
and they had no knowledge of any particular active support by the
Archbishop for it, but it seemed that what Dr. O Fiaich said was a
blessing of the IRA campaign. The London *Times* agreed. "Dr.
O Fiaich", it said, "could hardly have composed a more compre-
hensive endorsement of the Provisional IRA's position." The *Daily
Mail* termed the Archbishop's statement "an outrageously emotional
diatribe" and said that only the Archbishop's maker could say
whether he was "most pathetically gullible or most dangerously
blinded by prejudice."

As the examples given above of Protestant church leaders' attitudes were taken from an early stage in the H Block protest campaign,
I felt it advisable when preparing this book to seek the then current
views of the leading Protestant churchmen. They all responded cour-
teously to my letters—except for the Reverend Paisley who did not

reply—more or less saying the same thing: they would prefer not to
reply individually as there was a Protestant inter-church study group
examining the issue.

That group issued its report on April 15, 1980. It represented
the Church of Ireland, the Presbyterian Church, the Methodists, the
Moravian Church, the Non-Subscribing Presbyterian Church, the
Religious Society of Friends, and the Salvation Army. While recom-
mending a study of prisons all over Ireland "as a matter of urgency"
and acknowledging a legitimate Church concern about the H Blocks,
the group declared that Special Category could not be justified. The
way to end the protest was for the Provisionals outside to end their
campaign of violence. "This ought to be the prime aim of those concerned with human rights and the welfare of prisoners." The H Block
protest, making propaganda out of the largely self-inflicted conditions of the prisoners, was part of this wider campaign, attempting to
justify the Provisionals' acts of violence not as criminal behaviour
but as legitimate acts of war.

> Since 1975 the whole thrust of Government policy has
> reverted to dealing with all convicted prisoners as
> criminals.
>
> Any reinstating of special category status would
> be a major defeat for the Government and would be
> seen to give recognition to the claims of the Provisional
> IRA and other paramilitaries.
>
> There are also the strong feelings within the com-
> munity about the horrific nature of the crimes commit-
> ted by many of the men in H Block to be taken into
> account. The H Block protest cannot, therefore, be dis-
> cussed in vacuo.

The document discussed the question of whether or not a category of less favoured status for political prisoners was tolerable in
a democratic society. The group, while not accepting that the concessions which would accrue to special category prisoners could be

justified, did argue that there was a case for the then conditions of
ordinary prisoners to be improved.

The argument that the Diplock courts by using special methods
thereby conferred special status on the prisoners was not accepted.
The document also went on to express concern at the fact that the
British government's policy had had the effect of exposing prison officers to danger and death, and had also embittered the relationship
between the warders and the prisoners, but the Chairman felt that if
the prison service broke down the Northern community would find
itself in an even worse position than at the time of reporting. The document urged that the community should commit itself to the ending
of violence and to a just and law-abiding society in which the rights
of the prisoners as well as the public at large would be safeguarded.
All those concerned with these issues must redouble their appeals to
those involved to turn from violence and seek a more constructive
way. The document itself tried to take a constructive attitude towards
resistance in prison.

> Prisoners who continually resist prison discipline
> should be treated as normally as possible . . . However,
> the present prison rules have not been designed to deal
> with such an organised and continuous resistance of dis-
> cipline as the one in H Block.
>
> The abnormal factors in our society and in our
> prisons ought not to prevent the kind of review of prison
> rules and conditions which is continually taking place
> in Great Britain and other places.
>
> We accordingly, recommend that an official study
> of prisons, the methods of prison discipline and prison
> rules for all sorts of prisoners should be undertaken as a
> matter of urgency.

But to return to the reactions of 1978, when Tomás O Fiaich
issued his H Block statement. Predictably, he was attacked by Conservative, Unionist and Alliance Party spokesmen. Mr. Airey Neave,

then Conservative spokesman for Northern Ireland, later to be murdered by a Republican group, said the Archbishop's statement could be damaging to the security situation. His reaction also threw a strange light on what one would have thought would have been an English Protestant politician's reaction to the separation of Church and State. He said he was concerned because it seemed "there was sharp conflict between the Catholic hierarchy and the British government."

One would have expected the leader of the Unionist Party, Mrs. Anne Dickson, to have been critical of the Archbishop, and she was: "No matter what is said about the Maze, there must be no weakening by the government on the matter of political status. People who have been convicted of murdering and bombing are criminals, plain and simple, and should be treated as such."

Jack Anderson Enters the Fray

But the irony of Mrs. Dickson's sentiments lay in the fact that sometime earlier she had joined with the Archbishop in signing a protest at the treatment of Chilean prisoners. They were safely far away. Irish ones, however, always seemed to require an extra dimension of justification. However, the extra dimension of internationalisation which the Cardinal's visit and statement concerning the Holy See engendered—it also became known that the Papal Nuncio Dr. Alibrandi had been interesting himself in the affair—received an additional, and to the British, unwelcome fillip when on a visit to America a group of prisoners' relatives made contact with that contemporary master of the journalistic exposé, the *Washington Post* columnist Jack Anderson, and his resultant column set off a publicity bombshell across America on October 29, 1978. (He actually sent over a journalist to give a first-hand report of conditions inside the Maze prison, but his envoy failed to gain admission to the complex— a fact which makes the authorities' willingness to grant my own request for visits to Long Kesh and Armagh all the more remarkable.) Anderson's column managed to convey a graphic sense of outrage, as the following extract shows:

President Carter so far has ignored the protests of individuals and organizations concerned about the British army's abuses in the strife torn land.

But now critics with more political clout have urged the President to speak out on the situation. Outraged by firsthand evidence they have obtained on a recent fact-finding tour of Ulster, Representatives Hamilton Fish, R. N.Y., and Joshua Eilberg, D. Pa., sent a private letter to Carter asking that he do something about human rights outrages in Northern Ireland.

At the center of the controversy is the Long Kesh prison, a forbidding concrete fortress on the outskirts of Belfast. It is there that hundreds of Irish prisoners live in conditions of indescribable filth and physical deprivation.

Most infamous of all is the "H Block," or "hell block" as it is called by the prisoners. Its inmates, known as "blanket men," have been clothed only in blankets and towels since 1976, when British courts declared that IRA suspects were no longer to be given special treatment as political prisoners.

The few outsiders who have been allowed into H Block report that the walls are encrusted with rotting food, the floors are littered with excrement and an overpowering odor of decay is all-pervading.

One respected religious leader compared the horrors of H Block to the "tiger cages" of Vietnam, where American-trained South Vietnamese captors interrogated prisoners, or the North Vietnamese torture cells where American POWs were brutally mistreated.

Indeed Rep. Fish concluded that the conditions at Long Kesh were "worse than Saigon in 1968."

Hundreds of Irish prisoners in H Block, many of them still in their teens, were put there for signing confessions often extracted under torture by British security forces. Under the emergency suspension of Britain's honored legal system, anyone arrested may be held incommunicado for as long as seven days without even a formal charge.

It is estimated that perhaps 75 per cent of the political prisoners in Long Kesh have been convicted by uncorroborated statements or forced confessions made in Stalin-like kangaroo court procedures.

British officials tried to persuade the visiting congressmen and other dignitaries that Long Kesh is a model prison where inmates are treated with dignity in an up-to-date, humanely run facility. Almost no one swallows the official British line, however.

Several Ulster women have come to us with pathetic tales of the mistreatment being visited upon their husbands and sons, some as young as 16. They have been begging Congress for help, believing along with thousands of Northern Irish that only United States intervention can bring an end to Ulster's horrors.

An Ad Hoc Irish Committee of 119 members has been formed in Congress. But the committee's attempts to publicize the outrages being committed in Northern Ireland, along with the efforts of the Irish National Caucus, have been blocked by House Speaker Tip O'Neill and other congressional leaders who are reluctant to offend our British ally.

The initial letter from Fish and Eilberg was bucked to the State Department, whose bureaucratic response infuriated the lawmakers.

They fired off a second note to the President, in which they cited "incontrovertible evidence that the Northern Irish people, both Catholic and Protestant, earnestly and sincerely plead for United States assistance in achieving political and social stability."

The foregoing went down in the British Embassy in Washington like a Long Kesh turd in the salad bowl and the then Ambassador to Washington, Mr. Peter Jay, a son-in-law of the British Prime Minister James Callaghan, marshalled the official British arguments on the issue in reply.

When a columnist of Jack Anderson's eminence can be as utterly misled and misleading as he was in his recent column on Northern Ireland ("A 'Camp David' for Northern Ireland?" op-ed Oct. 29) the truth must be allowed a right of rebuttal. So let us ask candidly: Why was Britain involved in Northern Ireland in the first place?

When early this century London tried to give home rule to all 32 counties of Ireland, the Protestants in the North rejected this, threatened convincingly to fight, and retained the union of the 6 counties in Ulster with Great Britain in the United Kingdom. In 1969, the British government responded to the growing civil rights campaign in the province by disarming the "B Specials" police auxiliaries regarded by the Catholic community as a hostile sectarian force—and halting the discrimination against the Catholic minority that had grown up under the Protestant supremacy over the previous half-century.

Since then Britain's role has been totally different from what is still—and not surprisingly—enshrined in the bitter folk memories of millions of Irish Americans.

First, we believe that the ultimate status of Northern Ireland should be democratically determined by the people who live there. We will not retain it in the United Kingdom against its will. We will not force it against its will into union with the Republic of Ireland or into separate existence. In 1973 the people of Northern Ireland voted in a referendum to retain the present status.

Second, so long as a clear majority prefers to remain in the United Kingdom, we insist on certain fundamentals:

• All discrimination against the Catholic minority, whether in jobs, housing, civil rights or other freedoms is outlawed.

• Both parts of the community, Catholic and Protestant, must have a proper say in the government of the province; and until such time as elected representatives of Protestants as well as Catholics agree to this, the London government will directly and impartially administer the province.

• Proper standards of justice and law enforcement must be observed consistently with handling terrorism.

Third, we accept the responsibility of any government anywhere to protect ordinary citizens of all faiths from violent terrorists, Protestant or Catholic.

Fourth, we accept the responsibility to promote economic and social development, which, though starting from a low base, is now progressing well.

This policy has been successful enough for a recent poll conducted by the University of Strathclyde to show that direct British rule is favoured by 8 out of 10 members of the Catholic minority and 7 out of 10 of the Protestant majority.

Fifth, we would prefer Northern Ireland to manage its own affairs. Roy Mason, the responsible cabinet minister, recently restarted talks with the leaders of the political parties in Northern Ireland to discuss how this is to be achieved consistently with the British condition that the Catholic minority must have a proper say in the government of the province.

Meanwhile this political and economic progress is challenged by the IRA, a small group of armed terrorists whose declared aim is to overthrow democratic government in Ireland by violence. Their style of terrorism includes shooting, bombing, and other often singularly callous violence—like the napalm-type bomb thrown into a restaurant last January, killing 12 people, including families. Fortunately, such terrorism is now diminishing because its perpetrators have increasingly been brought to justice.

Since we believe in democracy and since the IRA's political representatives have systematically failed over half a century to attract any significant support from the electorate, Catholic or Protestant, we oppose by all legal means the armed takeover of the government, whether by the IRA or extremist Protestants.

When caught, suspects are charged within 72 hours in open court (exceptionally, with the express personal consent of the Secretary of State for Northern Ireland, within seven days). Accused persons are innocent until proved guilty. They are tried in open court and, if convicted and sentenced, held in jail. No one can be interned without trial. No one is imprisoned for his or her beliefs. Amnesty International lists no political prisoners in Northern Ireland.

As a result of the terrorist violence, Parliament has voted the government limited emergency powers, which must be regularly renewed or lapse. For example, jury verdicts are not required in cases where the jurors are exposed to the threat—a real one in Northern Ireland—of intimidation by murder or maiming.

In January 1978 the European Court of Human Rights found that torture had not been used in Northern Ireland, but that in 1971 some prisoners had been ill-treated. The Court noted with approval the measures taken by successive British governments since 1971 to prevent this recurring. Northern Ireland now has very elaborate safeguards for prisoners' rights.

Despite a systematic IRA campaign to discredit the police, every allegation of police brutality is thoroughly investigated and an independent prosecutor decides whether to charge the police officer involved. Any violation of human rights is illegal and absolutely condemned by the British government.

An Amnesty International report alleged maltreatment of suspects in Northern Ireland. In response, the British government set up an independent judicial inquiry to examine both interrogation procedures and the procedures for dealing with complaints against the police.

The government also undertook to refer all Amnesty's allegations to the independent prosecution where the evidence justified this. But Amnesty has so far declined to identify either the alleged victims or the police officers concerned, thus precluding verification of the facts.

Jack Anderson described the deplorable conditions in one Northern Ireland jail—the Maze. But those conditions have been self-inflicted by a group of prisoners, including over 70 convicted of murder and over 80 of explosives offences. The prison is modern, with good humane facilities.

In pursuit of their campaign for "political" status, IRA prisoners have elected to urinate in their cells, to smear their cell walls with excrement, to destroy property—even their Bibles—and to refuse exercise or normal prison work and recreation. Political status is not justified for criminals convicted under the law, least of all when open political expression is guaranteed and free elections (four since 1973) ensure democratic representation both locally and at the Westminster Parliament.

The propaganda value of this campaign is demonstrated in articles such as Jack Anderson's, especially at a time when the IRA, having failed to make any head-

way democratically in Ireland, is turning to the United
States in the hope of harnessing the traditional goodwill
here for Irish causes.

Ambassador Jay Dissected

Jay, formerly a noted journalist, was taken to task point by point in
a pamphlet produced by Fathers Faul and Murray. The priests' statement is also worth reprinting because it and Jay's statement give a
glance at both versions of contemporary Irish history, and particularly of the H Block version which Britain wishes to present and how
nationalist and Catholic campaigners for human rights on the ground
view this version. Both priests have detailed firsthand knowledge of
the H Block and Armagh jail situation to which Father Murray has
been the accredited official chaplain.

The priests were naturally concerned about the moral issue
raised by the Protestant "indications of fighting" statement but in fact
the main point about it is not that Protestants showed a willingness to
fight but that the British showed an unwillingness to confront them. At
the time of the Home Rule crisis mentioned by Jay, the British army
officer cadre virtually mutinied rather than proceed against their co-
religionists in Northern Ireland. The Loyalists' strike which wrecked
Sunningdale in 1974 could, its leaders now say, have easily been broken had not the army backed down. When, flushed with victory, the
Loyalists tried to repeat the performance two years later, a resolute
Secretary of State for Northern Ireland, Mr. Roy Mason, put sufficient
backbone into the army and RUC to crush the strike easily and appre-
hend the bully boys. It is the lack of consistency in impartial government that breeds the IRA. The priests' rebuttal was as follows:

> 1.   "The Protestants in the north threatened con-
> vincingly to fight." Mr. Jay suggests that the more con-
> vincingly you threaten the more you have right and
> legality on your side, and the more you are entitled to
> have your way. Does he not see the false morality

enshrined in this phrase? It is a perfect argument in support of the IRA or any group in the world who wish to achieve their aims by military methods.

2. He refers to the British Government at the present time as "halting the discrimination against the Catholic minority that had grown up under the Protestant supremacy over the previous half-century." Mr. Jay admits that the British government, including several Labour governments, totally neglected its duty to ensure human rights for all its citizens over a period of 50 years. Does this give us any reason that they will guarantee human rights for the Catholic people at the present time? In fact over the last 10 years there have been more serious violations of the human rights of the Catholic people of the six northern counties of Ireland by the RUC (police) and British Army than ever before and proportionately more than in any other country in the world.

3. "When caught, suspects are charged within 72 hours in open court." Mr. Jay omits to say what happens during these 72 hours (or 7 day period for which they may be held). "Caught" is a misleading phrase. Boys and girls are taken from their own homes. There is now abundant proof from medical evidence that many hundreds of people arrested under emergency powers were grossly and obscenely ill-treated from 1976 to 1979 in Castlereagh RUC Interrogation Centre and other interrogation centres and no policeman has been convicted or disciplined for brutality and torture. "Open Court"—the courts sit without a jury and some of the judges are ex-Unionist politicians or sympathisers and some are bitterly anti-Catholic. 90 per cent of the prisoners are convicted on the basis of statements taken under brutality or the threat of brutality.

4. "No one can be interned without trial." Many thousands of men and women are held for 3 days

and 7 days without trial and during these days they are
political prisoners. Many men and women have been
held for 16 months, 18 months and 2 years awaiting
trial in custody; then the charges are dropped or they are
acquitted for lack of evidence. This is imprisonment
without trial through a conspiracy of the RUC and the
judiciary to deprive innocent people of their liberty.

5.   "No one is imprisoned for his or her beliefs."
There is no doubt that many people are imprisoned in
the North of Ireland on extended remand (awaiting trial)
or sentenced, or held at seaports and airports in Great
Britain for periods of 7 to 14 days because their names
and addresses indicate that they are members of the
Catholic Church and have a united Ireland political
point of view.

6.   Mr. Jay says that "parliament has voted the
government limited emergency powers." In fact there
have always been emergency powers in Northern Ireland since 1921. The Northern State cannot exist without them. The Protestant majority cannot assert their
ascendancy without emergency powers to terrorise the
Catholic people and imprison them in large numbers.
Britain can never and will never hold any part of Ireland
without Emergency powers and torture.

7.   Mr. Jay is precise in not using the word
"torture" to describe the ill-treatment of prisoners in
interrogation centres. Why doesn't he use the exact
words of the verdict of the European Court at Strasbourg that in 1971 some prisoners (in fact several hundred) were subjected to cruel, inhuman and degrading
treatment? It is important to note that two of the
judges of the European Court found Britain guilty of
"torture" and the European Commission on Human
Rights at Strasbourg found Britain guilty of torture in
January 1977.

8. Mr. Jay, writing on November 19, 1978, says that "Northern Ireland now has very elaborate safeguards for prisoners' rights." Dr. Robert Irwin, a Government police surgeon, speaking on London Weekend Television, March 12, 1979, said that 150-160 men had been badly ill-treated in Castlereagh RUC Interrogation Centre and had come under his attention, and also Judge Bennett, in his Report of Inquiry into Police Procedures in Northern Ireland, February 16, 1979, lists 64 recommendations to try and protect prisoners. This makes a nonsense of Mr. Jay's claim, November 19, 1978, that prisoners were safeguarded.

9. Mr. Jay says that "every allegation of police brutality is thoroughly investigated and an independent prosecutor decides whether to charge the police officer involved." Nonsense. We have put in about 700 complaints against the RUC since 1971. Not one single complaint was upheld. No RUC man has been sent to jail for assaulting a prisoner. No detective from Castlereagh Interrogation Centre has ever been convicted for assaulting a prisoner.

10. "Amnesty has so far declined to identify either the alleged victims or the police officers concerned, thus precluding verification of the facts." This is completely false and misleading, because we know, and the British Government and the Director of Public Prosecutions know, that every one of the victims in the Amnesty International Report had entered complaints. The DPP has been up to his neck in very damning medical evidence during the 1976-78 period and he has done nothing about it.

11. Mr. Jay says the conditions in the Maze Prison, Long Kesh are self-inflicted. Our book shows that the British answer to a minor strike by the protesting prisoners was excessive punishments—24 hour

lock up, deprivation of physical exercise, fresh air and mental stimulation. The No-Washing, Non-Co-operation Phase was a result of the beatings of young prisoners and intensification of the harassment of the prisoners.[2]

How H Block Helps the IRA

That statement about Britain not being able to maintain itself in Ireland without emergency powers may seem melodramatic and ultra-nationalistic, but to thousands of people in the unemployment-ridden nationalist ghettoes of Northern Ireland, it matches the daily experience of life. Outside of these areas people may not care very much, but the people in them live out the grim and unfashionable reality of the situation that, to stay in Ireland, Britain must use laws and methods and countenance a situation like H Block which would never be countenanced in England. The brutalisation process thus engendered harms everybody—not least the IRA volunteers themselves. As Bishop Cahal B. Daly of Ardagh and Clonmacnoise put it in his address for World Peace Day on January 1, 1979:

> It does not come naturally to young people to kill. They have to be indoctrinated, brain-washed, made cynical, hard-faced and hard-hearted first. Something has to be killed in themselves first before they can kill others; and what is killed is what is most deeply human—compassion, sensitivity, humanity, what the older people called "nature." They should not continue to let their youth be stolen from them in this campaign.
>
> They are being exploited. It is just as foolish for young Irishmen to let themselves be made bomb-fodder by revolutionary fanatics today as it was in the past for young Irishmen to cross the seas to become cannon fodder for imperialist war-lords. It was imperial generals

and empire-building Colonel Blimps who, for their own purposes, created the myth of "the fighting Irish." It is pathetic to see young Irishmen today falling for that foreigners' myth.[3]

The Provisional IRA have, however, by an extraordinary paradox, received great help from an unexpected source—the mistakes of the British administration and the security chiefs, mistakes in which they have persisted with quite remarkable obstinacy in the face of the lesson of all Anglo-Irish history and all experience. The IRA was practically a spent and discredited force until they were handed the "H Block" situation as a propaganda gift. This, and the unnecessary army harassment of innocent people, especially young people, among the 44 "men of no property," are now virtually the only source of vestigial sympathy or of recruitment for the IRA. The IRA are exploiting the H Block situation with disquieting success. In the United States in particular, where the IRA propaganda effort had been very effectively neutralised, and the flow of money to them had largely dried up, there has been a notable new recovery of lost ground, a new upsurge of financial support on behalf of this Organisation. This is due entirely to their clever and unscrupulous manipulation of the "human rights" aspect of the H Block situation. This was entirely predictable and need not and should not have been allowed to happen.

The first thing to say about this situation is that men are suffering; men are suffering terrible degradation, in inhuman conditions. Their families and friends are suffering with them and for them. No matter what explanation or justification is given for this situation, and no matter how responsibility for it may be said to rest with the prisoners themselves, it must be declared that it is folly to refuse to review the situation which allows prisoners to

continue indefinitely living in such conditions. No matter
how the blame for the situation is apportioned, these conditions are objectively in conflict with all recognised
codes governing the environment in which prisoners are
to be allowed to live. These conditions are in contradiction with all enlightened contemporary penology.

But the Bishop's words had no more effect than anybody else's
in the situation. The British had themselves painted into a corner
where they must support the unsupportable, and persevere with a situation that in his heart of hearts no responsible decision-taker could
justify to himself.

1. *Church of Ireland Gazette*, January 1979.
2. *H Block*, by Denis Faul and Raymond Murray.
3. Author's note: The Bishop was quite right here. Ireland has never had con-
    scription since independence, except during World War II. Were it not for
    the Northern problem her army would only be half today's size and
    engaged solely in UN peace keeping duties abroad.

CHAPTER 14
Belfast, Dublin, Strasbourg

H Block was a single issue which involved many different groups, parties and even countries in its ramifications. As one of the key questions facing those concerned with the politics and future of Northern Ireland, it stood at the centre of an interlocking maze of interests and antagonisms. The previous chapter has taken us through the reactions of the Irish Churches, the American media and the British government. But what of the reactions of the Ulster Loyalist paramilitaries, whose opposition to their Catholic counterparts in the IRA was inexorably developing into opposition to London's policy as well? What of the Southern government, whose commitment to Irish unity sat awkwardly with its decision to co-operate with British security against the destabilising violence of the IRA? And what of the wider European scene, the forum in which so many political, social and even military problems are nowadays increasingly tackled? It is easy to become bewildered by the sheer diversity of the international debate, but if we take each component in turn and analyse it separately, an overall pattern does begin to emerge, as the H Block issue signalled a continuing failure of the existing package of policies, expedients and embarrassed alliances that led Northern Ireland to its state of impasse.

The Ulster Defence Association

The position of the Loyalist prisoners in relation to the blanket protest was, if their spokesman was to be believed, that of a pot coming to the boil. There was as yet little evidence of a widespread Loyalist reaction similar to the Republican one. But a leading UDA man told me, "It's coming." Point was given to his words by a riot amongst Loyalist prisoners in Crumlin Road on May 15, 1980 which wrecked several cells. But there were actually only five Loyalist prisoners "on the blanket" in that year. Seven came off the protest. Those five were the only ones whose relatives qualified for UDA welfare payments, and for whose families transport was provided in visiting times. The Loyalists had not yet embarked on the dirty protest but there were a series of other Loyalist protests in train. "The sort of things you associate with prisoners of war anyway," I was told. "Paint being spilled, small fires here and there, files being destroyed, that sort of thing.

"Our people get it very hard to shoot warders. It would be like Republican sympathisers in the South thinking of shooting guards. Personally I think there isn't enough of them shot—stupid misfits earning over £200 a week for beating people. What is happening though is that there are a lot of them getting beaten up that is not reported, and they get shot in the arms and legs and that sort of thing. You can take it, it is all going to get very interesting before it finishes."

The situation was quite different from that which obtained during 1978 when some Loyalists did embark on the blanket protest (for approximately three weeks). The UDA were aware that infractions of discipline in the compounds might lead to incarceration in the existing H Blocks, or in new prisons being built in Derry.

Andy Tyrie, then UDA leader, argued that compound prisoners have a kind of normalcy in their lives, more contact with their families, freedom to read, to do handicrafts and take exercise, and though there is a lack of privacy they can retire to their cubicles and shut out their neighbours for a time if they so wish. Such prisoners on release tend not to report back to their organisations be they Loyalist or Republican, "but the H Block men, they are full of hate. They want to get somebody. They come back almost as soon as they are let out."

Tyrie, under whom the UDA had moved away from sectarian assassination to a situation where some person or persons unknown still went after named Republican targets (because they were Republicans, not because they were Catholics), thought that the situation with the warders would deteriorate to the point where warders would end up living in estates of special houses provided for them, as they do in England, alienated from the community and hostile in attitude to it. Tyrie, a keen advocate of an independent Ulster solution—independent of both Dublin and London; indeed he was one of its principal architects—was clearly almost as anti-British as some of his Republican counterparts. He confidently expected that there would be a "big day," after which the British would depart. He acknowledged that some people were terrified of being left to the combined mercies of the UDA and IRA. But he didn't think that if a British departure was properly planned it would necessarily lead to a backlash, provided "Maggie Thatcher doesn't do something stupid, like trying to shove us into a United Ireland." That would get the UDA men out on the streets with their arms. He showed a good deal of respect for Charles Haughey in conversation:

> He is the boss. He has learned over the years what it's all about—like us. I don't mind all that stuff about the Arms Trial. I understand that. What was happening there was that some people were trying to get guns, handguns to their own people that were being attacked. Anyone would do that. We don't have to fear that. The sort of thing we have to worry about is the question of law and order after the British go. We are going to have the most corrupt police force in the world afterwards. They are used to such high wages with the overtime, £200 a week in their pocket to go chasing terrorists. What sort of police are they anyway who need overtime to go chasing terrorists—but you saw the case yourself there a while ago of the policeman that was on the charge. He gave up the £200 a week as an RUC man to take a job at £90 a week as a welfare officer and ended up stealing.

Tyrie of course was a figure much feared by rank and file Republicans and the average Catholic in the ghetto areas. But he was a disarming and oddly reassuring conversationalist, at least to someone from the South. He had personally driven members of the young Fianna Fáil students group around Belfast. After complaining that it was unfair that UDA men could join the British army for service abroad but were not allowed to join the UDR at home, he told me that I needn't have worried about being caught up in an Orange procession earlier in the week on the Shankill Road in a Southern registered car. "That's all over now, you would be all right. They only go after known Republicans." This sounded more reassuring in the surrounds of the Europa Hotel than it had been when I was watching "Up the UVF" signs give way to "UFF" and then slowing down to allow clumps of Orangemen to go by in their collarets. Then I must admit the thought had crossed my mind as to how one checked in a morgue as to whether one was a Republican or not. It was, after all, members of the UDA who bombed Dublin.

But Tyrie too had his pressures. Pressures that would affect not alone the Loyalists and H Block and whether the several hundreds of them elected to go on the blanket, but the whole course of events in Northern Ireland.

You know on our side it is not just the Army and UDR we have to worry about—sure we have friends in the UDR but they give us a bad time too. We have got to deal with the Democratic Unionist Party, the Official Unionists and the Orange Order." It is the push-me-pull-you interaction of each of these groupings, and their effect on what policy, or which compromise, is reached between them and the forces on the Catholic side, that will ultimately determine whether the Northern conflict ends relatively peacefully, as it could, or in a blood bath, as it might, if care, compromise and finesse are not employed, says Tyrie. "Sure it's no wonder you would be wanting to go in for a bit of aul devilment at times. It's only me family that keeps me right . . . There's no redundancy in my job you know," he chuckles.

Another UDA spokesman put their problems this way. "Look, I know the South. I know we've nothing to fear. I believe we can get certain guarantees. I believe also that the British will withdraw some day and that we must prepare for it—but you just try telling that to some woman up on the Shankill Road with the Doctor's photo up on the wall. . ."

It was these external pressures, invisible but potent, that played about the cells in H Block.

Southern Discomfort

Concern for the possible implications of a prison protest movement in Ireland, at a time when so many "subversives" were held in Southern prisons, had kept the Dublin government's responses more muted than many people felt they should be—one of those people being the former Fianna Fáil minister, then Independent member of the European Parliament, Mr. Neil T. Blaney.

In the Dáil on November 23, 1978, Mr. Blaney asked the Foreign Minister what steps he had taken or intended to take to bring to an end the treatment of political prisoners in Long Kesh. The then Minister, Michael O'Kennedy, outlined the government's attitude by first stating that since the prisoners had been convicted of criminal offences, many of them very serious ones, he could not accept that they were political prisoners. However, he did say that the situation gave cause for concern from a humanitarian point of view, but he was equally at pains to stress that those associated with the protest (the IRA) "had shown a cynical disregard for humanitarian considerations and were anxious to exploit situations if they could." He assured Blaney that "I and my department have been in constant contact with the appropriate authorities on this matter and I would welcome any further information which would enable me to express the concern of the government on humanitarian grounds."

On December 7 of that year, again in response to pressure from Blaney, he spelled out in more detail what this meant:

> On any and every occasion on which complaints or evidence from a reliable source are brought to me I will

pursue them at every appropriate level, as I said on the
last occasion. What I meant by "every appropriate level"
may not have been understood, but let me now clearly
put it on record. It means Ministers to Secretary of State,
where appropriate and where possible, and that has been
more than once. It means Ambassador to Secretary of
State; Ambassador to Ambassador; Minister to Ambassador. It means constant communication between my
officials on this and other issues. That is the way in
which these matters have been pursued.

The following month, in a speech on Anglo-Irish relations in
general, during which he appealed to Britain to encourage unity and
reconciliation, Mr. O'Kennedy said on January 5 at a Fianna Fáil
meeting:

The compounds and H Blocks of Long Kesh are testi-
mony to the futility of much of what has been done in
the last ten years. We all hope that a speedy and
humane solution can be found which will put an end to
the senseless suffering being endured.
    Many of those in Long Kesh were themselves
only children when the current violence commenced in
the North and this, of course, adds to the suffering now
being experienced by their families. While the crimes
committed in the North have been serious and horrifying, there is a particular tragedy in the suffering of
young people caught in a position they do not fully
appreciate and exploited by their own leadership for
propaganda purposes. In hoping that a proper solution
can be found, we should all resolve to do everything in
our power to prevent a similar corruption of today's
children and of tomorrow's.

The following month in London, on February 14 at a meeting

with Roy Mason, O'Kennedy specifically asked that a solution be found to the H Block situation. The *Guardian* report noted that "he pleased his British hosts" (Airey Neave was also at the meeting) by not pressing for an immediate solution to the Ulster problem.

O'Kennedy was of course responding to the policy directions of his Prime Minister, Jack Lynch, on the issue. In an interview on the Radio Éireann programme "This Week" on January 7, 1979, Lynch indicated what his personal views were: "We have always indicated our interest in the plight of these prisoners on humanitarian grounds, and through the Minister for Foreign Affairs, and indeed he has announced that several times, in the Dáil, the extent to which he has gone making his views and our views available and known to the British government. We believe that the plight of the political prisoners and of their families is being manipulated by the IRA and other paramilitary organisations for propaganda purposes and as long as that manipulation is being done, as long as that kind of propaganda is being used, it is going to be very difficult for our representations to become effective to the extent that they can be, but it's on purely—and I believe myself that Archbishop O Fiaich went on the same grounds—on humanitarian grounds that we had been interesting ourselves through the Department of Foreign Affairs through the Minister in this particular area."

The interviewer, Kevin Healy, asked: "Is there anything in your view that can be done at this stage to get these men to wear clothes and go back to normal life?"

Lynch replied: "I'd say myself that if these men were left to themselves and if this kind of propaganda manipulation from the outside and one might say control of their plight from the outside ceased, that they might be able to come to some kind of agreement that would ease their situation, but when you have the deputy-governor of that particular prison killed before the eyes of his own family, it would be very difficult to see, and no person inside did that job, it is very difficult to see how these poor men inside can ease their situation as long as they are being dictated to, as they seem to be, and certainly influenced as they seem to be, from the outside."

Healy then pointed out that Archbishop O Fiaich had said these men were not common criminals and they shouldn't be treated as common criminals. "The Northern Ireland Office says they are common criminals. What do you think they are?" he asked.

Lynch concluded by saying: "They are people who have committed very serious crimes and they have been convicted according to law, and well I know that some of them are young men. Some of them perhaps hadn't even achieved the age of maturity when the troubles started and some of them were caught up perhaps willy nilly in this series of violent activities but there is a certain amount of sympathy due to them from that point of view I agree."

Lynch was forced to resign before the year was out, largely because of opposition that centred around his Northern policies. His successor Charles Haughey said at the subsequent Fianna Fáil Ard Fheis that the North in all its aspects would henceforth be the number one priority of his government. Presumably this included the H Block issue, but by 1980 he had not made a statement on the matter. Pressed in the Dáil, however, by Deputies Blaney and Harte, the new Foreign Minister, Brian Lenihan, said on March 26 that he would raise the matter with the Secretary of State, Mr. Atkins.

Atkins, however, figured in an unsuccessful effort to resolve the imbroglio that very day, in the House of Commons in the unlikely setting of Budget Day, whether chosen to mask governmental intentions from his own public or that of the Unionists and the IRA was not clear. Nor was it clear whether his actual proposals were intended to solve the situation or merely for the record to prove that the government was attempting to be humanitarian. In all events after a few days' consultation within the prison amongst themselves, the prisoners rejected the Atkins proposals. These were:

1. The granting of regular exercise periods in "Regulation short-sleeved PT vest, shorts and plimsolls."
2. An extra visit a month.
3. Permission to write and receive an extra letter per month.

But these "gives" were accompanied by a "take," where it was proposed from the following April 1 (April Fools' Day) to phase out Special Category status altogether.

This meant that anyone charged and convicted before March 1, 1976, who might have wanted to claim Special Category status could now no longer do so. But the existing 429 men and 4 women with political status were to continue with that status until their sentences were served. The implication at least, if not the intent, appears to be that the numbers on the blanket were going to rise rather than fall—and of course the "no wash" aspect of the "dirty protest" made it highly unlikely that the prisoners were going to take the exercise carrot anyhow.

There had been high hopes that something more substantial was coming because Cardinal O Fiaich, this time accompanied by Bishop Edward Daly of Derry, had again visited Long Kesh on March 3, 1980 and in all spent ten and a half hours there speaking to "as many prisoners as possible." The short statement issued by the Bishops merely said:

> Either together or individually they spoke with and prayed with prisoners in all the H Blocks, including prisoners who are on protest and those who are not.
>
> They also met prisoners in the various compounds, including a number of Loyalists.
>
> In addition, the two Bishops recently visited Armagh women's prison where a protest similar to the H Block one is gradually building up.
>
> Feeling that no effort should be spared in attempting to avert the development of a second H Block situation, with all the tragedy and anxiety which this entails for prisoners, prison staff and the families of both, and wishing to ascertain if there is any useful role which the Bishops can play at this stage in seeking a resolution of the H Block impasse, they have sought a meeting with the Secretary of State, Mr. Atkins, at an early date.

But it was known in informed circles that the Cardinal, deeply perturbed and embarrassed by the situation building up in the women's prison in his own cathedral city, had had a long private meeting with Atkins in Armagh the week before the visit. The length of time the Bishops spent talking to the prisoners—two prelates being employed, meaning that any message or terms conveyed could be put individually to every prisoner—had seemed to be preparing the way for a new initiative, especially as the conference which Atkins had been chairing at Stormont on the future of Northern Ireland had just broken down, and a very senior cabinet committee, including Lord Carrington and William Whitelaw, were meeting the Secretary to plan something significant. Whatever those plans contained, nothing and no one had any hope of bringing peace to Northern Ireland so long as the H Block situation continued.

The Court of Human Rights

About ten days after the Cardinal paid his first visit to Long Kesh in August of 1978, a Belfast solicitor, Francis Keenan, acting on behalf of a group of H Block prisoners, initiated an action in Strasbourg before the Court of Human Rights seeking a decision as to what acceptable minimum standards should be employed to hold prisoners in a situation where there was dissidence on the part of the prisoners and a very difficult situation prevailing overall.

The action, which employed over a thousand pages of closely reasoned legal argument, alleged multiple breaches of various articles of the Convention of Human Rights and obviously if it succeeded would have had a terminal effect on the controversy. However, a number of points should be noted about Strasbourg and the action itself:

1.   The Court of Human Rights and the European Commission of Human Rights between them constitute a highly political forum.

2.   The Keenan picture differed from that of the Irish government in a number of essential respects:

    (a)   The Irish Government's case was of course taken government against government.

    (b)   It was alleged that the five techniques were used against men who were incontestably (i) not convicted of any crime and (ii) not criminals in any known sense. (Even the British government conceded this last itself by releasing many of them without further proceedings and later compensating them.)

However, Keenan's case was an independent petition. It concerned IRA men who were convicted as such, and it raised questions of international concern on a very different level to that of the Irish government's case. For if the IRA won against the British at Strasbourg there were implications for all sorts of other groups who use terror as a weapon, the South Moluccans *vis-à-vis* the Dutch government; the Baader-Meinhof grouping against the German government, and the Red Brigades against Italy. So, obviously, powerful interests could be stirred by this action.

In the case of the British and Irish government's case, it was possible for the court to go from issues of torture to those of ill-treatment in its judgement. As the grounds against Britain shifted so had the political situation. The Provisionals had risen in strength from the time of internment in August of 1971 to a point where they were challenging the British government, and the situation had got both that much more complicated and more deadly. However, in the H Block case for the reasons stated, the basically simple issue of minimal standards for prisoners had not altered in a way in which different types of verdict could be arrived at and (up to March 1980 at least) it wasn't possible to argue, as was being done in the Ireland versus Britain case, that a drastic remedy had been discontinued—i.e. internment.

But following on the Atkins House of Commons statement in the wake of Cardinal O Fiaich's visit, and the subsequent differing response of the Protestant churchmen, it came to be believed in Belfast that the purpose of the Atkins manoeuvre was so that it could

---

be argued that a domestic remedy had been made, a contention which the Protestant churchmen's report would tend to bear out, and that the Strasbourg case decision would have a different colouration to what it might have had. Only time would tell. But the reader should keep in mind such far reaching implications when he or she would hear, or believe, what appeared to be a straightforward approach on the issue. Things said or done in Belfast or Westminster may in fact be aimed at listeners in Strasbourg or other forums of influence, which one might not immediately think of.

CHAPTER 15

Eyewitness: Long Kesh

Now, as readers will be more than well aware by this stage, I have given the prisoners' view as to how they found themselves in their predicament. What about the view of the people charged with maintaining them in that condition? How did they see it? I had an opportunity to find out, on a visit to Long Kesh.

Firstly, it should be understood that for almost every charge, comment or view that a prisoner or a spokesman on their behalf makes or holds, there is an obverse mirror image on the official side. If readers cast their minds back to the revolting details of Maguire's description of H Block, the mirror search, the maggots etc., and imagine the situation as viewed by an official spokesman, they would find for every point he, or someone like him, makes there is a counterpoint.

For instance, the then prison Governor, Stanley Hilditch, denied completely that there were beatings and explained his control procedure whereby he argued it would be impossible for such things to happen without his knowledge. He made the point that the prisoners had handed out some savage beatings to warders, and that under the old compound system the debriefing of prisoners by their Loyalist or IRA officers after they had been sentenced often included torture—I mentioned the case of the Loyalist prisoner whose head had been fastened in a vice, but Hilditch cited other cases in which he averred prisoners had their nipples burned off with electric shock, were beaten and had poison administered to them.

He talked about cyanide being found, and in one case a quantity of strychnine being found in a Harpic bottle in the Loyalist compound. In another instance prisoners had used the handicraft facilities to make electric timing devices for bombs.

That's not the only thing the prisoners make. At one stage, until the authorities found the still, the best poiteen in Ireland was made by the IRA in Long Kesh, from oranges. This was an improvement on the alcoholic use to which oranges were originally put. They used to be injected with vodka, before being included in the prisoners' weekly parcels! Parcels play an important part, obviously, in prisoners' lives, but they also play sometimes a disproportionate part in their families' lives because some budgets of large families living on welfare are very badly strained by having to keep up the standard of parcel contents that the prisoners have come to expect. There's a sort of status attached to who gets or who gives the best parcel. Pondering on this schoolboy aspect of detention, or internment, I had an insight into what a social worker implied when she related to me the remark of a woman whose internee husband had been released not long before. Said the woman, "I thought I had only seven children, but when he came home I found out I had eight."

When one thinks that incarceration can have that effect even without a protest such as that in H Block being involved, one shudders to think of what the long-term psychological effects could be. By 1980, there were as yet no psychiatric studies done on any of the H Block men who had served their sentences (twelve in all at that time, but one, Martin McKenna, ironically the first to be freed, was killed in a car crash). However, the Department of Justice in Dublin reckons that on average a man becomes institutionalised to the point of being unfit for normal society after eight years in jail. Stanley Hilditch said in his experience this varies with the individual; some can take prison better than others. This is obviously true, but the notion of anyone spending a ten-year, twenty-year or even life sentence in H Block conditions does not bear thinking about. The place would just become a vast, shitty mental asylum—no matter which side was telling the truth. And the accounts are dramatically and diametrically opposed.

Nugent and Maguire both categorically stated that warders inserted fingers in their anuses and sometimes used the same fingers to examine their teeth; Hilditch—and other warders—denied this claim but made it another way saying that women had been known to bring tubes of cling wrapped writing materials and so on into the prison in their vaginas, remove the capsules in the toilet and pass them over to prisoners who then swallowed them. "You wouldn't believe some of the things that happen," a warder assured me.

The official side is one of a humane, cleanly efficient, long-suffering doing of one's duty. It was very hard talking to a random selection of warders to realise that these men were all under threat of their lives, and one could go through the other H Blocks in which the "non complaining prisoners" were sequestered without being aware that one was in anything but a modern and rather well-kept penal institution. Grass grew on the plots around the Blocks, and the place still had a shiny, freshly painted look about it, with shining kitchens, spotless surgeries and gleaming corridors to give the lie to the impression that the whole place was a hell-hole.

I had a number of specific questions to put to the Governor and to the officials I met, both before and after the tour of the prison, and broadly speaking I received answers to these, but in a way that made me feel that the H Block situation was a true microcosm of North of Ireland society. You could go through wide areas both of the larger societies outside the prisons and of the prison itself without realising that anything is wrong, but when one does come up against the hidden hideousness, the realities are unutterably foul.

My tour of the prison was prefaced by a visit to Stormont to see the political people in charge of running the prison and their civil servants. After a briefing I was taken on a tour of the prison complex, on the site of the old Long Kesh airfield, and broadly speaking I would have to say that I was shown everything I asked to see. However, both my visits to Stormont and to the prison were shot through with a mixture of propaganda, fair play, bureaucracy, straightforward bungling, duplicity, and even humour, that placed the whole H Block situation in its own, to coin a phrase, very Special Category.

The day began with a drive up the Newtownards Road from the centre of Belfast out to Dundonald and Stormont Castle. Because of heavy traffic it took three-quarters of an hour to accomplish what should have been done in ten minutes. So I had plenty of time to assess uneasily the large, denim-clad young men who stood around UDA headquarters and eyed my southern number plates. The traffic told one something of the problem. It was incessant and opulent. We were in the Protestant, or wealth owning, sector of the city. However, I got clear of the UDA headquarters and its environs without incident and with the May sun shining, literally giving everything a warm and cheerful look, I turned in the gates of Stormont. Carson stood in wrathful towering bronze silently proclaiming "not an inch," with his back to the imposing granite former Parliament building, that stands so huge and so compelling that it has often appeared to the disenchanted minority as being designed for a thousand years of supremacy.

However, this particular Reichstag was first closed down by the Provisional IRA's activities in 1972 and, when reopened, was closed down again in 1974 by the strike of the Provisional mirror image, the Loyalist UDA. Symbolically, via various security checks, I had to drive around to the right of the old Parliament to the smaller Stormont Castle where the Northern Ireland Office, as it is called, now conducts the affairs of the province. The mighty, if not fallen, are at least considerably reduced.

At the Northern Ireland Office I met a Top British Political Decision Taker (TBPDT), the senior civil servant in charge of prison administration, some press information officers, and a young man whose duties seemed to consist of (a) smiling at me and (b) taking down in careful shorthand everything I said to the TBPDT and everything the TBPDT said to me in reply. I had wanted my interview to be on record but I discovered when I was sitting down at Stormont Castle, having driven up from Dublin to make the discovery, that it was not to be. The other surprise of the morning was that I was not to talk to the prisoners or they to me.

The TBPDT was a tall, pale faced, grey suited Tory. This I

think I can safely reveal without breaching the seal of the confessional (his).

I asked him how he was going to get off the hook from the H Block protest. He replied that he wasn't on a hook. That the protest was not having that much impact; true, it might have if continental and other media took it up, but certainly he would have no difficulty in going into Parliament and defending the position of the government on H Block, at that time. He felt that the security forces were winning in the battle against the IRA. Statistics showed that violence was down and arrests were up. He was optimistic that if the detection rate in the South continued to improve then the IRA could be beaten. Co-operation in defeating the IRA was the only All Ireland dimension that the British willingly extend to the Irish. The South's role and responsibility in this activity is always strongly stressed. Of course, he had only been there for a year then and his time scale was too short to make any long term prognostications. He always referred to the Provisionals as PIRA. The Official IRA apparently were OIRA and we all laughed politely when I said this sounded very Irish. He expressed himself as rather surprised that the smell in the prison was not worse. When in England he had charge of mental institutions in which the secretions of years had set up a far worse smell and he said he was surprised at the good health of the prisoners.

"But"—I interjected—"they are very thin." The senior civil servant pointed out helpfully that lots of people paid large sums of money to get their weight off. We continued.

The Stormont party made the point that there was a good deal of coming and going on the protest. That some 150 had gone off it; when pressed it was agreed that there were something in excess of 350 continually on protest, as I had believed, but there was dispute over the number of Loyalist prisoners. "Yes, there may have been twelve in all but there are only five now." "No, we have not heard of Loyalists mounting any attacks on warders, or of special inducements for Loyalists to remain on the blanket such as payment of transport expenses to the jail."

In what later turned out to be a significant observation, making me question the worth of some of the intelligence reaching decision takers connected with the H Block issue, the TBPDT remarked with a little laugh that Martin Meehan—a famous Belfast Provisional who had been jailed after being convicted through rather mysterious circumstances a few weeks earlier—had not lasted very long on the protest. "In fact he had come off after a few days." And, another little laugh, "he was supposed to be one of their leaders . . ."

Could the British, I asked, not take a leaf out of the Southern government's book and find a formula as in Portlaoise to defuse the situation. To this the TBPDT answered that in the South the position was different, and the population as a whole supported the government in arranging a face-saving compromise. This consensus would not exist in the North. At this stage we began a conversation like a man crossing a river by stepping stones with the TBPDT disputing my contention that this in effect meant they were afraid to move because of Unionist opinion by one argument after another. He said, no, this was not fair. That the fact was, a mistake had been made at one stage in the conflict when, because there was not sufficient prison accommodation, Special Category status was introduced.

At the risk of digression I feel that the point about Unionist reaction should be stressed. When Marian Price was released the reaction of the then official Unionist Party leader, James Molyneaux, was to threaten to raise the release in the House of Commons, and a spokesman for Ian Paisley's Democratic Unionist Party, the Reverend William Beattie, termed the release "incredible" saying that Miss Price could easily have been treated in prison. Such reactions tend to justify Daniel O'Connell's famous but seemingly sectarian remark: "Over their tea and their tracts, the Orange faction would delight to shed your blood."

I asked about the other mistake which put a considerable strain on prison resources—the introduction of internment. For a moment a mood of "now, old boy, you are being mischievous" darkened the atmosphere of sumptuous carpeting, sunlight and bloody marys.

But we pressed on. I asked did not the fact that Stormont no

longer stood as a Parliament indicate that there was no consensus in
the Province, and that this could have a bearing on both the numbers
and the condition of the prisoners involved. The TBPDT fetched up
on a final stepping stone from which he said that the will of the people as expressed in the Parliament (at Westminster) "at which of
course the Province was represented" (of the twelve MPs at the time
only two, Frank Maguire and Gerry Fitt, were Catholic) was that
criminals such as the men who had done the things that had landed
them in the H Blocks were being fairly treated under the prison rules,
their plight was a self-inflicted one, and there could be no question
of conceding Special Category. The position regarding a hunger
strike, should one occur, was as outlined, by the then Home Secretary (Mr. Roy Jenkins) in July 1974, in which he said in effect that
hunger striking if pursued would inevitably lead to the prisoners'
deaths, because the British government were determined that there
could be no further concessions to that form of protest.

I asked whether there was not validity in the prisoners' claims
that their protest was rather like that of trade unionists who went on
strike to have a benefit, which had been conceded after an earlier strike
but then withdrawn, returned to them. A Press Attaché earned his pay
by suggesting that they had already had their concession bought back
from them by the offer of a fifty percent remission of their sentences.

But if they were being treated in a special way and being sentenced in special courts on the basis of confessions extracted by special methods was it not already officially conceded that these men
were *de facto* special, I enquired. This was not a fact in the eyes of
the TBPDT. In addition, I suggested, would not the Special Powers
Act further cut across the normal rules by conferring a form of martial law on the province? Again there was a touch of the "now, now,
old boy," routine. But in the ghettoes surely this was what the Act
amounted to, I suggested. Well, perhaps the ghettoes were different,
said the TBPDT, but certainly not in the rest of the province.

We talked about the underlying problems which gave rise to
people joining the IRA in the first place—the unemployment statistics in Belfast and so on—and the TBPDT agreed that these were

very wearisome but said that there was no way one could force industrialists to site factories in areas where they didn't want to go. (Places
like the Falls Road, Strabane, Derry, and Fermanagh, which have
Catholic majorities.)

Somehow the difficulties of getting the security forces out of
parts of the province in which it was fairly obvious a sizeable section
of the Irish population did not want them to be was not touched upon.
One difficulty the TBPDT did discuss and discounted was the question of the position of warders; the campaign of the IRA against them
was not hurting the prison service, he claimed. They were finding no
difficulty in getting numbers to join and it was proving easier to protect those who did join. Of course there were "some inducements" to
entering the prison service, he did concede. How much in pounds,
shillings and pence would these inducements amount to, I enquired.
"Well, I am not prepared to say, actually" was the answer. From other
less reticent sources I learned later in the day that the average prison
warder's income in the North of Ireland prison service at that time
was of the order of £10,000 per annum.

After that friendly but not very illuminating encounter, the
TBPDT and I agreed that when next he came to Dublin we would
break bread together, and I went off on the last part of my Odyssey,
suggesting to the TBPDT that Mr. Alison, the Secretary of State with
responsibility for prisons in Northern Ireland, might like to issue an
official statement to me which I could include in the book so as to
give, on the record, the official British view, and thus prevent a "one-
sided IRA tract appearing."[1] One of the hitherto silent press officers
stirred himself. "And would that prevent the one-sided IRA tract
appearing?" he asked hopefully.

We drove to the nearby golf club at Knock to have a sandwich,
and conversation switched to my mother's novel, *The Big Wind*. Evidently in compiling a dossier on me which included all my published
writings, articles, books and so on, they had also studied my mother's
literary output. I mentioned that she had also written a book about
Knock, meaning the Knock in the west of Ireland where the Blessed
Virgin appeared, I explained.

Said my guide and interlocutor, laughingly but with feeling: "I can tell you it's very unlikely she will appear here!" Indeed it was very difficult to visualise the upper-class Unionist Protestant membership of the plush golf club we sat in receiving a visitation of that sort. Who knows, I thought profanely, perhaps in a United Ireland.

After the lunch we drove to Long Kesh, where the Governor was waiting for us in his office to explain to me, with the aid of a wall chart, the layout of the prison. Apparently arrangements had been put in train for me to have a full guided tour of the workshops, the kitchens and the rest of the prison apart from the Blocks on the dirty protest.

The Press Attaché pointed out, however, that I was rather less interested in handicrafts than in the protest. It was decided that I should be allowed to pick at random two Blocks, one of prisoners not on protest and one where the protest was in progress. I was to pick two cells at random in each Block but I could not talk to the prisoners. At Stormont Castle I had been told that the talking to the prisoners was a matter for the Governor, and at the prison the Governor said that his terms of reference would not allow him to permit me to speak to the prisoners. Ping Pong.

However, I must say that within the parameters laid down for the visit, Hilditch, albeit from his side of the argument, spoke openly and helpfully to me about any matter I raised. He was then a steely-eyed, well-preserved man, with a pale face, in his early fifties who liked to walk very fast, and a background of ministry to the Protestant religion, before he entered the prison service.

The various questions which had been put to me as stumbling blocks he answered fairly enough, and what he didn't reply to, the senior civil servant in charge of the prisons, who had motored on from Stormont Castle while we were at lunch, to be at the prison before us, spoke up on. I raised issues like the lack of privacy in the design of the toilets, the lack of furniture in the cells, the allegations of beatings, the procedure of the mirror search and so on.

Either the Governor or the senior civil servant countered by responses such as "every point in the prison has to be within the Governor's purview, that includes the lavatories. There can be no question

of my going to a coroner's inquest after some psychiatrically disturbed prisoner has taken his own life, and say that there are parts of
the prison which were out of my control and that I couldn't answer
for them for hours on end.

"We would be glad to leave furniture in the cells but the prisoners [the protesting prisoners] smash it up and use it to wreck the doors."

The Governor himself demonstrated to me what was required
of the mirror search. He made it seem simply a gentle flexing of the
knees so as to part the buttocks over the foot square mirror set in
foam rubber on the floor. To my question as to why was it only
protesting prisoners who were subjected to this form of search after
a visit—making it look like a punishment, not a necessary search—
the answer was to the effect that the prisoners sometimes got very
dangerous objects smuggled into them after visits. However, I must
point out here that any Republican prisoner (or Loyalist for that matter) is likely to try to get something smuggled into him during a visit.
The fact that only the protesting prisoners were subjected to this form
of inspection, which they manifestly detested, did look suspiciously
like harassment. My query as to why the Board of Visitors didn't
publish their annual report, as is done in the Republic, was shrugged
off with "Oh yes, we might look into that. There is no particular reason why they shouldn't be, but of course they are not all that well
written, you know."

That a general regime of continuous punishment and diet deprivation existed was denied or countered by allegations of the prisoners' misdemeanours. Hilditch never referred to beatings, always
speaking of "the allegations" and he said that "the allegations were
growing less as the level of aggro in the prison falls." This I could
believe. It paralleled a situation outside the jail. The army generally
only used saturation tactics and harassment of the population as a
counter to IRA activities (overlooking of course the fact that instead
of countering them, they were changing the peoples' attitude in the
district from condemnation to encouragement).

There were other factors also—the continuing efforts of the
Cardinal through the Secretary of State, Humphrey Atkins; the

Strasbourg case; the growing pressure generated by the campaign
itself; the fact that to both the authorities' and the IRA's dismay it
had spread to Armagh and the women prisoners; even the fact that
this book was being written. All of these seemed to have produced
an at least temporary easing of the prison situation generally. Marian Price was released on May 1. She had been very ill for three
years and could have qualified for release at any time during that
period, so some other consideration obviously prompted the move.
On the deadly chessboard of Northern Ireland neither side moves
their pawns gratuitously.

However, in general, as during my tour of the southern prisons
at a time of political controversy over their condition, I was aware
that to a large extent my tour would be a scenic railway exercise and
that unless something unusual happened I would have no direct way
of establishing for myself the truth or falsehood of either sides' allegations. A visiting journalist need not expect either prisoners to lay
on a riot for him or warders to beat up a prisoner during his tour of
inspection. However, as we drove and walked around the sprawling
prison complex I was able to form an impression which was probably valid enough.

The actual Long Kesh site (or Maze prison as the authorities
term it) is a mixture of military installations and normal prison.
Armed uniformed soldiers stand at the gates. High watch towers
adorn the walls, in the background the sound of barking guard dogs
can be heard, and entrance to each section of the prison is effected
through carefully controlled iron gates and high wired fences. The
system of passes and checks employed as one goes from one area to
the other, whether on a visit like mine or as a normal visitor, makes
escape virtually impossible—at least from the H Block areas—
though there have been some breakouts from the compounds.

In the handicrafts area Hilditch spoke enthusiastically and
authoritatively about the welding and handicraft facilities available,
showing them to me with pride. They were undoubtedly first-class,
for a prisoner who had come into conflict with the law in the ordinary way and wanted to rehabilitate himself—but not for one with a

burning sense of injustice who might be tempted to make other use of the facilities.

The prison hospital was obviously designed to the very latest modern standards as were the dental facilities and so on. The kitchen too was large and hygienic. A number of prisoners were cleaning out the floor, in an effort to keep it that way. This was part of the prison work that the protesting prisoners refused to do. In an effort to draw my attention to the excellence of the diet, Hilditch remarked with apparent surprise on the presence of a large container of cauliflowers in the kitchen. "Cauliflowers at this time of the year! Where did they come from? They must have come from some place foreign."

"No, Sir," interjected one of the warders, "they come from the South." End of cauliflower interlude.

The warders were friendly enough to me as we entered one section after another. At each gate the warder in charge of each wing repeated to the Governor the number of prisoners under his control. One of the vital tasks laid on a warder is to know at all times who he has and where. I didn't have much opportunity of talking to them but when I did, they tended to make light of the problems of security: "Well, in one-third of the province approximately, if you are a drinking man you have to be careful where you go. But other than that it's all right." The men who accompanied the tour party were probably hand-picked as they were visibly brisk, efficient, disciplined men. But here and there I did notice glowering pot-bellied specimens whom I certainly would not like to be under the control of.

The best description overall for the differing categories of prisoners, like their counterparts outside the jail, is probably "Protestant" and "Catholic"—though neither side abides much by the teachings of their churches, which the Protestants, be they Church of Ireland, Presbyterian or Methodist, rarely visit, and against whose priests and bishops the Catholics are often very bitter and anti-clerical. However, though the Church leaders like to say that the struggle is not religious, because of its embarrassment to them, religion at least in its cultural conditioning is a vital determinant. Much more so than saying "Loyalist" or "Nationalist."

To an outsider the prisoners look alike and they sound alike, but they come from profoundly different backgrounds. Someone trained in the tribal divisions would have no difficulty in picking up the nuances. The Protestant will talk about "Londonderry," the Catholic will call it Derry. (The ancient city of St. Columbcille known in Irish as Doire came to be known as Londonderry after the Catholic siege led by King James was beaten off by the Protestant defenders who swore allegiance to William of Orange, Good King Billy). The Catholic if he discusses sport will probably discuss Gaelic football, or hurling. While a ban imposed by the Gaelic Athletic Association (GAA) on foreign games, i.e. rugby, soccer, cricket and hockey, was removed on April 12, 1971, he would almost certainly not have had any sporting encounter with his Protestant compatriots who went to Protestant schools learning largely English history. And the British army acknowledged the importance of Gaelic games in the Catholic tradition and sense of identity, in the most important way of all: they harassed GAA clubs and sometimes as in the case of Crossmaglen GAA Club damaged the grounds and buildings. If the playing fields of Eton built an Empire, the playing fields of the GAA were recognised as having shaped many a Republican.

At his school the Protestant learned English history. The Catholic by contrast learned Irish history and also the Irish language. The Protestant very likely saw a Union Jack in his church on Sunday probably adorning a plaque to Ulster Protestants who died in one of Britain's wars. Possibly too his church stained glass windows showed a soldier in British uniform dying "pro patria." Certainly his house in the Shankill Road, indistinguishable from the red brick kitchen houses in the Falls Road area, would be likely to have a picture of the Royal family displayed. By contrast the Catholic adjoining him would have a framed facsimile of the 1916 Proclamation or a Long Kesh harp. The differences are as much cultural as religious. One is a "Loyalist" but he is not quite as certain as he was that the Crown he is loyal to is that concerned with him. Certainly if he is in prison for an excess of Loyalism, i.e. shooting or otherwise putting down the treacherous Fenian Catholic, he finds his sense of identity under a severe strain as he looks out through barbed wire at British uniforms keeping him there. In the old days of the Tory Unionist alliance some of his forebears got jobs and houses through similar activities.

I found the UVF compounds particularly sad and ironic in this context. Their huts were all called after World War I battlefields in which their forefathers distinguished themselves—"Ypres," "Paschendaele," "Thiepval Wood" and all the other brave wasteful futilities. Today's UVF are one of the withdrawal pangs of empire. They reminded me of Australian ex-service men I met in Sydney talking on Anzac Day about Gallipoli, the Borneo Campaign and all the rest of the glorious military past and then with some disenchantment having to contemplate a present and a future in which the mother country had abandoned them for the Common Market.

The UVF compounds were also the neatest with little litter boxes for cigarette butts and orange peel affixed to each hut. One hut was unusually adorned—with a large cage of singing birds, which one of the prisoners bred in the manner of the Birdman of Alcatraz. "It seems to have a good effect on him," remarked the Governor.

There were few of the prisoners to be seen as we drove around because the snooker championships were on TV. The only sign of activity around the sprawl of barbed-wire enclosed Nissen huts that housed the UDA were two UDA men jogging and chatting amiably to each other as they ran around in bright singlets and shorts as if they were circling a university playing field.

The only ones actually using a playing field were the Provisionals who had two teams engaged in a lively and expert game of soccer. Too expert. Watching their expertise, and admiring their uniformly neat jerseys and shorts I realised that behind the vigour and skill displayed—of the level of a top class Irish soccer club—there must have lain several hundred hours of pent-up energy channelled into learning to control a soccer ball on asphalt and behind barbed wire. That was how soccer, control of a ball by foot, first grew up in the back-streets of industrial England. Skill and control were essential in such confines and watching the players again I thought of Sean

McDonnell's remark about going from the confines of a larger prison to a smaller one.

Hilditch understandably showed himself reluctant to talk about his personal security as we drifted on to one of the sorest topics of all raised by the H Block protest, the shooting of warders. "All the terrorists want," he said, "is a nice soft target, and an easy way of escaping. Then they'll strike all right." Obviously for a man in his position these killings must be a matter of deep emotion. To give but two examples which horrified me, there was the case of the retired warder who, with his wife, also in her sixties, was shot dead in their home in Belfast, their bodies only being discovered much later by their son.

In the second instance Prison Officer Cassidy was attending a family wedding with his wife and was at the church holding his three-year-old daughter by the hand when the assassins arrived. Only one shot him at first and he fell to the churchyard path, releasing his child's hand, then the other who had stepped around the group surrounding Cassidy emerged through the startled screaming guests to stand over the squirming man, pumping bullets into his head.

To Hilditch, the most horrific shooting was that of his former colleague, Assistant Governor Jones. "He used to sit there in that chair you're in," he said during our talk in his office—causing me to shift position a little uneasily. "If you only knew what he used to do for prisoners. The interest he used to take in them, both in the prison and when they got out. He knew their fathers when they were in, in the forties and fifties. He really was a model jailer. Jailer isn't a word used much now, but it's the proper term—and he was a proper jailer in every sense of the word."

In some ways I felt, though I didn't say it to him, that that description of the murdered Governor more than anything illustrated the gulf between the men behind the bars and the men who kept them there. "Knowing their fathers" would only have increased the IRA's mistrust of Jones; he knew too much about them. I remember one night talking to an IRA family about the arrest of the son of the house at the time of internment because a warder who lived nearby had given him away. The son, who was subsequently released after being subjected to the "five techniques" was telling his father that he was surprised at the betrayal. "I always found him a very decent sort," he said.

"Then you're a fool," said his father. "Didn't I always tell you a screw was a screw? He was doing his job as a screw. There's no such thing as a good screw or a bad screw. Just screws."

The warder in question was shot dead one day. The exchange between father and son serves to illustrate why even before H Block started, elements in the IRA had been seeking to have the warders declared "legitimate targets." A friend of mine said of Falls Road people once, "They're lovely people, but they're like alsatians: you never know when they'll go for your throat." Certainly as far as the conflict between the IRA tradition and the Unionist and British one was concerned, he was right. They've been raised in an alsatian society.

The atmosphere in the non-protest Block I visited was quite peaceful, certainly a lot less tense than Portlaoise when I visited it, though I don't think I was being fanciful in detecting an undercurrent of resentment. The men appeared to be in good physical shape and were actually having a meal when I arrived. One of them seemed to recognise me (from TV) and smiled at me and I nodded back. Hilditch brought me into a number of the cells and they were clean, in some cases adorned with pin-ups, in others with family snapshots. The quality of reading material varied from the *Daily Mirror* to works on sociology, politics, and literary works of all sorts. I spoke to one prisoner who turned out to be a Loyalist. As we were chatting about a model boat he was building, the Governor told him I was a journalist and he said laughingly but with some force that "if I'd known that I wouldn't have let you into my cell—you're only after propaganda." Evidently he thought that since the Northern Ireland Office had sanctioned my visit it must necessarily have been designed to further the official line. As we went from that section to one of the Blocks on the dirty protest, the Governor asked me what I had made of the prisoners and their general attitudes. I told him that although they seemed cheerful enough, in good condition, there was an element of tension underneath.

"You know," he replied, "they are the same people that are doing the killings outside. You remember that one who smiled at you? He seemed to know you. Well, I could tell you a story about him and things about him but it would be a breach of professional integrity. But I can tell you that he attacked a warder once and I have seen beatings in my time but I never saw anything like what he did to that warder, before he was . . ." he paused, searching for the word, and then finished, "dealt with."

I don't know what condition the warder was in then but the prisoner didn't show any signs of ill effects. As we came near the protesting Block the atmosphere in the tour party grew more tense. I noticed that my companions' breathing seemed to become heavier, conversation grew less easy and that we seemed to be making little forays here and there to inspect aspects of the prison that the Governor wanted to show me, almost as if we were postponing the evil hour.

I wanted to know if I could have a word with Gusty Spence, the UVF leader, while I was in the jail, but the Governor said his terms of reference did not allow me to talk to the prisoners.

We had a general discussion about penology north and south of the border. So far as facilities were concerned the new H Blocks were well in advance of anything in the South. But facilities are not the sum of man's existence. When we got to the dirty protest Block, the Governor pointed out to me the fittings outside each window which allowed air in through the use of grilles but prevented the prisoners from dropping their faeces and urine out into the yard.

There were some shouts and incomprehensibilities as we walked across the yard. The Governor warned me that there might be some form of outburst as I came in, and standing on the polished entrance hall, I was allowed to take my choice of any wing I wished and any cell I chose. I picked a wing and stopped about two-thirds of the way down picking a cell at random. The door was opened; the Governor asked me to wait a moment, stepped inside and said a word to the two occupants.

All I could catch was the admonition "no conversation"; as if to underline this, two enormous warders, either of whom would dwarf me (and I am not a small man), entered the cell and stood behind the cell's occupants. They were then aged twenty-one and twenty-two, as I afterwards learned, serving ten and twelve years respectively. When the cell door opened they both looked frightened and looked anxiously at us for a moment. They were pallid and naked except for a blanket draped over their shoulders. They stood silently, fear hardening into defiance, I felt, as we looked at the cell.

It was covered in excrement almost to the ceiling on all four walls. In one corner there was a pile of rotting, blue moulded food and excrement and the two boys had evidently been using bits of their foam rubber mattress to add to the decor as we entered. There wasn't much of a smell but the light was dim and the atmosphere profoundly disturbing and depressing. I felt helpless and angry as I stood and looked at these appalling and disgraceful conditions, prevented by bureaucracy and by history from talking to two of my fellow human beings who had brought themselves and been brought to this condition of self-abnegation.

There just didn't seem to be anything to say. I had thought about giving them cigarettes but in the circumstances of no talking and no contact I didn't know what sort of situation the gesture might provoke. Their last state might be worse than their first so I just stood looking at the two boys; one of them had long curly red hair; both were bearded, of medium height. They tried not to appear cowed or to meet anyone's eyes. Eventually after a few minutes of this I said thank you and left. Someone in the party said, "Well, you certainly picked a good one. I have never seen anything like that. That's the worst one I have ever seen." I just couldn't speak for a few minutes.

The only time I have ever experienced a sensation like it was on being briefly locked into one of the punishment cells used for Irish Fenian prisoners in Tasmania. The prison village is still preserved at Port Harcourt, and one can still see the flogging triangles, the isolation cubicles in which they sat in silence to attend Church services—and the solitary confinement cells designed so that no light entered them. Food was placed in a corridor outside the cells and could only be groped for when the warders withdrew. Prisoners kept themselves sane by devices such as dropping a button in a corner of the cell and crawling around until they found it. On emergence they had to wear hoods over their eyes for several days because they would otherwise have been blinded by the light.

I had gone to Port Harcourt out of a long term interest in the history of Irish political prisoners and when I emerged blinking from the dark I for a moment relived and empathised with the hate and horror of that ancient chapter of the story that was then being written in H Block.

Similarly in H Block I was so overcome with emotion that for a moment I neither could, nor wanted to, speak with my escort, but just felt a blind sickening feeling that someone, somewhere, somehow was going to have to answer for this, whether it was the IRA or the authorities who were responsible.

Someone rabbitted on about steam cleaning processes which would remove what I had just seen from the walls one of the days, until the prisoners were transferred back and dirtied it up again, and mentioned that already after only a couple of years the effects of the steam cleaning were beginning to crumble the walls. As I was trying to pull myself together and cope with the notion of a twenty-one-year-old facing a decade in those conditions, I heard somebody in the party remark that the TBPDT seemed to have not been so well informed after all. "I see Meehan is still on the protest"—and I remembered what I had been told earlier in the day about Martin Meehan apparently giving in under the protest after a few days, so for my second cell visit I opted for a visit to his cell.

Everyone was slightly taken aback. Meehan was not the type of person that they would have chosen, left to themselves, for me to see. The senior civil servant and the Governor looked at each other questioningly for a moment. Eventually the civil servant said, "Why not?" As we walked towards Meehan's cell I had an opportunity to ponder on the rather less than perfect rapport which must have existed between the permanent civil servants at Stormont and their political masters, that must have prompted the man who made known Meehan's actual circumstances as opposed to what the TBPDT had said.

Even though he was clearly out of sympathy with the prisoners' protest, he was not a hundred percent in tune with his boss either. I could not image a southern Irish civil servant in the same position drawing a similar circumstance to my attention, were we touring a southern prison.

Meehan, a low-sized man with a fringe beard, was wearing a towel around his waist, and was apparently trying to achieve a variant on the wall patterning with his faeces. So far as I could make out he seemed to be drawing palm trees on the walls.

As soon as we entered the cell he began to tell the Governor he had been framed. The Governor countered by saying that the circumstances of Meehan's arrest and sentence were not a matter for him, and for a few minutes the two had quite an argument.

Meehan had just begun (at Easter) a twelve-year sentence for conspiracy and the false imprisonment of a seventeen-year-old boy, Stephen McWilliams. He had already served three years for IRA membership, was a former OC of the Third Battalion of the Provisionals in North Belfast, escaped from the Circular Road jail in 1971 and had a list of exploits behind him for which the authorities were greatly delighted and relieved at having him behind bars. As he said himself he was "no saint," but he could well have been telling the truth about his conviction.

The McWilliams youth was forced to become an army agent after being caught in a burglary. He was kidnapped by the IRA in July 1979, admitted after beatings that he was an informer and would have been shot had the army not raided the house where he was being held. He claimed that he had caught a fleeting glimpse of Meehan at Oakfield Street as Meehan allegedly drove a car, acting as "spotter" for the one ferrying him. He denied knowing Meehan to see, but later in the hearing he admitted to having been shown a photo of Meehan the last day before his kidnapping. A taxi driver gave evidence, as did the man who hired the car, that the car described in court as Meehan's had been out on hire that day. Meehan, for his part, claimed that he had spent the day at a Folk Museum with his girlfriend and her children, and the night at home.

The Judge, Mr. Justice Gibson, said that McWilliams' identifying evidence was of "poor quality." Another part of it was proved false, resulting in the acquittal of another defendant, Kevin Mulgrew. Nevertheless he preferred McWilliams' story to that of the taxi man and his family and said that the presence of Meehan's car in the Oakfield area was corroborative proof of the "poor quality" evidence. So Meehan went off to the H Blocks to draw palm trees from his own faeces and young McWilliams remained in fear of his life in army custody. It was said that he was going to join the army, the only way that he could hope to escape the vengeance and execution that the Irish traditionally visit on that most hated of figures, "an informer."

In an effort to cut off Meehan's protestations of innocence, the Governor asked him what he was doing to the wall. Meehan replied: "I don't know but it's well beneath me anyhow."

The Governor, a man obviously ingrained with the tenet that "cleanliness is next to Godliness" and equally obviously repelled by the nature of the protest, replied with some heat, "To me it's beneath any human person. I don't know how any civilised man could do this sort of thing." I felt that conversational rules or not, I had to make some gesture of humanity in this "diamond cut diamond" situation and stepped forward to introduce myself to Meehan. He transferred the piece of foam rubber he had been using to make his "pictures" to another hand, and we shook hands without giving any sign of squeamishness. Meehan was "delighted to meet me." The Governor regained his professional detachment and we left the cell, the door closing on Meehan standing looking after us, a towel around his loins, passing his piece of foam rubber from one hand to another.

Meehan subsequently went on hunger strike to draw attention to the circumstances of his imprisonment, coming off the blanket to do so. It was feared that his gesture might precipitate a mass hunger strike, but, at that time, the other Block OCs prevented this.

As we walked across the yard outside the Block to the exit gate, a medley of sounds came from the prisoners who during our tour had kept up a spattering of shouts and interjections in a form of Irish that sounded incomprehensible to me. But now I thought I caught some instruction in English directed at the Governor which if complied with would have required a high degree of physical and moral flexibility.

I asked one of the warders what the prisoners were saying. "I don't know, sir," he said diplomatically, "they have an argot of their own." They have. It means hate.

As I left the prison one of the warders saluted me and asked in friendly fashion if the badge on the front of my car meant that I was a member of the Royal Lifeboat Institute. I replied that it did, and he beamed as he gave me a cheerful farewell salute. Obviously anyone belonging to an institute with the word "Royal" in it had to be all right.

1.   Perhaps the closest thing to such an official statement would be Michael Alison's reply to Fr. Reid in Appendix I.

CHAPTER 16

Eyewitness: Armagh

Armagh jail is surprisingly inconspicuous, standing in the centre of Armagh town. It looks like one of those old warehouses one sometimes sees in city suburbs, and one would have to notice the signboard saying "Armagh Prison" to realise that it is a jail. Once inside, the bars, the searches and the caution about opening gates soon make the nature of the institution plain. However, from the outset one is aware of a marked difference in the atmosphere compared to Long Kesh. There were no armed soldiers in evidence, for instance, and the presence of women prison officers immediately strikes a different chord to the sombre atmosphere of the Maze. Armagh prison is built on the old nineteenth-century pattern of a central hall from which radiate wings easily surveyed from the hall itself. Its main draw-back is that it has no place to grow, being confined by the city all round it, and there is almost no greenery to be seen. However, within this limitation and that of its age, the workrooms, recreation facilities, laundries, kitchens, bathrooms etc. are as bright, clean and up-to-date as could be expected in the circumstances.

I was met by the then Governor, Mr. George Scott, and taken first to one of the workrooms to have an opportunity of seeing the kind of prison work that the ordinary prisoners do. A small group of women were making overalls, for use in the prison service generally, in a classroom-like work area. I was encouraged to walk around and talk to the women, who talked freely to me. One was a Republican prisoner who had come off the protest because of her children.

Another was Chrissie Smith who was in the prison indefinitely because of the Ogilby murder described earlier. She was a slight, small, black-haired woman who said she got on very well with her Republican fellow prisoners and apparently still maintained her UDA associations. She said that "the troubles" had opened her eyes about things generally and made her more politically aware—she was sixteen when sentenced and was then twenty-three. She kept herself well and could have been an office worker in a typing pool anywhere. After talking with the women, I went next to the exercise yard where a group of Republican protesters were exercising. They were quite friendly to me also. At first they spoke to me through their leader, Síle Darragh, but then talked to me generally and freely. Like all the Republican women on the dirty protest, they had just benefitted from a change of clothes which they had agreed to accept once every three months, but they had not washed since February. I commented on how clean they looked and some of them showed me their necks and chests and there was much laughter and joking. Their places of origin told the initiated all one needed to know about the background to their presence in the jail—Twinbrook, Oldpark, Derry, Strabane, Ballymurphy, Short Strand. All are places in Catholic areas where unemployment has created both the Republican ethos and the larger prison of which Sean McDonnell spoke. They seemed completely unafraid of the Governor and his party and discussed openly with me topics from the shooting of the warders, which they agreed with, the IRA campaign outside the jail, their own attitude to force, to the prison regime and to the state of their health and the medical attention provided.

They said what they had to say as if the Governor and the others were not present. Propagandist, but with no bravado or cheekiness, just a very strong determination to continue their struggle to the end. They had obviously become politicised and quite bitter, particularly about the treatment of the men at Long Kesh. Their view of life was partially the straightforward IRA one and partially a blend of Catholicism with an anarchist, nationalist admixture, in which their religion, their social background, group solidarity and the support they had derived from the Irish language and Irish history buoyed them up. I asked them what they thought of the meeting between the British Prime Minister and the Irish Taoiseach and they replied that it meant nothing. The British were too hypocritical, nothing would come out of it. To them the existing system only meant continuing unemployment and more struggle. They didn't think that the established parties held any relevance for them. They made no strong claims against the prison regime apart from retelling their version of the events of February 7 and the "chicken search" that began the protest. One girl complained that she wasn't being properly treated for her duodenal ulcer. It was only when she mentioned that she had an ulcer that I noticed she was paler than the others, but she was just as cheerful and highly motivated.

The most striking feature of the group to me was their youth. The average age was early twenties and the duffel coated, bejeaned group could well have been in the yard of a training college or a university campus for all the distinguishing characteristics that separated the women from their contemporaries walking up and down outside in the streets of Armagh town. But the charges which brought them there covered everything from explosives and possession of arms to charges of murder. The common denominator that linked them with all the Republican prisoners I was to meet during my tour, which in all lasted nearly six hours, was a burning sense of injustice at the "system" and, in particular, Castlereagh and the "conveyor-belt." At the end of the tour the one thing I could say with certainty was that none of the women I met, on the Republican side anyhow, would have been in trouble with the law had the troubles not broken out in 1969. The Governor and his staff, whilst they would obviously not agree with all the women's claims about the regime, seemed to be agreed on this point also.

After talking to the exercising group in the yard, I was then taken to inspect A Wing where the dirty protest was in full swing. This was sickening and appalling.

Tissues, slops, consisting of tea and urine, some faeces, and clots of blood—obviously the detritus of menstruation—lay in the

corridor between the two rows of cells. At first the Governor proposed to show me a clean cell—the cleaning process employed at
Long Kesh had just been used at the jail ("They tidied the place up
for you," the women told me). He was overheard making this suggestion to me and, from a locked cell, came a woman's voice shouting, "Show him one of the dirty cells!"

I saw the clean cell first. The clean cell was a clean cell. Next
door was an empty dirty one smeared to the roof with faeces. The
women had also worsened their condition by refusing sheets, lying
only on blankets. In one space not covered with excreta, someone
had written:

I am one of many who would die for my country
I believe in fighting the fight to the end
If death is the only way I am prepared to die
To be free is all I want and many like me think the same

That last sentiment I certainly found to be the case. Across the
corridor I spoke to Katrina Pettigrew whom I mentioned earlier [see
Chapter 9]. As the windows were shuttered from the outside to prevent them throwing their slops out into the street, the cell was dimly
lit and Katrina's pale face seemed particularly pale and sickly. I could
understand why her parents were worried about her but she was quite
cheerful and determined to continue with the protest.

A little further on in the wing, I met the prisoners' leader
Mairéad Farrell, and her cellmate Sinéad Moore. We talked about the
Haughey/Thatcher meeting which neither of them held out much
hope for, "unless Mrs. Thatcher bends a little." Like the women in the
exercise yard they too were wearing comparatively clean clothes. As
they had them on for a week, though, they were beginning to smell
a bit. In fact I found the smell in the girls' cells far worse than that
at Long Kesh, and several times found myself having to control feelings of nausea. Dinner had been served shortly before I came and the
women had plates of chicken and chips in their cells. They all said
this was for my benefit but didn't seem to be particularly hungry.

Even though I urged them not to let me delay them in eating, they seemed keener to chat than to eat. Given the surroundings, this was, I thought, understandable.

Mairéad complained, as had some of the other women, that at night some of the prison officers threw bricks at their boarded up cells and shouted obscenities at them to keep them awake. I asked the Governor what he had to say about this and he at first said "it doesn't happen," and then he asked the women where were the bricks in the morning and Mairéad pointed out to him that as the windows were boarded up, they couldn't see where the bricks lay. The Governor conceded this point and allowed that there might be one or two warders who behaved in this way. Like the women elsewhere in the prison, Mairéad and Sinéad talked openly in front of the Governor about many complaints they had, their opinions on the general struggle, the shooting of warders and the men in Long Kesh. The women, I noted, seemed to relate the campaign against the warders to the treatment of the Long Kesh prisoners. They did not seem to be aware that the IRA had threatened to shoot warders over the abolition of Special Category during the negotiations after Feakle [see Chapter 4]. But while the women did not seem to be aware of this background, the Governor was. Mairéad, apart from being the prisoners' leader, was also conducting the Irish classes. There again the struggle and the solidarity of the other women on the protest was obviously keeping them going.

One of the things one realises about prisoners is that despite one's preconceived notions of them, they look exactly like their counterparts on the outside. Mairéad and Sinéad could have passed for two typical well-reared Belfast women in their twenties were it not for the fact that they were in a narrow cell barely wide enough to allow in two beds, which was covered from top to bottom in their own excreta, and in which they were determined to stay until they were released through death, the ending of their sentences, or the concession of political status.

Mairéad said, "We are in a war situation. We have been treated in a special way and tried by special courts because of that war, and because of our political activities we want to be regarded as prisoners of war."

After leaving A Wing we went to B Wing, a three-storey edifice with Republican and Loyalist prisoners on the first two landings and remand prisoners awaiting sentence at the top. There was one remand prisoner, Jeanette Griffiths, on the first floor, because she had her baby with her. The prisoners in B Wing were not on the dirty protest.

Like the men prisoners, the women had come to jail via Castlereagh and similar interrogation processes. Most of the women on remand had been waiting for trial a very long time—a year was nothing out of the ordinary—and the women regarded this as internment by another name. Several of the women in the prison denied completely having committed the crimes with which they were charged. I realise of course that this is a common claim in prisons, but their denial was balanced by the fact that some other women did tell me they had done the things for which they were sentenced. Others said that they had broken after two or three days under interrogation, and signed to stop the interrogation continuing.

One girl, for instance, had cracked up after being shown photographs of her dead brother, whose body was taken from a lake three months after he was last seen alive in an RUC police station where he too was being interrogated. This girl told me, "They kept shoving the picture in my face. It looked like a big lump of rotting meat. They told me I'd look like that because they would hang me, so I signed. I would have signed anything to make them stop." When she received the depositions later on in the prison and saw what she had admitted to, she attempted suicide and was saved, after slashing one wrist, by a fellow prisoner.

Here again readers will realise the significance of the statistic I noted earlier relating to the high percentage of convictions obtained in Diplock Courts on the basis of confessions.

I met Ettie Cowan who was sentenced with Chrissie Smith for the Ogilby murder. We joked for a time about her smartly tinted hair which she had set herself with the aid of another sister who had joined her in Armagh on an arson charge. The whole atmosphere in B Wing was different to that of A Wing and light years removed from that of Long Kesh. One slender, ladylike blonde girl of twenty-two, Rosie Armstrong, who was doing fifteen years on charges arising out of the destruction of the Brooklands Hotel, invited me in to have a cup of tea with her cellmate, Linda Quigley. Rosie and Linda had been on the protest in A Wing but came off it. Their cell was brightly painted and furnished and lightened by feminine touches like the teddy bear on Rosie's bed. Were it not for the bars on the window I could have been sitting in a women's hostel. They also made tea for the Governor and the rest of the party, and obviously enjoyed "the crack" of having the Governor in to tea.

If one studied Rosie closely, one noticed that she trembled slightly, and had a pallor, but otherwise she seemed a cheerful, normal woman with a highly developed sense of fun. On their landing there were facilities for cooking, apart from electric kettles in the cells, so that the women could cook food supplied by their relations outside. As the women all wore their own clothes and went to a lot of trouble with their appearance I frequently found myself forgetting I was in a prison at all, such was the intensity of the effort they made to keep up their own morale.

Prisoners' relatives had made some complaints about an article in the *Belfast Telegraph* which made conditions in Armagh seem pleasant and the women well-treated. I could understand how the author (Sandra Chapman, 18.4.80) got a generally benign impression, because leaving all questions of the author's viewpoint to one side, the women did make a tremendous effort to keep up their morale—too tremendous, I felt at times. What tensions did the bright manners conceal? What crack-ups might lie in the future?

Jeanette Griffiths, for instance, the girl with the baby who was awaiting trial on a triple murder charge that she vehemently denied, was a fine-looking, well-developed, brown-eyed woman with close-cropped, stylish hair, looking more like a young model housewife than an inmate of a prison. Only Pauline McLoughlin from Derry (whose health condition I described earlier), of all the prisoners in B

Wing, looked like a prisoner, because of her pallor and pitifully thin appearance. Whatever caused Pauline's malady, seemingly some form of nervous spasm, the result was that she could not keep food down and vomited up everything she ate within minutes. Chips apparently stayed down longest. Her companions on the protest persuaded her to come off it when her weight reached six and a half stone. I promised her that I would ask the medical staff about her condition because she felt that she was not being properly treated. She gave me permission to discuss her condition if I wished, as otherwise this would be a confidential matter.

In the prison hospital wing—again, as well appointed and staffed as one could reasonably expect—the staff all knew about Pauline but could offer no explanation for her trouble, which apparently had been a lifetime condition. But I was assured with a wealth of circumstantial detail that everything possible was being done for her.

The women on remand were on the top floor of B Wing. One of them, Josephine McCready, had five children. She was a small, gentle, worried woman with black hair. She showed me the mark of a bullet on her back. She received this wound when police fired on a car she was driving one night, after two young men to whom she was giving a lift had jumped from the car on coming to a roadblock.

The spokeswoman for this group was Jennifer McCann, who wore a bright striped football jersey and jeans and looked like somebody on her way to a disco. She was on a charge of attempted murder. We discussed with the Governor the possibilities of giving them extra recreation in the yard. The women wanted to be allowed out when Jeanette Griffiths was wheeling her baby under supervision of a prison officer but the Governor argued that he didn't have the staff to watch them as well. Jeanette, because of her baby, was unlikely to try to escape or make contact with the outside, whereas the probability of the women on remand doing so could not be overlooked. However, he promised that he would try to let them out and one of the women said, "Now if you don't do that, Mr. Scott, we'll write to the *Irish Press* . . .!" The same woman complained to me that someone had stolen lollipops from a parcel her mother had just sent her. I interceded with the Governor afterwards to be sure and keep his promise, and he said he would if he could at all.

In its own way this interlude was a revealing insight into the cost of the prison service. Even a small thing like an hour in the fresh air costs money in terms of supervision, although it seemed to me that since there were prison officers on duty on the landings where the remand women were being kept, these could just as easily have watched them at recreation as in their cells. Another complaint this group had was not being allowed to make use of a mini-canteen facility similar to the women on the lower landing. In each cell we entered the women had some request to make to the Governor, who completed my tour by bringing me to the section of the prison where the three women who actually had political status were kept.

These were Dolours Price, Pauline Derry and Chris Sheeran. This was C Wing, which housed the Special Category prisoners on an upstairs floor, and downstairs the young offenders. There was only one of these at the time of my visit: a woman on a fatal baby-battering charge, an increasingly common occurrence in Belfast since the troubles.

The Special Category wing was fitted out like a suite in a hotel, with a TV room and a particularly well-designed, brightly decorated and furnished kitchen-cum-dining room, which the women themselves had helped to decorate. Again if one overlooked the bars, and the fact that the three occupants of this "suite" were young women who, if they had to serve their sentences in these surroundings, would be there until past middle-age, this was quite a pleasant place.

I talked with Dolours Price for a while. She was a particularly intelligent woman. Like her sister Marian, who was released, she suffered from anorexia nervosa, giving her a lemur-like air, though she counteracted the effects of the disease by dressing tastefully and attending carefully to her hair and manicure. She was obviously keeping depression at bay with some effort. The forced feeding apparently destroyed the metabolic relationship between her body and eating and she found it difficult to keep up either her painting or writing because of the lack of stimulation in her surroundings or of any real incentive. "One tends to forget what it's like on the outside. . ."

She had a very highly developed political and artistic sense and was obviously widely read. I asked her would it be a fair assumption that the real problem was not the regime imposed by the Governor and his staff but the issue of political status, and she said this was a fair assessment. The Governor and his staff were in general as humane and reasonable as one could expect—Scott had previously been described to me as a "Hitler and a tyrant who keeps the women locked up twenty-four hours a day in their cells and won't let them go to the lavatories."

Dolours and her two companions were lively, friendly women who reacted to me as would their sisters on the outside had I dropped in to a suburban house unexpectedly on a visit. They were slightly restricted in their movements, because they would not exercise with the women on criminal charges, and were remaining indoors on a fine summer's day of their own choice while the other prisoners took the air.

The situation in Armagh jail, like that of the world of Northern Ireland outside it, was deceptively pleasant. The sun was shining, and if one had not been through A Wing and sat in the filthy cells talking to the women, one could have imagined oneself in model prison sur-roundings. But I had sat in those cells. The Governor reckoned that after six years in normal prison conditions, a woman began to suffer permanent physical and psychological effects. What A Wing could do to the women was anyone's guess. Over a meal with the Gover-nor I talked with him about how he felt to be continually under threat of death from the friends and associates of the women I had met and joked with earlier. Obviously conditions in A Wing took a toll on more than just the prisoners. Just outside the window of the prison canteen where we sat was the main prison entrance where one of the female prison warders had been shot dead and some of her compan-ions badly injured not long before. These are the realities which con-tinually lurk in the shadows outside the pleasantries of Northern Ireland.

Governor Scott, who would himself be a prime target should hostilities against the warders be renewed, took only a cup of tea because he suffered from a bad stomach. He attended a Presbyterian church, and knew little of the South, which he felt it was not safe for him to visit.

No matter how humanely intentioned he was (and although the women accused him of niggling, petty tyrannies, I would accept that he was humane), still he had to cope with the obvious cultural divergencies between himself and the women. Apart from these cultural divergencies, there was also the difference between the attitudes of today's prisoners and those of their predecessors. Scott, a man with over twenty years in the prison service behind him, remembered IRA men who were household names serving out their sentences comparatively peacefully. "I remember Joe Cahill working in the kitchen in the Crumlin Road—you used to see him going around with a big knife." Another anecdote he had concerned a prison officer who suddenly found himself face to face with an IRA man he had got to know through having his brother under his charge, as rioting and stone-throwing erupted in a Catholic district. But instead of betraying him to the rioters, the IRA man led him to safety.

It was not likely, however, that in the atmosphere engendered by the H Block and Armagh protests, such an encounter would have a similar outcome in 1980.

Actually, nowhere in Northern Ireland more than in the yard of Armagh jail did the Special Category issue seem more unreal. Unlike the male prisoners in the Northern system, the women already had their own clothes—unlike the Republic, Northern male prisoners normally wore a uniform—and could circulate with considerable freedom as in B Wing. It would mean only a minute adjustment to the women's situation to find a formula on the lines of the Portlaoise model, and to end the Armagh protest, and hence the threat to life and health of all those involved, with no further ado.

The reality was, however, that despite the cheerfulness and good hairdos and clean clothes, it was the intensity of feelings generated by the women being on the "dirty protest" which was likely to have the worst effect of all. It was too easy to think that because the situation was less tense than in Long Kesh, the Armagh position was not highly dangerous. In fact it was a highly combustible element, with the threat of further danger. Not alone was it manifestly obvious that the women involved in the protest and their colleagues in B Wing would never have come within miles of any prison were it not for the troubles, but the plight of the protesters had served as the focus for a protest which might have in fact increased their numbers.

Beginning on March 8, 1980, a group called "Women Against Imperialism" staged a picket outside the jail to highlight the condition of the women inside. Eleven were arrested and refused to pay their fines, and because of this refusal two of them, Margaretta Darcy, a playwright, and Liz Lagrua, went on to serve sentences in A Wing with the Republican prisoners. If these demonstrations were to continue, and there was every reason to believe that they would, more and more protesters would thus be found to swell the ranks inside. Ways should have been found to defuse, not heighten, this situation.

CHAPTER 17

Where the Warders Stand

The people caught between the hammer of the Provisional IRA and the anvil of official reluctance to concede on Special Category were of course the warders. Since eighteen of them had been killed by 1980, the reluctance of individual warders to talk about their problems, or to comment openly on the prisoners' allegations, was understandable. However, a spokesman for the warders did agree to see me and talk to me at length, but only on condition that his identity was kept secret. His friend and predecessor, Officer Des Irvine, was shot dead on the steps of the Wellington Park Hotel in Belfast after attending a meeting which he himself should also have been at had he not been diverted instead to deal with a problem at Long Kesh that morning.

He attributed the fact that recruits were still coming forward in good numbers for the prison service, to the publicity campaign mounted by the Northern Ireland Office to attract new staff, and to the general unemployment and redundancy situation which made the relatively high pay-scales offered by the prison service attractive, despite the dangers of the job.

For instance, he himself had a son in the service. In 1980, the scale of pay varied from an officer, ordinary class, earning about £8,500 plus overtime, to £13,000 for a senior officer, up to Governor status which carried a salary of approximately £16,000, plus fringe benefits such as holidays, canteen service, pensions and—ominously—life insurance benefits. I would reckon that the widow of a prison officer would stand to receive between three and four times as much in benefits as would the widow of a Republic of Ireland soldier killed on UN peacekeeping duty in the Lebanon.

The recruits were drawn mainly from the existing services: British Army, UDR, RUC. In fact, after a spell in the service some of these recruits left and rejoined the army or the police. There were some young people around the twenty mark joining, who did not have a background in any force. These must be assumed to come predominantly from the Unionist population, in the absence of any figures to the contrary, although my informant, in common with the Northern Ireland Office, would deny any flavour of particularism in recruitment. The actual training period was quite short, a total of twelve weeks in all, and roughly half of this took place "in house," as it were. So after a training period of four to six weeks, recruits came into contact with prisoners directly. The major qualification for a prison officer, I was told, was "common sense."

Before joining the prison service, the spokesman had been a senior executive in charge of the sales division of an important North of Ireland firm. His main reason for leaving industry was that in order to get to work each day, he had to "run the gauntlet of one set of paramilitaries"—the Catholic set—"and my lads were teenagers at the time, so you could see where that would lead. To another set of paramilitaries"—the Protestant set.

So, as he didn't want to join them, he decided to jail them, taking advantage of one of the few employment opportunities on offer at the time, by joining the prison service and leaving behind his pension rights and all the entitlements of the old job. Becoming a warder was just a job to him. "I had no thought of the prison service, or anything like that, at the time."

My informant told me that he was one of the strongest opponents of the introduction of Special Category status and one of the strongest advocates of its abolition. He had just returned at that time from the annual Prison Officers Association Delegate Meeting in England where he had met William Whitelaw, and he and his Northern Ireland colleagues had told Whitelaw in no uncertain terms what they thought of his introduction of Special Category in the first place. Despite the attrition, the spokesman disdained the idea of making any concession to the prisoners because of the H Block and Armagh protests. It was difficult to know exactly how the prison officers broke down on the issue. For every one whom one met who was determined to fight on, one met another who thought the game was not worth the candle and felt that the issue should be conceded.

My informant, who carried a firearm off duty, argued on quasi-professional grounds:

> When I was on Magilligan [earlier in the decade when prisoners were confined in compounds at the Magilligan camp prior to their transfer to Long Kesh] you weren't a prison officer, you were only a guard. Only a senior prison officer or Assistant Governor could talk to the Prisoners' OC, not directly to the prisoners themselves. Some of them were quite nice to the staff. You would often hear of them asking an officer that they dealt with in for a meal. They would fry up steak or something from their food parcels. The next day the same fellow would be coming at you over the wire with a big hook trying to split you. There was no control in those days [circa 1974]. I remember the army were called in nearly every day to Magilligan. They wouldn't eat the food. I remember chickens being thrown over the wire. In the Blocks, the cellular system, an officer can go into a man's cell, say if he is doing handicrafts or something and he can admire his work and pay tribute to it. A prison officer in the eighties should be more than a turnkey, opening grilles and cell doors. That has to be done of course by somebody but an officer should have a knowledge of sociology and that sort of thing. At the moment we have sixty young officers on courses.
>
> I think we should withstand this campaign by pure determination and never allow ourselves to be turned

---

away. But ideally there should be mutual trust between
the prisoners and the officers. Prison is for prisoners
after all, not for the officers. The officers should be
closer to the prisoners on welfare schemes and rehabilitation and such matters.

I question the motives of some of these allegedly
politically motivated people. Going out and shooting a
policeman doesn't further a cause. You had those
Shankill Butchers. I was in H Block 8 recently. There
are 149 inmates and two-thirds of them are serving sentences in excess of twenty years. Some of the Butchers
were there, and I had a long talk with them. They are
very nice fellows, but they would tell you that there is a
'political characteristic' to their activities—and look at
the litany of tortures and murders they committed. How
can you have a divided house on an issue like law and
order? Half the prisoners doing their own thing and half
conforming. The prison officers themselves have to wear
a uniform. You can't have discipline without it. In America they are finding out that the harsher type prison
regime has to be restored. The open prison approach, the
do-gooders, they are not getting anywhere.

Take the present position with clothes and work.
Prisoners don't have to work on a Saturday or Sunday.
After tea every day they are free to wear their own
clothes and even if they are out working during the day
and a visitor comes—I mean a visit they are entitled
to—they can be brought back to their cells, given facilities for a shower, and then they can put on their own
clothes for the visit. I mean there is an alternative to
everything. They don't have to subject themselves to the
condition they are in.

We hear that there are talks on between different
people. We are not told anything, but we understand
that if the talks break down we will know about it,

because we may pick up the paper and see that four or
five warders have been shot. We are under non-stop
pressure. There are threats, and a very restricted social
life. There are places here [we were talking in Col-
eraine] where the Loyalists would kick my head in but
there are other places, Strabane, Newry, where the Provisionals would set me up. I went into a pub not so long
ago with my wife and I saw two former Special Category prisoners sitting in a corner. They didn't do anything themselves but you would have to guard against
one of them making a phone call. . . The other day the
Special Branch men went to an officer's house at mid-
night and said, 'Bob get you dressed and move *now*, not
tomorrow, *now!*' Not in five minutes' time either. They
had information that he would have been shot. That's
the sort of thing you are up against.

My informant, a low-sized, dapper, disciplined man, obviously
derived part of his resolution from a reluctance to let himself be
bested. He was very Irish in his Provo-like tenacity. And in fact as
our acquaintance progressed and the barriers came down I noticed
that he ceased referring to the Provos as PIRA and began calling
them Provies. When we parted he shook hands very warmly with me
as a "fellow Irishman" and said he thought privately that the long-
term solution to the problem of Ireland was some form of unity and
a British withdrawal. "Ireland is one country, after all. But the South
will have to change—and the Church of Rome will have to change.
All those thousands of women going to England for abortions, and
they just ignore them. They just don't want to know."

He strongly emphasised a point which I came across again and
again in researching this book—the utterly appalling nature of the
dehumanising effects of the whole Northern Ireland situation on
young people.

"You have young fellows of twelve to fifteen years coming on
all the time, and they've never known anything else except violence

and the troubles. You can imagine what they are like." I can indeed.

He gave an interesting insight into how some Unionists view the implications of the Rhodesian settlement. "They think because the British have arranged majority rule in Rhodesia, now they'll come and give us majority rule in Northern Ireland." That would mean rule by Loyalists. For his own part, however, he would favour an administration that would share power between Catholics and Protestants.

He clearly mistrusted the British. This was partly over the expediency of the introduction of Special Category. "Whitelaw now knows he made a mistake. He admits it," he said. But he also felt that the British would go one day when it suited them, and leave people who had struggled to uphold the system to take the consequences. And he quite candidly admitted that the South had done very well out of the EEC through being able to negotiate independently as a sovereign state for her own interests, not as an appendix to Great Britain depending on British civil servants and politicians to take up the Northern case once the UK mainland's interest had been got out of the way.

In politics he said he would have supported Terence O'Neill's blend of liberal unionism, but he tried to go too far too fast. The Irish, he believed, were slow in any part of the country to make changes. In religion he had a Plymouth Brethren background on his mother's side, but attended a Presbyterian church. "I haven't got anything against Catholics. In the service now, I never ask a man's religion— although," he laughed, "one of my colleagues happens to be black and told me that he was a Catholic into the bargain—as if he didn't have enough trouble being born black without being Catholic as well. I could take you to my own native village and I could show you there that if anything the bias is against Protestants. If you could see the homes. The way the Catholics live. I tell you this much, that if fifty years of Loyalist rule taught the Catholics anything it was to fend for themselves. And they have fended for themselves, very nicely."

The prison officers' spokesman was in part institutionalised in his approach, in part imbued with that pride in "the service" that one often finds in armies, and in part a shrewd trade unionist who realised that the troubles in Northern Ireland had at least provided one burgeoning growth industry—employment in the prison service. And he was determined to make the most of it, for himself and his colleagues whom he represented. We discussed problems like getting mileage allowances for prison officers who had to drive to the Maze and Magilligan prisons, which he said would lead to industrial action if it wasn't solved.

One of the murdered warders whom we talked about was Albert Miles, whom he admired: "Bert was a militant man, a militant man. If he wanted something and they wouldn't give it to him, he just called all his colleagues together and they sat in the canteen until such time as they got their way."

It was odd to hear of the prison service and even facets of the H Block protest being discussed in trade union and productivity terms. For instance, the spokesman had, not long before, been doing an experimental turn at the cleaning out of cells with the steam cleanser used to remove the faeces from the H Block walls, to determine what the rate for that job should be. "A hundred pounds a week wouldn't pay you for it." He corroborated at least part of Maguire's statement [see Chapter 1] about the maggots. "Before the steam cleaning was introduced the maggots were skipping up and down the corridors, never mind the cells. If they hadn't brought in the steam cleaning they would have had to give way on the Special Category because the medical people were on the point of closing the whole thing down as a health hazard. "

He described an occasion when, on a visit to the H Blocks in the pre-steam cleaning days, a group of official visitors chanced to witness a group of "dirty protesters" being bathed. "They didn't have much stomach for their lunches after they saw that sight, I can tell you," he recalled with a grim chuckle.

On other matters raised by Maguire, Nugent and the prisoners' relatives, such as the beating of prisoners by warders, he was more guarded, but not dishonest in his approach. Like most Ulstermen, Protestant or Catholic, he had a basically straightforward approach.

I have always found interviewing Northerners preferable to dealing with Southerners. Northerners tend to answer yes or no, and either tell you what you ask or say straight out that they won't tell you, but they don't beat around the bush, and you were never in much doubt as to how you stand in a Northerner's esteem.

I put it to him that after a tour of Long Kesh in which the Governor had done everything to impress me with the cleanliness of the place and the quality of the food, and where episodes of prisoners being beaten by warders were described as "allegations," not factual happenings, I then found in the *Irish News* an uncontested statement by Father Faul that prisoners' food had been urinated in, that one of the blanket men had witnessed this, and that when he complained he had been placed on punishment as a result.

"Yes, you will get occasions of that sort of thing," he said, "but let's take the other case. I remember in Magilligan that for a few days the food was uneatable. It turned out that a Republican orderly was putting washing powder into the porridge and that sort of thing, until he got a few days on the boards for his trouble. But the prison disciplinary code is strict. I have to go along when people have broken the rules, and sometimes I can tell you that it's a purely mechanical exercise. I wouldn't stand by some of the things that happen."

Such as?—I pressed him.

"Well, you might have a prison officer going on the piss and attacking a policeman, or you get one or two, both staff and prisoners, who have an opportunity to abuse privileges. There is always some degree of truth in allegations that has to be recognised. The prison officers are under a good deal of pressure, I mean apart from the campaign, and we are told now that because of talks between people that we don't know about, the attacks have ceased, but I can tell you that the threats haven't. I have high level intelligence available to me because of my position on a daily basis and recently I discovered that the IRA not alone had my movements taped but they had my son's telephone number and the address of another son who is in the RUC. But the threats, the phone calls, that goes on all the time.

"As to the nature of the job itself, I recall a period from April to September in '74 when we worked right around the clock. From '74 to '77 before the Blocks were built, and even after it, was a period when seven days a week, twenty-four hours a day was nothing out of the ordinary. No social life, nothing. The only thing the men had was drink. It was one massive piss-up. I have seen marriages and homes split up, people leave the service. You can imagine the sort of thing that atmosphere breeds."

However, the prison officers' spokesman stressed that the prison rules were there and would be strictly enforced—if specific cases of brutality by warders to prisoners could be taken out of the realm of "allegations" and substantiated.

The spokesman had known all of the warders who were shot by the IRA and filled in details about some of their killings.

Graham Fox, I worked with him for three years. He came over here in the army, stayed on in the prison service. He liked Ireland. He was a really good bloke. A fine man. He was shot not far from Magilligan. He drove into a little field to get away from them. . . but they found his body next day, some of his colleagues found him in fact.

Peter Cassidy. He was a Catholic and he went to his sister's wedding. He had his three-year-old child with him and the child fell on top of him when he was shot. Of course it was well publicised in the area that he was coming to that wedding. I went to his funeral. I remember the parish priest was very strong on the murderers. He blamed some people locally, who he said could have been sitting in the church at that moment, for his death, for giving the intelligence to the IRA.

The women at Armagh, they had made a practice of getting takeaway food in a restaurant near the prison. I had warned against that practice. Habitual use of any premises like that is dangerous. They opened up on the group with an Armalite and then threw a grenade in on top of them when they had them down. P. O. Wallace was killed, the others had terrible injuries. I knew them all. I know their widows. We try to be as good as we can to them.

Northern Ireland people are traditionally generous to their next of kin. The Prison Officers' Association tries to ensure that in the first day or two after her husband had been murdered, the one thing the widow knows she won't have to worry about was money. I remember one case where they shot a man in the door of his home as he went out to pay the insurance on his new bungalow. We got a senior counsel to fight the case and even though he hadn't got to paying the premium the insurance company were induced to give the widow the bungalow.

The one that hit me hardest though was Des Irvine. He wasn't only a colleague, he was a close friend. My wife and his wife were friends. I often think about him and how I should have been with him that morning . . . they cut him to pieces with the Armalites. I remember once being on duty in a certain prison and it came over the TV that two warders had been shot that night in Belfast. The prisoners were taking their tea and everything was quiet but when they got the news they jumped up and sang and cheered and danced on the tables. We exercised restraint, showed no emotion and just got them back to their cells.

Our conversation ended with some very frank talk about the likelihood of the British staying or going, and the position of the warders if the then talks between Cardinal O Fiaich and Secretary of State Humphrey Atkins failed to bear fruit. Even though he did bitterly resent Special Category being conceded, the spokesman was very clear about the dangers then arising. While the IRA had not attacked any warders since those talks began towards the end of January 1980 (the shooting which occurred in late May was the work of Loyalists) it was known that they had used the time to improve their intelligence on the warders, and the spokesman's estimate of perhaps four warders being shot in one night was probably well under the likely toll in such an event. We talked about the possibly illusory nature of the prison building programme and all the other seemingly permanent steps being taken by the British. "Some of the facilities," he assured me, "are better than the Europa Hotel. Hydebank Wood, a new jail for young offenders, is the most modern in Europe. Magheraberry and some of the other facilities at the new prison complexes going up in and around Northern Ireland are unbelievable."

But despite all this, he acknowledged that there was a difference between that type of investment and, say, spending on a resource like a gold mine or an oil well, which might induce a power like Britain to remain in a country. The builders of the jails and prison complexes, after all, had received their pay. The money was spent, and there was no further return on it.

He viewed the future with hope rather than confidence, determined not to be intimidated but to do his duty as he saw it, and to go on getting the best bargain that he could for himself and his colleagues, in the process.

Whatever the uncertainty of his future, there was no mistaking the sincerity and warmth of his handclasp as we parted—in his own words—as "fellow Irishmen."

EPILOGUE

Towards a Solution?

By this stage readers have, I hope, a good general outline of how the H Block problem arose and developed. The question then became how to get everybody off the horns of the dilemma thus presented—the prisoners, the warders, the relatives and the British, from their different points on the spectrum. Both the prisoners and the authorities had painted themselves into a corner in which a climate of opinion had been built up where compromise was virtually ruled out. The British were unwilling to concede because to do so would be to cut across their Ulsterisation, Criminalisation and Normalisation policy, and their other general counter-insurgency policies of the moment.

A number of factors had conjoined to bring the issue to a head. Firstly, overall there was no immediate prospect of any long-term solution emerging from Westminster. The proposals which had leaked from Mr. Atkins' Constitutional Conference envisaged neither an Irish dimension nor power-sharing, and come so close to the policies of Dr. Paisley as to be utterly unacceptable to the Dublin government and to the SDLP. They were unacceptable to such an extent, in fact, as to make one wonder if the whole exercise was not solely designed, as the anonymous Whitehall source quoted by the *Economist* [see Chapter 3 above] hinted, to keep the Northern Ireland issue out of the American Presidential campaign of 1980. Coincidentally, if nothing more substantially in terms of linkage, the Atkins proposals were leaked in London, by the same briefing methods used with the *Economist*, on the very day when it appeared that

Senator Edward Kennedy had finally lost the primary race—and raised the Irish issue for the first time at a rally in San Francisco—on June 4.

Certainly, in 1980, in the absence of any evidence to the contrary, informed Dublin opinion felt that then current Tory policies would accelerate violence, not diminish it.

Meanwhile, the percentage of teenage to adult males from the minority community in Northern Ireland who had come into abrasive contact with the "conveyor-belt" system, the security forces, or prison—whether on remand, or actually in one of the protesting H Blocks, or serving out sentences in one of the North's numerous other cell blocks—was then over five per cent of the total. The cumulative effect of this, in the interlocking web of relationships that makes up the Northern minority community, could scarcely be exaggerated.

There was on the one hand an ever-growing alienation from "the system," from "their" notion of "law" and "their" order; and on the other hand an ever-swelling tide of sympathy with the prisoners.

Castlereagh, despite all denials, continued to function. I had an experience as I completed this book that sent me right back to Lord Diplock's original report, which in its consequences has had the ironic effect of making Protestant Northern Ireland a more truly "confessional" state than the Catholic South. I spent an evening with a couple who had come South on a short holiday to enable the wife to recover from the effects of three and a half days at Castlereagh. Beginning with being taken from her home at six o'clock in the morning, her ordeal included a non-stop tirade of insult directed at her two most vulnerable points: her religion and her sex life—which last, being a North of Ireland Catholic mother, she would not normally bring herself to discuss with anyone. But for days on end she was subjected to that peculiarly debased form of sub-pornographic linkage between sex and religion which one so often encounters in the North. This included lurid fantasies about priests and nuns, and speculations about her own proclivities and those of her husband.

When she finally emerged, she was bruised about the breasts and forearms from incessant poking, but was not otherwise subjected to physical maltreatment. However, the psychological sectarian assault was visibly sufficient to affect her and her family very powerfully. She was not charged with anything; the object of the "interrogation" was to get her to admit that her house in Andersonstown had been used by the IRA to hide Dr. Niedermayer, the kidnapped German Consul who died in IRA hands. The woman was of course quite innocent of the suspected harbouring.

But what struck me most forcibly about the episode, which in its own way epitomised the clash between the ruling and minority cultures of the North, was the gulf it revealed between the official versions of what was said to be happening in the North and what actually happened.

Lord Diplock, having stressed that in order to save life, power would have to be given to the security forces to question suspects, described how these investigations would be conducted:

> The whole technique of skilled interrogation is to build
> up an atmosphere in which the initial desire to remain
> silent is replaced by an urge to confide in the ques-
> tioner. This does not involve cruel or degrading treat-
> ment. Such treatment is regarded by those responsible
> for gathering intelligence as counter-productive at any
> rate in Northern Ireland, in that it hinders the creation
> of the rapport between the person questioned and his
> questioner which makes him feel the need to unburden
> himself.

The type of "rapport" which was in fact being established, long after Lord Bennett's report was supposed to have cleaned up Castlereagh, was one of hatred, mistrust, and a desire for vengeance that crystallised around the H Block issue. The British made high-sounding statements of principle about the reasons why a compromise on H Block could not be arrived at, why there could be no return to Special Category, and yet they continued to administer a system which depended on "special" offences (i.e. scheduled ones) being dealt with by "special" courts on the basis of confessions obtained in a very "special" way. The contrast was glaring.

One of the principal arguments advanced against the concession of Special Category was that it would encourage a move towards seeking an amnesty. Yet the British had already built a "half amnesty" into the debate with their offer of a fifty per cent remission of sentence, which must surely be reckoned as going a very long way indeed on the road towards an amnesty. So that argument was easily disposed of.

But the rancour inside the prisons was not. As the quibbling continued, a number of ominous developments were taking place. Inside the jails moves were afoot, which according to my information meant that (1) mass hunger striking was only a matter of time; (2) the campaign against the warders was likely to recommence and intensify, making use of the fact that the IRA used the lull in attacks to build up intelligence dossiers on the men and women concerned; (3) savage bombing attacks both in Northern Ireland and very possibly spreading to England might be expected.

By 1980, one would have thought the British and Irish had tortured each other long enough over the preceding decade without continuing with this particular source of anguish. But it had to be remembered that, more and more, the IRA were reacting to the feelings of the ghetto dwellers who, while they fuelled the Organisation with an ever flowing source of manpower, also brought to it the preoccupations and the resentments of those areas. They didn't take a larger view of the two islands. Their horizons were bounded by concepts of "an army of occupation" and "their law and their order," with the functioning of the "conveyor-belt" system to heighten this impression. Where that was not sufficient there was the outrage over "official versions" of last week's shootings or yesterday's interrogation.

Hitherto the world was not greatly concerned as to who was correct when it came to a dispute between the army and local incidents in Ballymurphy, Andersonstown, Twinbrook, Short Strand or South Derry as to whether or not the dead X was an IRA gunman or an innocent sixteen year old. By 1980, the dimensions of the H Block problem meant that the results of this outrage could be felt far out-side the ghettoes to a degree that could have a destabilising impact on Irish society as a whole, bringing a very great worsening of Anglo-Irish relations and a very great increase in the already appalling toll of human suffering that is daily being added to in Northern Ireland.

The British may have felt that they could disregard constitu-tional Irish national sentiment, go for a purely military solution, and reduce violence to a semi permanent "acceptable" level. This is a fal-lacious policy. The violence, whether institutional or otherwise, would not be acceptable to the people around whom and on whom it centred, the ghetto-dwellers of the minority in Northern Ireland. They had the will and the tenacity to make their outrage felt, either in Ireland, or in a resumed bombing campaign against purely civil-ian targets such as the London tubes. This thought was too ghastly to be further elaborated on, but neither could it be entirely overlooked.

If the British believed that the H Block issue was such an embarrassment to the IRA that it might eventually create a split or weakness in the movement, making it worth persevering with the strong line, then I believed that they were wrong. By 1980, there were more people on the H Block protest than were picked up in the internment roundups of 1971—a very dismal indictment of the poli-cies followed in attempting to solve the Northern Ireland crisis. But just as the Coalition in the South mistakenly persevered with an unenlightened "security" policy when the rest of the Sunningdale package of which it formed a part had long since been abandoned, so too were the British persevering with the "No Special Category" policy long after the 1975 package of which it formed a part (truce, "incident centres," a Convention that was supposed to yield an over-all political solution) had vanished. This policy was doomed, as was the Coalition policy, particularly its prison policy, and the fact should have been recognised.

It became too easy to die in Northern Ireland, particularly in the ghettoes, and so many have died that it was easier to contemplate join-ing the majority. In 1980, the OCs in the H Blocks were collecting the names of volunteers who were prepared to embark on the final desperate course—hunger strike. Prison psychology was taking an ever-increasing hold. If the solution could not be delivered from outside, and if the prisoners were not convinced that outside support was tending towards a solution, then a solution would be attempted from within. I was told of this grim prognostication by one prisoner: "In Ireland they never take note of anything until you hit them over the head with dead bodies. This thing will go on until we start coming out those gates in coffins."

If the problem were not solved by negotiation, the H Block prisoners had only three choices:

1. to come off the protest;
2. to face the prospect of completing their sentences in their then condition;
3. knowingly and willingly to risk their lives in taking the one final step open to them to bring about a solution.

But what were the chances for a negotiated solution? As Mr. Atkins had already indicated a willingness to compromise on the issue, we need not disturb ourselves too much about the question of principle involved. The solution did not have to be called Special Category—Long Kesh was one place in the world where a rose by any other name would smell as sweet! Moreover, within the existing prison regulations it was possible to find a solution compatible with the prisoners' demands. These Rules provided for a type of Special Category for political prisoners in so far as security considerations were concerned. There should have been no difficulty in enlarging on this principle, arriving at a policy on holding the prisoners rather than trying to humble them as well.

Both the IRA and the British should have isolated this one issue, independently of any larger solution in which the problem could be subsumed (i.e. an Anglo-Irish agreement on Northern Ireland), and like opposing armies who mutually agree that a certain town or terrain be excluded from the war, they should have removed the issue once and for all from controversy.

In my view both the Portlaoise settlement and, more pertinently, the report of the Protestant churchmen which I quoted in Chapter 13, pointed the way forward. The Churches' group spoke of the need to look at the problem of dissident prisoners, and at the overall prison situation, in a new way. They were absolutely right. In this spirit the issue of prison clothing, for instance, could have been disposed of on the grounds both of economy and flexibility by asking: why should the State of necessity have to supply expensive prison clothing anyway? If the prisoners have their own clothes—let them wear them!

The IRA should have undertaken to avoid any triumphalism, or any efforts to make political capital out of a settlement. Just as the situation in Portlaoise was defused without any fuss, and kept that way by both parties, it would be all the more appropriate to do so in Northern Ireland, which had far greater resources of security and containment than were available in the Republic. The Republic showed itself flexible and humane enough to move with the times, having earlier proved itself determined enough to withstand Republican demands when these could be shown to be inimical to national security during the Second World War. A defused prison situation would not threaten Northern Ireland; rather, it would bring some balm to that sorely troubled area.

It would have been quite possible, given good will, to hammer out agreement on individual problems within the conflict between the prisoners' "five points" and the official attitude. (The five points, as stated in Chapter Four, were the right to wear one's own clothes, to abstain from penal labour, to free association, to education and recreation, and to full remission of sentence.) For instance, the prisoners would do what was now termed "prison work"—keeping their cells tidy and so on—if they were being instructed to do so by their own leaders. The H Blocks could have been run efficiently, and prison life made as bearable as long-term loss of freedom ever can be.

By 1980, there had been no psychological studies done on the effects of the dirty protest on prisoners, but the long-term effects must be harmful, particularly for prisoners with sentences of ten years or more. After all, the evidence from the prisoners in this book was of necessity based on the experiences of short-term men who were released since the protest began. Could a western European nation in 1980 envisage men being on the dirty protest for periods of twenty years or more? And there was also the situation in Armagh jail to be considered. (The then Church of Ireland Primate of All Ireland, Dr. Armstrong, demonstrated his concern by making a personal visit to the prison.)

The talks between Cardinal O Fiaich and Mr. Atkins were of necessity shrouded in the utmost secrecy, but a sense of disappointment that more had not emanated from them spread amongst the prisoners and their relations. This disappointment had progressed from such questions as "Why doesn't the Cardinal make another statement?" to actual preparations for a hunger-strike, as I described above.

The IRA of course bore a responsibility, and a heavy one, in this situation. The existence of the Diplock courts and "conveyor-belt" system came about in response to their own ruthless methods. Both were produced by a faecal society. It must be conceded that those disposed to argue that the scales of Law needed to be tipped in the direction of Order à la Diplock received a particularly telling fillip, when the Provisional IRA claimed responsibility for kneecapping a forty-five-year-old father of a family, Mr. Patrick Gallagher, in Donegal, because he had given evidence against IRA men charged with armed robbery before the South's Special Criminal Court.

But could they not, even at such a late stage, have called off the protest? The answer, so far as I have been able to sift it from the evidence, appeared to be not at that stage, after nearly four years. The avalanche was moving downhill. In fact the IRA leadership was under severe pressure from supporters of the "blanket men" to respond not with negotiations and efforts to head off hunger strikes but with a spectacular outburst of deadly violence. I described how the Armagh protest escalated outside the control of the IRA leadership. The H Block protest had gone on for several years and had acquired a momentum and volition of its own. For both the IRA and the authorities, prison in general and the Special Category issue in particular had assumed a size and significance that they neither foresaw in the past nor could control in the present.

As I tried to show in the early part of this book, the physical force tradition in Irish history had given to prisons a place in the Anglo-Irish problem which had to be taken into account as one of the basic realities. It was there and would not go away.

I do not subscribe to the belief that it is the karma of England and Ireland to torture each other forever. The two countries can and should, I believe, work out a destiny of mutual respect, interdependence and, at the same time, independence. There was no hope of doing this while the problem of the prisons in Northern Ireland remained unresolved. Solving the issue of the H Blocks and Armagh would not of itself immediately lead to an all-Irish solution. Not solving it, however, rendered any hope of progress, towards any form of peace, utterly impossible.

Tim Pat Coogan
June 5, 1980

Postscript

The negotiations and hopes described in the Epilogue did not yield a solution. Mrs. Thatcher proved that she wanted a win, not a compromise. The prisoners did go on hunger strike. But they called it off just before Christmas 1980 because they believed a compromise was on offer and it seemed that one of the strikers was about to die.

All was euphoria that Christmas 1980. The spin doctors of both Charles Haughey's Dublin government and those of Mrs. Thatcher were each presenting the outcome as a triumph for their respective endeavours. But the one man in the world who knew better, Fr. Brendan Meagher, a Redemptorist priest stationed in the Clonard Monastery in Belfast, was not euphoric. He called to my home in Dublin on Christmas Day to relax a little. He had spent the previous months enmeshed in an unimaginably racking peace shuttle between the prisoners and the various principals involved outside.

In the event, neither of us relaxed all that much. Fr. Meagher feared that the prisoners had been conned. The "five demands" had not been conceded. Only the appearance of concession had been created. He was right. The New Year would usher in one of the most explosive periods in Irish history.

First, anger and despair spread through the prisoners and their supporters as they realised that they had been tricked. Then, inside the prison, the prisoners re-grouped themselves and elected Bobby Sands as their leader. He decided to go on hunger strike, beginning on March 1, 1981. Colleagues followed him at phased intervals. Sands died on May 5, 1981. It is estimated that a hundred thousand people attended his funeral in Belfast. In all, the strike lasted for 217 days, ending on October 3, 1981 as members of the hunger-strikers' families began exercising their right to decide that the prisoners should receive nourishment after they had lapsed into unconsciousness.

And so the British won the battle of the bowels but lost the war for the hearts and minds. In time, the prisoners achieved all the concessions they sought, in effect the Portlaoise type solution which I advocated earlier in these pages. And the ten young men who died on hunger strike have passed into an honoured place in the history of the Irish race.

On a visit to Australia in 1996, I found them engraved on one of the largest Irish Republican monuments in the world, the Waverly Cemetery Memorial outside Sydney. The hunger strikers appear alongside Wolfe Tone and the 1916 leaders. Their names are: Bobby Sands, Francis Hughes, Ciaran Doherty, Joe McDonnell, Tom McElwee, Martin Hurson, Kevin Lynch, Mickey Devine, Patsy O Hara and Raymond McCreesh. In their lives these were unremarkable, mostly working class young Irishmen. By the extraordinary protracted self-sacrificial nature of their deaths it is safe to say that each of them produced a thousand IRA Volunteers (whether they were actually accepted or not is another matter).

Apart from those who died on hunger strike, others whose names readers will have encountered in these pages either did not live to profit from Sinn Féin's political gains, or ended up back in prison. Joseph Maguire, for example, the subject of the first interview in this book, was amongst these. The dead include Mairéad Farrell, whom I met leading the women protesters in Armagh Jail, and who was shot down in an SAS ambush in Gibraltar. Pauline McGeown's husband Pat went on hunger strike but survived when Pauline ordered him to be taken off it after he had lapsed into unconsciousness. Pat went on to become a prominent member of Sinn Féin but died in 1996, his health undermined by both the hunger strike and the strain of trying to maintain the IRA ceasefire which was declared on August 31, 1994. So ended a marriage that began when the couple were each seventeen.

The story of the ceasefire really begins with the Irish general election of 1981. Sinn Féin were revitalised by the hunger strikers. Outside the jail, their supporters mounted one of the greatest publicity campaigns ever seen in Ireland. Haughey's government fell in the emotional vortex of the times. H Block candidates in key constituencies took crucial Fianna Fáil seats. One of the victors, Ciaran Doherty, did not live to enjoy the fruits of his victory. He was one of the "ten dead men" as the hunger strikers were known in a phrase that became a Republican mantra. Out of all this there emerged a new and powerful Sinn Féin Party which threatened to become the largest Nationalist party in the Six Counties.

The rise of the Republicans so worried the Dublin government that it set up an all-party Forum to chart a new course for Ireland and England which it was hoped would stem Sinn Féin's rise and restore the fortunes of John Hume's SDLP. Mrs. Thatcher, the British Prime Minister, however rejected the Forum's findings in her celebrated "out, out, out" speech of November 19, 1984. In this, she rejected the three proposals which the Forum had come up with, after more than a year's discussion involving all the Republic's political parties and the SDLP.

The proposals were for either a Unitary state, a Confederation of both parts of Ireland, or Joint Authority over the six counties by both Dublin and London. Mrs. Thatcher's peremptory dismissal of Nationalist Ireland's painfully teased out formulae provoked such a reaction both in Ireland and America that Mrs. Thatcher was forced to concede that she had erred and in November of the following year (November 15, 1985) she signed the Anglo-Irish Agreement with the Republic's Taoiseach, Garret Fitzgerald. Under this Agreement, Dublin gained some small, but symbolically important concessions on sovereignty from London.

Dublin now raises matters of concern to Nationalists at an Inter-Governmental Conference set up by the Agreement. Dublin civil servants now staff a secretariat at Maryfield in Belfast to which Nationalist politicians have easy and frequent recourse. Lastly, and galling to the Unionists, the Irish Tricolour which was once banned under the Flags and Emblems Act now flies proudly over the secretariat building.

Parallel to these political developments, a savage IRA campaign continued. This was countered both by orthodox military methods on the part of the British and by under-cover assassination squads who indulged in an officially denied "shoot-to-kill" policy. Loyalist paramilitary efficiency also increased—some say with covert assistance from British counter-insurgency units—to a point where, by the time the ceasefire was called, the Loyalists were out-killing the Republicans by a ratio of roughly two to one.

However, behind the mayhem and the political posturing, peace efforts began and continued, largely initiated by one man, Fr. Alex Reid of Clonard Monastery to whom this book is dedicated. He was the guide and interlocutor who made my research possible. The strain of the events described herein took their toll on him, as they did on anyone who came in touch with the happenings of those years. I myself did not write about Northern Ireland until seven years had passed.

But Fr. Reid continued his efforts. He realised that the increasing politicisation of Sinn Féin offered the possibility of a political path opening for Republicans as opposed to a purely military one. He initiated contact between John Hume and Gerry Adams, and through me, between the Dublin government and Sinn Féin. A new Taoiseach in Dublin, Albert Reynolds, put the North at the top of his priorities and, with the help of White House pressure, succeeded in negotiating the Downing Street Declaration of December 1993.

In America, a powerful Irish-American lobby built up, led by Niall O'Dowd, the publisher of the *Irish Voice*. It included some of the most successful Irish-American businessmen of the century including Bill Flynn, Chairman of Mutual of America and Chuck Feeney, the originator of the duty-free shop idea, who donated his billions to charity. Jean Kennedy Smith, President Kennedy's sister, was appointed American Ambassador to Dublin, and, with her brother Senator Ted Kennedy, became a major player in the peace process, helping to secure a visa for Gerry Adams to visit the US. President Clinton also took a personal interest in the Irish issue.

With all these different forces coming together, Fr. Reid's initiative began to bear fruit. Gerry Adams had become convinced that with Irish-American help, a ceasefire would do more to advance the goal of

Republicanism than militarism could ever hope to achieve. The granting of the visa was a tangible proof of this and he succeeded in persuading his colleagues to declare a ceasefire on August 31, 1994.

However, it unfortunately foundered in the welter of Westminster politics. Faced with a revolt within his own ranks over the European issue, John Major, the British Prime Minister, became dependent on the Ulster Unionists for his survival. Barriers were raised to Sinn Féin's participation in peace talks. "Decommissioning" became a *sine qua non* for eligibility to the peace table. In other words, the IRA were to disarm in advance of talks.

The ceasefire broke down on February 9, 1996, thus creating a further obstacle to Sinn Féin being admitted to discussions chaired by the former Senate Majority Leader George Mitchell which continued for most of 1996. In the absence of Sinn Féin the talks were not so much *Hamlet* without the Prince as without Shakespeare. At the time of writing, the violence continues though at low intensity level. But for how long this state of affairs may be expected to last is anyone's guess.

The hope is that after the forthcoming British general election, a strong administration will emerge, presumably Labour, which will not be dependent either on the Conservative Right or the Unionists. But after the experiences of the last decades, in particular those detailed in these pages, one can not be too optimistic.

The British now refer to Long Kesh as the Maze. The term would be better applied to the situation within the Six Counties and the external triangular London-Dublin-Washington relationship which has grown out of the happenings in the prison.

How it will all pan out we do not know, but it can be said with certainty that without benign and sustained American intervention, not on the lines we have seen so far in Ireland, but in Bosnia and the Middle East, where the United States took an interventionist, arm-twisting role, the people of Ireland will remain trapped in that maze.

Tim Pat Coogan
Dublin
January 31, 1997

APPENDIX I

The Reid-Alison Exchange

Correspondence between Fr. Alex Reid and Mr. Michael Alison, Minister responsible for Northern Ireland prisons

Clonard Monastery
25.8.79

Dear Mr. Alison,

I am writing this letter as a priest who regularly helps Father Toner in his ministry to the prisoners in the Maze Prison. My reason for writing is the concern which I and many people feel about the problem of the protesting prisoners in the H Blocks there.

I know that you will share this concern because of the suffering and hardship which the situation imposes not only on the prisoners themselves but also on their families and relatives, on the prison staff and their families and also because of the tragedies that have already resulted and may result in the future from the tension and violence that the situation in the prison tends to engender in the community outside.

The first thing I would like to say concerns the conditions under which the protesting prisoners are now living. Briefly it is this, there is or at least there seems to be a serious disproportion between the faults the prisoners are committing in refusing to obey prison regulations and the punishments they are suffering as a result.

As you know, the protesting prisoners insist that the offences for which they were sentenced had a political dimension because, from their point of view, they were connected with the political troubles that have already affected Northern Ireland for the past fifty years and especially for the past ten years. They want this political dimension to be recognised by the authorities and because the authorities are refusing to do so, they have gone on protest. In practice, this protest means that they are refusing to obey certain prison regulations especially those that relate to the wearing of the prison uniform. (The wearing of the prison uniform is, as I understand it, the crunch issue in the whole protest).

For this refusal to submit to prison discipline, they are being punished by the full loss of remission on their sentences and also by the loss of certain privileges relating to visits, letters, parcels and the wearing of leisure clothes. But in addition to these punishments, the discipline being applied to them at present also means that they suffer the loss of any access to fresh air, any form of physical exercise, any form of normal occupation or mental stimulation, any form of association or recreation or any means of relaxing like television, radio, newspapers, light reading, cigarettes, tobacco etc. Most of these activities and facilities would normally be regarded as necessary for the physical and psychological health of prisoners.

They are also subject to search procedures which, as far as I know, are not normally practised in prisons throughout the United Kingdom and which most people would regard as repugnant and objectionable.

It is a principle of human and British justice that the punishment should fit the crime and that true justice is always tempered by mercy. When one looks at the situation in the Maze Prison one wonders if this principle is being fully and properly applied. That is why many sensible and moderate people, who would in no way condone the offences for which the prisoners have been sentenced,

----

are seriously concerned. They ask themselves, is there a serious and indeed an unjust imbalance between the action of the prisoners in disobeying prison rules and the action of the authorities in imposing a discipline that deprives them of facilities that are normally necessary for health? Are the rights of the prisoners being infringed? Is the policy being followed in breach of a moral law that is far more fundamental and far more important than any prison rules being broken by the prisoners?

Whatever the answers one may give to these questions, it is fair, I believe, to say that it should be possible for the authorities to devise a system of discipline that would not impose the kind of deprivation on the prisoners that the present system is imposing. For example, regarding fresh air, physical exercise and association, would it not be possible to allow the prisoners to exercise in the open in leisure clothes or wearing an athletic outfit or even to walk in the cell corridors? Regarding occupation, could permission not be given for serious and light reading material, for some form of handicrafts? Would it not also be possible to provide some facilities for relaxation, for example, some card games, some access to television, some ration of tobacco and cigarettes?

I make these suggestions with respect because I know the situation is a very difficult one. The main suggestion I would make is that steps should be taken now to ease the tension and the sense of confrontation that is in the situation by the adoption of a more open, a more positive and a more compassionate approach. I believe that this is needed more than anything else—the creation of a new and better atmosphere which would ease the atmosphere of deadlock and open the way to progress.

Related to the concern about the conditions under which the protesting prisoners are living is the concern which many people feel about the composition of the prison staff. The problem here is common to Northern Ireland because of its political composition. In general it means that when people of one political tradition have power over people who belong to the other political tradition in Northern Ireland, there is always the danger that prejudices, discrimination and hostility will enter in and that justice and fair-play will suffer.

Applying this to our prison situation, the danger is that members of the staff who belong to a political tradition that is bitterly opposed to the political tradition represented by the prisoners, may be emotionally hostile to the prisoners and inclined to take a prejudiced attitude to them. Here I do not wish to be unfair or to pass a blanket judgement on the prison staff because I know from my own experience in the prison that their work is very difficult and that many of them do their best to be fair and reasonable in their approach. All I wish to do here is to draw attention to the danger that, because of their own community and political background, members of the staff may be emotionally conditioned to take a hostile and prejudiced attitude to the prisoners and especially in the prisoners' point of view.

This hostility and prejudice could emerge in the day to day treatment of prisoners, in the reports about the conduct of prisoners that are given to the authorities by members of the prison staff and also in the advice about policy that is given to the authorities by the staff or its representative body, the Prison Officers Association.

My own impression is that the Prison Officers Association does have a considerable influence on the policy that is being adopted towards the protesting prisoners and, because of the dangers of prejudice inherent in this situation, many people fear that this influence would tend to be negative and hardline and even hostile.

The concern that is felt about the composition of the prison staff and its representative body also pertains to the composition of the Prison Visitors Committee and the Civil Service staff that advises the Government authorities about prison policy. In so far as this committee and this staff have a membership drawn from Northern Ireland, the same fears about prejudices and hostility towards the protesting prisoners and their political attitudes would exist.

The Visitors Committee and the Civil Service staff have a great influence on the policy that is being adopted towards the prisoners and again the fear would be that this influence is not always as positive or as fair or as neutral as it should be.

I can express these fears in another way by saying that they would hardly exist at all if the prison staff, the Visitors Committee and the Civil Service involved in prison administration, had memberships drawn mainly from England or Scotland. Then people could be reasonably satisfied that the advice on prison policy which these bodies would give to the authorities would be positive and fair and reasonable. My own feeling is that if our prison administration were completely outside the influence of Northern Ireland attitudes, the policy towards the protesting prisoners would not have been as harsh in its results as it has been to date.

I believe that the concern I am expressing about the danger of political prejudice affecting the administration of our prison service is reasonable given the political background of Northern Ireland and I trust that the Government authorities are aware of this danger and that they always keep it in mind when taking advice on prison policy and also that they have an effective system of checks and balances to counter it and to ensure that their decisions on prison policy are based on fair and objective assessments.

The day to day treatment of the protesting prisoners is for me an area of special concern because, in attending the prison over the years, I have regularly listened to complaints and allegations about the abuse of prisoners by members of the prison staff.

This alleged abuse could be physical in the sense that it would involve beatings or the use of undue physical force towards prisoners, sometimes in their cells, sometimes during wing changes and, most often, during search procedures before and after visits.

The alleged abuse could be verbal in that it would involve insulting or derisive remarks, the singing of party songs, or the use of threatening and intimidatory language. The abuse could also be in the form of harassment, for example, interfering with the prisoners' food, soaking their mattresses with water, using overheated water in forced washings.

How is one to judge these allegations? In general, my own opinion is that many of them are substantially true. Over the years I have come to know many of the prisoners personally and I believe that I now know them well enough to be able to judge the trustworthiness of anything they might say to me. I also believe that I make a genuine effort to be fair and objective in my approach to those allegations and I know that I am not motivated by any desire to discredit the prison staff or any member of it. I am well aware of the dangers that attach to their work and I would not be party to any propaganda that might heighten these dangers or the tensions that affect their families. Knowing that there are two sides to every story I try, whenever possible, to check complaints with the officer in charge.

It is also worthy of note that one seldom if ever gets complaints in one or two of the protesting H Blocks while one regularly gets them in one or two of the others, often about the same wing or the same officers. I think that this fact is significant and that it supports the opinions I have formed about the prisoners' allegations.

I believe that everyone who is concerned about the situation in Northern Ireland has a duty to listen carefully and to take seriously any complaints that come from the protesting prisoners. There is already enough tension, enough potential for trouble and enough suffering in our situation without adding to it unnecessarily. If it is true that prisoners are being abused and that the necessary steps are not being taken to prevent it, then another ingredient for trouble is being allowed to fester and to put the day of peace further away. One has only to remember what happened regarding the interrogation centre at Castlereagh when complaints about interrogation methods were apparently resisted for too long a period even though they were being made by responsible and reputable people. One would hope that the same thing does not happen regarding complaints about the ill-treatment of prisoners.

I know that there is an official complaints procedure and that in normal circumstances it should be adequate. I would be the first to tell the prisoners to use it and have done so on several occasions. I have found, however, that the prisoners are reluctant to use it, not because they are unwilling, but because they believe that the procedure is loaded against them and that it would be very difficult for them to obtain justice. They fear, for example, that the evidence of prison officers would always be given more weight than their evidence and that prison officers would tend to support each other against them.

As they see the situation, it would be most unlikely that any prison officer would feel free to support any of their complaints because even if he wanted to, he would be under severe moral pressure not to do so. This moral pressure could come from his colleagues but even if it did not, it is already there in the whole situation. Given the political connotations of the prisoners' protest and of any accusations they might make against prison officers and given too the whole context of their bad relations with the prison staff, it would be very unlikely that any prison officer would feel free to support a complaint.

The prisoners also believe that the general attitude of the Prison Visitors Committee would in the same way be biased against them and that consequently their complaints would not receive a fair hearing or decision.

Another reason why the prisoners are reluctant to use the official complaints system is because they are afraid that if they make accusations against the prison staff they will suffer reprisals from the staff for doing so. They have expressed this fear to me on several occasions when I was urging them to use the official procedures. They told me that if their complaints were not accepted as proved, they would be open to the charge of making false accusations against prison officers and to the punishment that could follow and that in fact several prisoners had already been charged and punished in this way.

Even if we believe that the reluctance of the prisoners to use official procedures is unjustified, we must accept that it is a fact and that these procedures have therefore broken down. One must also keep in mind that the protesting prisoners live in very abnormal conditions and, as a result, are under great strain and tension. These circumstances heighten their fears of official procedures and especially their fears of reprisals from the prison staff.

As I see it, this breakdown in the arrangements for dealing with prison complaints stems from the politically divided nature of

Northern Ireland where political prejudice or the fear of it, constantly tend to enter in and to upset the processes of administration. It is the reason why direct rule is necessary, why there are problems about the acceptability of the police service and why, in the past, there have been problems about local administration.

The government acknowledges this general problem in its policies for Northern Ireland. It accepts in principle that special administrative arrangements and safeguards are necessary if the rights of all its citizens are to be properly protected and ensured.

Applying this to prison administration, it follows that special arrangements and safeguards, not necessary perhaps in other parts of the United Kingdom, are necessary here if the rights of the protesting prisoners are to be properly protected and the prison administration is to function in accordance with the principles of justice and compassion.

This would mean, for example, taking practical steps to counter any partisan influence on the part of the prison staff or the Visitors Committee on the procedures for dealing with prisoners' complaints so that these procedures are seen to be fair and independent of prejudice. This would have the effect of encouraging the protesting prisoners to use them and of removing the concern which people feel about the present procedures.

I believe too that the whole situation regarding the protesting prisoners needs to be reviewed to ensure that the disciplinary policies being adopted towards them at present are not being improperly influenced by discriminatory or prejudiced attitudes, and also to examine the possibility of improving, on humanitarian grounds, the conditions under which they are living.

In writing this letter I have tried to look at the situation in the Maze Prison and the effects it is having on the community outside from the point of view of Christian compassion for everyone who is either directly or indirectly involved in the suffering it is causing. I have also tried to throw some light on it by giving the point of view of someone on the ground and also by pointing out some aspects of the problem that are causing serious concern to many people.

For the past ten years, I have lived close each day to the troubles of Northern Ireland and I know from this experience, the horror and terror and the anguish of mind and heart that they have brought and are bringing to so many people in Northern Ireland and throughout the United Kingdom. I believe, therefore, that everyone has a serious responsibility to do all in his or her power to ease and to end any source of tension that may be inflaming the conflict or heightening the danger of further horror and tragedy. I am certain that the situation in the Maze Prison is such a source of tension and further trouble, that it is leading to a hardening of attitudes, damaging the prospects for peace and making the task of those who are working for peace more difficult and frustrating.

I trust, therefore, that our new Government will treat the problem of the protesting prisoners as a matter of urgency, that they will bring all their wisdom and compassion to bear on it, and that they will maintain a constant effort to alleviate and, as far as possible, to end the tensions and the sufferings it is causing.

Mr. Gerry Fitt, MP, has kindly agreed to give you this letter for me.

Yours sincerely,
A. Reid C.Ss.R.

Clonard Monastery
23.10.79.

Dear Mr. Alison,

I recently sent you a letter about the situation in the Maze prison through Mr. Gerry Fitt MP. Trusting that you will bear with me further, I am now writing a second letter because there are still some suggestions and observations that I would like to make.

I realise that the problem of the protesting prisoners is a very difficult one, so difficult indeed that one is tempted to despair of being able to do or to say anything that might help towards a solution. I believe, however, that trusting in the grace of God, one has to keep trying and that is why I am writing this letter.

There is one fact at least that gives encouragement. It is the prison situation in the Republic of Ireland, where the same basic problem exists and where it appears to have been solved.

Certain prisoners in the Republic claim political or at least special category status for the same reasons that the protesting prisoners in the Maze Prison claim it. The authorities in the Republic refuse to grant it just as the authorities in Northern Ireland refuse. But the authorities in the Republic have managed to avoid the kind of confrontation that we are experiencing here. I believe, therefore, that the approach of the authorities in the Republic is worthy of careful examination because it may be possible to learn from their experience and even to copy their example.

As far as I know, the key to the solution of the problem in the Republic has been the abolition of the prison uniform for all prisoners or at least the freedom to wear it or not.

I mention this matter of the prison uniform because, when the problem is viewed in concrete and practical terms, the obligation to wear it is the central and the crucial issue. If it can be sorted out, all the other issues can, from my information, be easily resolved.

While I realise that you understand the situation in the prison, I should like in this letter to give my own impression of it in the hope that it will throw some extra light on the problem.

The protesting prisoners are refusing to accept the present prison discipline because they believe it is designed to categorise them as common criminals. They absolutely refuse to think of themselves as common criminals and therefore reject the policy which, as they see it, seeks to treat them as such.

To them, a common criminal is a person who was motivated by considerations that were private and personal to himself when he committed the offence for which he was sentenced.

The offences for which they themselves were sentenced were, to their way of thinking, motivated not by private but by political considerations. Their offences, they would maintain, arose directly from the political situation in Northern Ireland, and should not, there-fore, be classified as common crimes. In support of this contention, they quote the nature and the circumstances of the legislation under which they were arrested, interrogated, tried, convicted and sen-tenced. This legislation is special to Northern Ireland and was enacted because of the political situation here.

The conviction that they are not common criminals runs very deep and gives rise to a determination that they will not submit to being treated as such, no matter what happens. The evidence of this determination is their willingness to endure and to go on enduring the appalling conditions which they have created for themselves by refusing to co-operate in such elementary matters as wearing clothes, washing themselves, slopping out their cells etc. The danger in this determination is that it will lead to further extremes in which many of the prisoners may refuse even to eat. If this happens, the conse-quent escalation of tensions inside and outside the prison will lead inevitably to further violence, suffering and tragedy.

I would like to draw special attention to this danger of a hunger-strike. One cannot be certain how the situation in the prison will develop over the next few months but anyone who has his ear to the ground and who knows how tensions are building up, will be aware that the danger of a hunger-strike is real. I believe, therefore, that everyone who is concerned about what may happen in the future has a duty to assess this danger now because prevention is better than cure and later on it may be too late. Here I am thinking, not only of the hunger-strike itself, but also of the consequences it would natu-rally tend to have in terms of an escalation of violence outside the prison.

In assessing the danger of a hunger-strike, one must take account of the mental and physical strain under which the prisoners have been living, many of them for several years. This strain may impair the balance of their reasoning and lead some of them at least to desperate decisions about escalating their protest.

The fact that the protesting prisoners are isolated from normal communication with one another and with people outside increases the danger that their thinking will become isolated from reality and that it will be impossible to reason with them.

One must also remember that the protest and the confrontation with the authorities have now gone on for a considerable period of time, up to three years in some cases, and that during this time the situation has deteriorated into a state of complete deadlock. Some of the prisoners may feel that the only thing to do now is to escalate the protest by going on hunger-strike.

The commitment to their course of action, the determination and the ability to endure severe hardship, which many of the prisoners have shown, must also be taken into account as one tries to assess the likelihood of a hunger-strike and the consequences it would have. These attitudes indicate that at least some of the prisoners would be prepared to go on hunger-strike and to pursue it regardless of consequences.

I have no wish to add to the anxiety one naturally feels about the H Block situation or to give a false credibility to threats and rumours about what might happen there, but as a priest who is close to the situation and who can see the way the wind is blowing, I feel a responsibility to make my concern known to those in authority. If a hunger-strike were to develop and to have serious consequences, I would feel that I had failed in my duty if, knowing the danger, I had not forewarned the authorities about it.

Obviously, you will have to assess the danger for yourself and I would respectfully ask you to do so and to remember that about two months ago a decision to go on hunger-strike was taken by some of the prisoners and was only rescinded when people from outside intervened.

The attitude of the prisoners then, as I understand it, is not that they refuse to accept their sentences or that they are unwilling to submit to prison discipline but that they refuse to submit to a discipline which, as they see and experience it, categorises and treats them as ordinary criminals.

Their essential claim is not for greater privileges than those given to other prisoners but for recognition, at least in some symbolic way, of what they see as the reality of the situation, namely, that the offences for which they were sentenced arose directly from the political situation in Northern Ireland and have therefore a political dimension or at least a dimension that places them in a different category from the offences for which people are normally sent to prison.

Here I would like respectfully to make some suggestions which may prove helpful.

First, the problem of the prison uniform; this, as already noted, is the crunch issue because to the prisoners who are on protest the prison uniform symbolises what I shall call here, "the status of the common criminal". I am satisfied that if this issue were sorted out, the other issues would be more easily resolved.

My suggestion here would be that, as part of a normal and developing policy of prison reform, the whole question of prison dress should be reviewed in principle and in practice so that consideration could be given to adapting the rules by which the principle is applied. If, under a heading of adapting prison rules in a developing policy of penal reform, the obligation to wear the present style of prison uniform were removed for all prisoners and a greater freedom of choice given to them in the matter of prison dress, the door to a solution of the problem of the protesting prisoners would, I believe, be open.

Another suggestion would be that permission be given to all prisoners to wear, during working hours, a form of clothing which is normally worn by people at work, for example, overalls or boiler-suits.

It would be a great pity if, at the end of the day, history were to record that the sufferings and the tragedies arising from the situation in the H Blocks were allowed to continue and even to grow worse because the main practical issue preventing a solution, namely, the obligation to wear the prison uniform, was not tackled with sufficient wisdom and compassion. I would ask you therefore to give special attention to this issue because I believe it is the key to the whole problem. I understand that, as a concession, female prisoners are not obliged to wear a prison uniform and this indicates a flexibility of approach on the part of the authorities which might also be applied to the Maze situation.

Prison work is also an issue in the present protest. In so far as this work would involve the cleaning and maintenance of the prison blocks and the areas where the prisoners live, the preparation of food, vocational training courses and educational courses, there would, I believe, be no great difficulty. My impression is that, with a little flexibility, this issue could be resolved.

Another request of the prisoners is "freedom of association" but if the problems of the prison uniform and prison work were solved, any difficulty about this matter would in practice disappear.

A final suggestion I would like to make, again with respect, is that the authorities should consider approaching the situation in the Maze Prison in the way that they approached the situation in the Castlereagh Interrogation Centre when allegations were being made about the ill-treatment of suspects and the Government decided to set up a committee of enquiry.

The constant allegations about the ill-treatment of the protesting prisoners, the concern expressed by so many responsible people about the extreme consequences and even about the morality of the policy being adopted towards these prisoners, their concern too about the conditions under which the prisoners are living and the effect they could have on their psychological and physical health, the fear that the discriminatory and prejudiced attitudes which have tended to bedevil the administrative processes of Northern Ireland are also affecting the prison situation, the danger of an escalation of tensions, are all factors which indicate to my mind the need for a special inquiry and report.

The work of such an inquiry could also be seen as a follow-up to the report of the Bennett Committee which raised doubts about the justice of some of the sentences now being served by prisoners because of the methods used to obtain confessions on which convictions and sentences were based.

Like the other priests who attend at the Maze Prison, I am deeply concerned about the situation there because of the suffering

----

it causes especially to relatives and also because of the tensions it engenders in the community. I trust therefore that you will give due consideration to the observations and the suggestions I have made in this letter and that you will comment on them as soon as possible.

I am forwarding this letter through Mr. Gerry Fitt MP.

With kind regards,
Yours sincerely,
A. Reid C.Ss.R.

Mr. Alison's Reply

Northern Ireland Office
Stormont Castle
31 December 1979

G Fitt Esq MP

Dear Gerry,

This is in reply to the letters which you passed to me from Father Alex Reid of Clonard Monastery about the prisoners at Maze who are protesting against the refusal of special category status.

I should like to say, at the outset, that I recognise the sincere concern which prompted Father Reid's letters. I understand and respect his pastoral interest in the prisoners taking part in the protest, and in the anxieties of their families.

I have noted Father Reid's views on the various aspects of the protest, and will keep them in mind. You will not, I think, expect me to comment specifically on all the aspects to which he referred in his letters, but I should like to make a number of points arising from what he says.

First, as regards the punishments which are awarded to the protesting prisoners. There is a measure of confusion in the letters between those privileges which the prisoners lose as part of the disciplinary awards (for example three privilege visits a month over and above the monthly statutory visit) and those facilities which they themselves decide not to take up because they are not willing to put on prison clothing—for example exercise and access to books and newspapers.

I cannot accept that the punishments are unjustifiably severe, given the nature of the protest action. The disciplinary procedures used are in accordance with Prison Rules. It would be totally unfair to those prisoners—the great majority—who comply with the Rules if due action were not taken against those who persistently and deliberately seek to make the prison ungovernable.

Father Reid suggests that the wearing of prison uniform is the "crunch" issue. This does not seem to us to be the case, nor does it accord with statements which have been made on behalf of the protesting prisoners. Uniforms, track suits for exercise, relaxation of punishments—those are not what the protest is about. Any concessions in these areas would be seen by the protesters and those who support them merely as forerunners to others; they would not be regarded by the paramilitaries as meeting their demands.

The objective of the campaign is to secure a form of special status, whatever this might be called. This would carry with it the implication that an amnesty would be granted to the prisoners once the violence had ended. This, in turn, would be a direct encouragement to the paramilitaries to continue with their campaign of terror and to try to recruit new members, particularly among the young. The Secretary of State has said on many occasions—the last in the House of Commons on 11 December—that the Government is not prepared to make any concessions on the special category issue.

In regard to the close body search, I accept that the procedure is unpleasant for prisoners and staff. However security considerations make it necessary because of the determination with which the protesting prisoners have used smuggled materials to cause further damage and disruption. A considerable number of potentially dangerous items have been discovered through these searches, and I have no doubt that smuggling on a considerable scale, and including highly dangerous articles, has been averted only by carrying out the searches.

Father Reid also mentions the attitudes of prison staff. I regard his sweeping and generalised criticisms as totally without foundation.

Prison officers do a difficult job in demanding circumstances; often as we have seen, they put themselves and their families at risk. They are not selected on the basis of their political beliefs and anyone meeting the entrance requirements can apply. The selection procedure is careful and impartial to ensure that as far as possible only candidates with the right qualities of integrity and good character are recruited. Moreover they are carefully trained and are required to carry out their duties within a code of instruction and discipline.

Prison officers are required to treat all prisoners properly and in accordance with Prison Rules; they continue to perform their duties humanely and well despite the unique provocations—including 17 murders—to which they have been subjected. As the Secretary of State said in the House on 11 December, prison officers are not in any way concerned with the circumstances of the offences for which the men and women in their charge were sent to prison.

Father Reid's assertion that the Prison Officers' Association is able to influence the policy which we adopt towards protesting prisoners is entirely misconceived. The POA is a staff association and, as with any body representing the interest of staff, it is afforded the opportunity to present its case on matters relating to the terms and conditions of staff. It is not in any way involved in the policy as regards the handling of the protest. I am also satisfied that Father Reid's criticism of the Civil Service staff involved in prison administration is without foundation.

I have noted his remarks about the attitude of the Boards of Visitors. Every effort is made to secure a balanced Board for each establishment, with proper representation of the two communities and the various geographical areas of Northern Ireland. I believe—as did the independent Committee under the chairmanship of Mr. Justice May which recently reported on its review of the United Kingdom Prison Services—that the Boards of Visitors are vital institutions and an important part of the prison system. I am satisfied that they perform their duties impartially and with a proper degree of thoroughness; in particular I do not think that it would be right, or helpful, to consider appointing members of Boards from outside Northern Ireland.

In conclusion, I think I should make the fundamental point once again. It would be a gross abdication of responsibility for the Government to accept that those who commit (in a society where there is ample freedom to express all political views and to demonstrate within the law) criminal offences of the gravest kind in the course of a campaign of killing, maiming and terror, should receive any special form of treatment or concessions in prison.

Yours,
Michael Alison

APPENDIX II

Republicans in British Jails
in 1980

To conclude our historical survey of Republican endurance and prison protests, we may briefly return to the then current scene in the UK "mainland," as it is sometimes called in Britain.

Between the time of O'Donovan Rossa and Seán Russell's campaign, nothing had changed in the attitudes either of warders to their prisoners or prisoners to them. A report dating from the fifties, on an IRA man, Joseph Collins, serving twenty years in Parkhurst prison, illustrates this point:

> . . . very little chance of becoming law-abiding . . . a
> very difficult case and a confirmed rebel, both here and
> in Ireland . . . There's no change in the prisoner's politi-
> cal ideas . . . is apparently unmoved by getting 20 years
> . . . P.S. It's most doubtful whether this man will ever
> lead a law-abiding life.[1]

Nor did they change subsequently. The average Englishman is uninterested in political causes or the doings of governments. England has, after all, been involved in a lot of troubles in faraway places. But when, in the seventies, bombs started going off in pubs in Guildford and Woolwich and Birmingham, or in a bus on the M6 killing women and children, then it was a different matter. There was a wave of outrage against the evil monsters who do such things, and who not alone do them but demand special consideration in prison into the bargain.

In Britain, as in the Northern Ireland prison system, a very sharp distinction was made between what were known in official circles as ODCs (Ordinary Decent Criminals, also referred to as HACs, Honest Average Criminals) and IRA men. And these distinctions found their outlet in continuing reports of brutality towards Irish prisoners in English jails as the seventies wore on. The treatment, in particular, of those arrested for the Birmingham bombings gave rise to well-founded feelings that ill-treatment was systematically being meted out to persons charged with IRA-type offences.

One of the most celebrated of these cases occurred at Albany prison on the Isle of Wight and gave rise to such persistent and lurid accounts of what had happened that it was investigated by Amnesty International, the Howard League for Penal Reform and the National Council for Civil Liberties. The London *Times*, giving the first public account of the incidents, reported as follows on September 25, 1976:

> Five IRA men involved in an incident at Albany maximum security prison, on the Isle of Wight, a week ago appeared before the jail's Board of Visitors yesterday accused of prison code offences, including mutiny and gross personal violence.
>
> Two of the men were sentenced to 570 days loss of remission and 91 days confinement to their cells, exclusion from association and privileges, and loss of pay.
>
> Two others received sentences of 690 days loss of remission and 126 days confinement, loss of privileges and pay, and the fifth man was sentenced to 690 days and 133 days respectively.
>
> The five, with a sixth who is still in the prison hospital recovering from injuries, were said to have barricaded themselves into a corridor and demanded the

release of another prisoner who was being segregated.
Two prison officers who went to break up the barricade
had to be treated for injuries.

It later emerged that several protests about the treatment of the
prisoners were being made by relatives and interested parties such as
Mr. Frank Maguire, MP, a man of strong Republican views. One of
the most unusual complaints emerged from a source normally hostile to the IRA prisoners: one of the HACs. This man described what
happened in a letter to the *Guardian* on September 29, in the following terms:

Sir,

Prisoners have very little sympathy for IRA terrorists.
However, the treatment that the six IRA protesters
received in Albany has outraged and alarmed most prisoners.

These six men were not armed and announced that
they were making a peaceful protest. They had blocked
off a small spur by placing a table across the entrance.
The gate to this spur could have been locked and these
men posed no danger to the prison security i.e. escape.
They would have soon got tired and hungry and would
have given themselves up.

However, prison officials decided to deal with the
situation in a way which very nearly started a riot (if it
had been any other inmates other than IRA there definitely would have been a riot) and with one prisoner
ending up in hospital with broken or fractured ribs, five
other inmates needing to be stitched up and one warder
with a bad leg—which he did himself by accidentally
getting in the way of another officer's club.

All inmates were locked away as usual at 9 p.m. At
9.30 p.m. twenty officers entered the wing in riot gear—

they were supported by another thirty men who were not in riot gear. They went to the spur and battered these six men to bits. All of us who were locked up could hear the clubs and screams. It was sickening. Violence breeds violence; if this is the policy being adopted to deal with peaceful demonstrations how long will it be before someone gets killed. The next peaceful demonstrators may have knives to protect themselves from this baton wielding riot squad. Surely the most sensible solution would be a non-violent ending to any demonstration.

Yours,

A long term stay prisoner

P.S. I would like to point out that these men have lost a total of 10 years remission without any legal representation.

On September 30 Mr. Maguire told the *Guardian* what one prisoner, Sean Campbell, had suffered:

After visiting four IRA men in prison yesterday Mr. Frank Maguire, the Independent Northern Ireland MP, said he was horrified at the injuries he had seen.

Mr. Maguire said he would seek a meeting with the Home Secretary Mr. Merlyn Rees, to ask for an explanation of injuries received by six IRA men in Albany prison two weeks ago. Mr. Maguire said that in one case he put down the injuries he had seen to "the most savage and sadistic beating I have ever seen handed out to a prisoner by prison warders." Sean Campbell was then in the prison wing at Parkhurst, where Mr. Maguire said he was being treated for a broken arm, two broken fingers, a broken leg, and fractured ribs.

He also saw two other prisoners who were injured, Father Patrick Fell, who has a broken nose, eight

stitches on his forehead, and severe body bruising, and
Cornelius McFadden who has bruising and stitches in
his head.

In Father Fell's case the loss of privileges also meant a prohi-
bition against his saying Mass for several months.

Whether or not the prisoners brought a good deal of their mis-
fortune on their own heads is a hotly debated one, by now readers
should have a fair insight into the IRA men's prison attitudes on
which to base an opinion—but the Albany episode does indicate the
type of incident which the presence of IRA men in English jails can
and does generate.

1.   Published by J. Bowyer Bell in *The IRA*, Academy Press, Dublin 1980,
       page 182. (The report incidentally was prepared by a Catholic priest, a
       Father Lynch, for the authorities.)

APPENDIX III

Prison officers killed 1976–80

Name	Rank	Date killed
P.C. Dillon	P.O.	April 8, 1976
J.D. Cummings	P.O.	April 19, 1976
R.J. Hamilton	P.O.	October 8, 1976
T.G. Fenton	P.O.	June 22, 1977
D.E. Irvine	Principal Officer	October 7, 1977
A. Miles	Deputy Governor	November 26, 1978
J.M. McTier	Clerk	December 14, 1978
P. Mackin (retired)*	Former P.O.	February 3, 1979
M.C. Cassidy	P.O.	April 16, 1979
A.J. Wallace	Woman P.O.	April 19, 1979
G. Foster	P.O.	September 14, 1979
E.D. Jones	Assistant Governor	September 19, 1979
T. Gilhooley	P.O.	November 5, 1979
D.W. Teeney	Clerk	November 7, 1979
G.F. Mulville	P.O.	November 23, 1979
W. Wright	Chief Officer	December 3, 1979
W. Wilson	Senior Officer	December 17, 1979
G.F. Fox	P.O.	January 18, 1980

*Mr. Mackin's wife was also shot dead.

INDEX